SAINT PAUL

Saint

New York

Paul

A STUDY OF
THE DEVELOPMENT
OF HIS THOUGHT

BY CHARLES BUCK
AND GREER TAYLOR

Charles Scribner's Sons

To Charles Lincoln Taylor

PREFACE

This book is the product of a happy collaboration. As originally planned it was to be two books, one a study of the Pauline chronology by Charles Buck and the other, growing out of that, a study of Paul's legal theory by Greer Taylor. As the two works progressed, however, it became increasingly apparent that they necessarily covered much of the same ground and could be combined in a single presentation. So extensive was the agreement between the two, in fact, that the process of bringing them together turned out to be largely mechanical.

The debt which each of us owes to the other is greater than the foregoing would indicate. One cannot deal with the chronology of the letters without treating the development of Paul's legal theory, nor can one trace the development of the legal theory without reference to the chronology. Over the years we have repeatedly discussed these questions, and each of us has made suggestions which have influenced the thinking of the other, so that in a number of areas we now find it impossible to remember which of us was the first to express this or that idea.

Our debt to others is large. We began this study at the Episcopal Theological School in Cambridge, and it was the Dean of the School at the time, Charles L. Taylor, who encouraged us to persevere in our attempts to trace the development of Paul's thought, a line of inquiry which older Pauline scholars had pronounced fruitless. Encouragement and help came from many others, chief among whom was Sherman E. Johnson, then Professor of New Testament at the Episcopal Theological School and later Dean of the Church Divinity School of the Pacific in Berkeley.

Each of us in addition would like to acknowledge a number of individual debts. In the case of Buck these are to W. H. P. Hatch, whose approach to the study of Pauline theology is constantly reflected here; to the late N. B. Nash, whose trenchant criticism of the parts of this book that were written before his death led to their being completely rewritten; and to H. J. Cadbury, without whose guidance the chapter on Acts could not have been written at all. In the case of Taylor they are to the late Alfred Putnam Lowell, association with whom in the practice of law was an education in legal theory and in the relevance of law itself to the sort of practical problems that Paul had to deal with, and whose influence is reflected in every contribution that Taylor has made to the present study; to Robert Tomson Fortna, who as a colleague on the faculty of the Church Divinity School of the Pacific was an indispensable partner in the shaping of many of the principal ideas expressed here; and to Bruce Hargreaves Kennedy and Stuart Schlegel, who as students at the Church Divinity School contributed both interest and insight to the working out of those ideas.

Practically all of the material in the book first saw the light of day in the form of lectures to students, those of Buck having been delivered at the Episcopal Theological School and at St. John's Theological College, Suva, Fiji Islands, and those of Taylor at the Church Divinity School of the Pacific and at Vassar College. The portions which have appeared in journals are identified in the notes.

CHARLES BUCK
GREER TAYLOR

Boston

CONTENTS

Preface . . . . . *vii*

Introduction: The Sources and the Problem *3*

PART I : THE EVIDENCE OF THE LETTERS · *21*

1. I Corinthians, II Corinthians 1–9,
   and Romans *23*

2. The Previous Letter, the Corinthian Reply,
   and I Corinthians *31*

3. I Thessalonians *46*

4. Eschatology, Christology, and the Law in I Corinthians
   and II Corinthians 1–9 . . . . . *53*

5. Philippians *68*

6. Galatians 82

7. II Corinthians 10–13 103

8. Colossians and Philemon 115

9. Ephesians 124

10. II Thessalonians 140

11. Absolute Dates 146

12. Summary: The Order of Events
   in the Letters 163

PART II : THE EVIDENCE OF ACTS · 177

13. The Acts of the Apostles 179
   Jerusalem Visits and Missionary Journeys 181
   The Sources of Acts 190
   The Last Chapters 205
   The Chronological Sequence of the Pauline Sections
      of Acts 211
   The Datable Events 211

PART III : SYNTHESIS · 217

14. The Man Who Had Seen the Lord 219

Index of Scriptural Passages 263
Index of Subjects and Authors 271

SAINT PAUL

INTRODUCTION

The Sources and the Problem

The sources of our knowledge of the life of Paul are two in number: a collection of his letters preserved among the New Testament epistles, and an account of his missionary career in the Acts of the Apostles. These documents provide the sole basis for his biography.

Fourteen of the New Testament epistles have at one time or another been attributed to Paul. They fall into three classes. The first class consists of a group of ten letters: Romans, I Corinthians, II Corinthians, Galatians, Ephesians, Philippians, Colossians, I Thessalonians, II Thessalonians, and Philemon. The second consists of the three Pastoral Epistles: I Timothy, II Timothy, and Titus. The third has only one member: the Epistle to the Hebrews.

The ten epistles which make up the first class seem to have been published as a collection sometime in the last quarter of the first century. They are considered by a majority of historians and literary critics to be the work of Paul. The Pastorals, on the other hand, are no longer thought to have been written by Paul. These three letters, which did not appear until the early years of the second century, are now recognized as the work of a later writer. Their author may have incorporated into them a few genuine fragments from unpublished letters of Paul, but these are impossible to identify with any assurance and therefore cannot be used as sources. As regards the Epistle to the Hebrews there is no problem. Originally published as an anonymous treatise, it was only subsequently attributed to Paul by uncritical readers. Competent scholars, both ancient and modern, are unanimous in denying its Pauline authorship.

We are left, therefore, with the letters of the original collection. As copied in the manuscripts and published in modern Bibles these appear to be ten in number. As originally published they seem to have numbered only eight, no distinction having been made at first between I and II Corinthians and none between I and II Thessalonians. The familiar divisions between these letters were made by early editors, who noticed that in each case more than one letter had been included under a single heading. We are at liberty to ask, therefore, how well these early critics did their work.

In the case of Thessalonians the task was simple and the traditional solution is doubtless correct. What had appeared as "To the Thessalonians" was actually two letters, which even the casual reader could separate with ease. On the other hand, the material that had appeared as "To the Corinthians" was not so easy to divide into its component elements, and the traditional solution seems to be only partially correct. The major break between what we now call I and II Corinthians was obvious, and a division could be made at that point without difficulty. A second important break in the material, however, went unnoticed. It occurs between chapters 9 and 10 of II Corinthians and it marks the end of one letter, of which the final greetings are missing, and the beginning of another, which now lacks a formal salutation. Thus there are at least three letters to the Corinthians with which the historian must deal separately.[1] Of less importance is a

---

[1] A small fragment of still a fourth letter may be found in II Cor. 6:14–7:1. Attempts to divide the Corinthian correspondence still further have been numerous. The most

similar undetected break in Romans, the last chapter of which appears to contain a separate letter, possibly to the church in Ephesus. Our traditional ten letters, therefore, are probably at least twelve in actual number.[2] It is with these, and not the other epistles attributed to Paul, that the historian of Paul's life has to deal.

Over against the letters stands the book of Acts. This history of the primitive church is a companion piece to the Gospel of Luke and is the work of the same author, whom tradition identifies with "Luke the beloved physician," a friend and fellow worker of Paul (Col. 4:14). The date of Acts is not known. Some critics have sought to place its composition in Paul's lifetime, seeing in it a documentary defense of the apostle's activities intended to be introduced as evidence at his trial. Others incline to a date in the final quarter of the first century. A few even view it as a second-century work. For our present purposes neither the authorship nor the date of the book is of primary importance. We are chiefly concerned with the character of the work as a source of information about the life and thought of Paul.

As a historical document Acts is clearly a secondary source. Although its author may well have been an eyewitness to some of the later events which he narrates, he was not an eyewitness to the events of the earlier years of Paul's missionary career. His knowledge of these earlier happenings depended on the records and recollections of others rather than on his own personal experience. Even in the latest sections, which may well contain first-hand reporting, it is often extremely difficult to form an opinion as to the extent to which he is

ambitious of these to appear in recent years is that of W. Schmithals (*Die Gnosis in Korinth*, Göttingen, 1956). Schmithals' work, which combines the principal partition theories of its predecessors, reconstructs the Corinthian correspondence as follows:

Letter A: II Cor. 6:14–7:1; I Cor. 9:24–10:22; 6:12–20; 11:2–34; 15:1–58; 16:13–24
Letter B: I Cor. 1:1–6:11; 7:1–9:23; 10:23–11:1; 12:1–14:40; 16:1–12
Letter C: II Cor. 2:14–6:13; 7:2–4
Letter D: II Cor. 10:1–13:13
Letter E: II Cor. 9:1–15
Letter F: II Cor. 1:1–2:13; 7:5–8:24

[2] For a discussion of the widely held theory, which the present writers do not accept, that Philippians is actually two letters, see below, pp. 76–91.

speaking for himself.[3] That being the case, Acts must be treated as of secondary rank throughout as compared with the letters.[4]

Such a distinction between primary and secondary sources amounts to an axiom of historical study, for it is universally recognized that whenever information is transmitted at second or third hand the possibility of inaccuracy is greatly enlarged. In the study of Paul's life, however, this principle has only on rare occasions been consistently applied. Historians, assuming Acts to be a trustworthy biography of Paul, have often taken it as their principal source and treated the autobiographical material in the letters as so much extra detail with which to fill out the Acts narrative. At many points, where Acts agrees with the letters, this process of harmonization has yielded satisfactory results. At other points, however, Acts and the letters are so contradictory that they can be harmonized only by means of a most complicated and unnatural exegesis, and in these cases a critical presumption in favor of Acts has often relegated the letters to the status of secondary documents, to be followed when they agree with Acts and explained away when they disagree. That this method belies the canons of sound practice in historical research needs no demonstration. That it has failed to yield satisfactory solutions to the main problems in the life of Paul is evident to every serious student in the field.

But although Acts is clearly a document of secondary rank, it is nevertheless of great value. It agrees with the letters more often than not, and it gives every indication of having been composed by a historian of more than ordinary skill. Although it undoubtedly presents a biased account of some events, the bias seems to be that of the sources, which the final author was honest enough to allow to speak for themselves. Acts may not stand on an equal footing with the letters, but it is by no means to be regarded as a work of slight importance.

[3] See H. J. Cadbury, "The Purpose Expressed in Luke's Preface," *Expositor*, XXI (1921), 431–441; "The Knowledge Claimed in Luke's Preface," *Expositor*, XXIV (1922), 401–420.

[4] This point has been made by a number of recent writers. See J. Knox, "Fourteen Years Later: A Note on the Pauline Chronology," *Journal of Religion*, XVI (1936), 341–349; "The Pauline Chronology," *Journal of Biblical Literature*, LVIII (1939), 15–29; *Chapters in a Life of Paul* (Nashville, 1950); D. W. Riddle, *Paul, Man of Conflict* (Nashville, 1940); P. S. Minear, "The Jerusalem Fund and Pauline Chronology," *Anglican Theological Review*, XXV (1943), 389–396; C. H. Buck, Jr., "The Collection for the Saints," *Harvard Theological Review*, XLIII (1950), 1–29.

If it is a mistake for the biographer of Paul to treat it as a primary source, it is just as serious a mistake for him not to treat it with respect.

The problem that these sources pose is basically one of chronology. The letters do not contain a great deal of explicit chronological information, but such information as they do contain conflicts with Acts in such a way as to make it extremely difficult to determine the order of events in Paul's missionary career. The most important of these conflicts involves the date of Galatians.

In Galatians, Paul states that he had visited Jerusalem only twice between the time of his conversion and the writing of the letter (Gal. 1:18; 2:1). This can only mean, if both Acts and Galatians are reliable, that Galatians is the earliest of the letters, since all the other letters were written to churches which were founded, according to Acts, after the third visit to Jerusalem. Some of these other letters, however, notably those to the church in Thessalonica, seem to reflect a stage in the development of the church, and in the development of Paul's teaching, which is earlier than that reflected in Galatians. Indeed, so marked are the doctrinal and literary differences between Galatians and the Thessalonian letters, and so strong are the affinities of Galatians with such admittedly later letters as II Corinthians and especially Romans, that it seems most unlikely that Galatians could have been written before I and II Thessalonians.

But if Galatians is not the earliest of the letters, how is the problem of the Jerusalem visits to be met? One possibility, long ago suggested by Lightfoot, is that Galatians may have one visit too few: Paul may have omitted to mention a third Jerusalem visit in Galatians for the reason that it was unimportant to his argument. This would allow Galatians to be dated after the third visit after all, along with the other letters which it most closely resembles. Another possibility is that Acts may have one visit too many: Acts may contain two separate accounts of a single Jerusalem visit, so that what now appears in the Acts narrative as the third visit may be only a doublet of the second. This would accomplish the same purpose by allowing the founding of the European churches to be dated before the third visit, in the same period that produced Galatians.

Either of these solutions would do away with the discrepancy in the number of Jerusalem visits, but neither of them deals at all satisfactorily with the related problem of the date of the Jerusalem Council relative to the composition of the Corinthian correspondence and Romans. According to Acts the Jerusalem Council, which settled a controversy over the authority of the Jewish law for Gentile Christians by decreeing that they need not observe the whole law but must "abstain from what has been sacrificed to idols and from blood and from what has been strangled and from fornication" (Acts 15:29),[5] took place before the founding of the European churches. On the other hand, several of the letters, notably II Corinthians 1–9 and Romans, which were written after the founding of the European churches, deal at considerable length with the authority of the Jewish law for Gentile Christians, and these letters give no indication that this question had been previously decided, either along the lines of the decree of the Council, or indeed along any other lines. Instead they appear to have been written while the controversy over the law was still at its height. This would seem to suggest, unless the whole account of the Council and the decree in Acts is to be dismissed as a fiction, that the letters in question, and hence the founding of the European churches, must be dated before the Jerusalem visit when the Council took place rather than after it. But if this is so, then the entire relationship which Acts sets up between the Jerusalem visits and the Missionary Journeys is wrong, and the generally accepted order of events in Paul's missionary career collapses.

Even within this generally accepted order of events there is little agreement with regard to dates. The conversion, for example, has been dated as early as 29/30 (Goguel) and as late as 38 (Renan); the Jerusalem Council has been variously placed anywhere between 44 (Wellhausen) and 52 (Weiss); and Paul's arrest in Jerusalem has been put as early as 53 (McGiffert) and as late as 59/60 (Jülicher).

The problem of the Pauline chronology, in other words, has yet to be solved. Since it apparently will not yield to the standard method of attempting to fit the letters into the framework of Acts, a new ap-

[5] The text of the decree is corrupt: "from what is strangled" is probably a gloss on "from blood."

proach would seem to be called for. John Knox was the first writer to insist on the necessity for such a new approach, and in his *Chapters in a Life of Paul* (Nashville, 1950) he demonstrated that the order of events during a considerable period in Paul's career could be determined on the basis of the evidence of the letters alone.

But although Knox's new approach to the problem was admittedly the only one that could be completely justified in principle, and although it clearly pointed the way toward a far more satisfactory solution of the problem of the Pauline chronology than had been achieved before, it was not widely adopted in practice. Nor could it be, for if the chronology of Paul's life is to be based on the evidence of the letters, it is necessary to know beforehand the order in which the letters were written, and once the framework of Acts is dispensed with, some of the letters are extremely difficult to date even relatively. As we have seen, it is still possible to debate whether Galatians is the earliest of the letters. Similar questions can be raised as to whether II Thessalonians was written before or after I Thessalonians, and whether II Corinthians 10–13 was written before or after II Corinthians 1–9. The position of Philippians in the series is perhaps the most difficult of all to determine. It is still an open question whether it should be dated before or after the other prison epistles, and it is not even certain that it was written from Rome rather than from Ephesus, or possibly Caesarea. If Knox's approach is to succeed, therefore, what is needed is some method of establishing at the outset the order in which the letters were written. The present study is an attempt to devise such a method of dating the letters on the basis of the development of thought which they reflect.

Hitherto most Pauline critics have taken the position that it is impossible to trace a development in Paul's thought. Johannes Weiss may still be taken as a spokesman for this point of view. Speaking of the early years of Paul's missionary activity, before the surviving letters were composed, he writes, "It cannot be too much insisted upon that the real development of Paul both as a Christian and a theologian was completed in this period which is so obscure to us, and that in the letters we have to do with the fully matured man. . . . By contrast, the 'development' which some think they can discern in the period of the letters—ten years, at the most—is not worth considering at all." [6]

This statement, quite apart from its unquestioning assumption of the reliability of the Acts chronology, which alone forbids the dating of any of the letters in the earlier years of Paul's ministry, seems to assume also that development of thought is not to be expected in a "fully matured man," and that ten years would be too short a period to accommodate such development even if it did occur. The facts of history, however, tell us otherwise. The Luther of the three treatises which appeared in 1520 is scarcely recognizable as the Luther who had published the *Exposition of the Seven Penitential Psalms* in 1517. Nor do such changes occur only in the comparatively young. Cicero was in his sixty-second year when he produced his philosophical essays, which are so different in thought from the rest of his writing as almost to seem the work of another man. These essays were written for the most part in a single year, 45–44 B.C. "It is the work of this astonishing year," writes Mackail, "which, on the whole, represents Cicero's permanent contribution to letters and to human thought." [7] Developments of this kind, in short, do occur, and it is precisely in those lives that are most deeply involved in struggles over great issues that history teaches us to expect them.

Paul's was such a life. He is unique among New Testament writers in conceiving of his own experience as forming a part of the gospel he preached. The gospel was not, to him, primarily a record of past happenings or a system of religious thought and practice. It was, rather, the disclosure of a divine event which was even then in progress and in which he had been chosen to participate. He was at once, therefore, the recipient of the divine revelation and also the chosen instrument of its communication; the divine event included both what God had done for him and what God was doing through him. As he puts it in Philippians, "What has happened to me has really served to advance the gospel, so that it has become known in the whole praetorium and to all the rest that my imprisonment is for Christ" (Phil. 1:12–13). He is even more explicit in II Corinthians: "If we are afflicted, it is for your comfort and salvation; and if we are

[6] *History of Primitive Christianity* (Eng. trans.), Vol. 1, p. 206.
[7] *Latin Literature*, p. 72.

comforted, it is for your comfort, which you experience when you patiently endure the same sufferings that we suffer" (II Cor. 1:6). In other words, the revelation of God's purpose to Paul, and through him to others, was continually taking place in the experiences he underwent.

The consciousness that he occupied a divinely appointed place in history explains many of the most noticeable features of Paul's letters. Not only are they autobiographical to an extent not approached by any other New Testament writing, but they also betray a presumption of personal authority on the part of the writer which is quite unlike that of any other New Testament author. Paul alone among New Testament writers can add to a commandment of Jesus a commandment of his own, and justify his right to do this by saying, "I think that I have the Spirit of God" (I Cor. 7:40). He can also change his mind, even on important subjects, if new circumstances or further reflection on his part dictate such a change. In one famous instance he tells his readers that he has even changed his way of thinking about Christ: "From now on, therefore, we regard no one from a human point of view; even though we once regarded Christ from a human point of view, we regard him thus no longer" (II Cor. 5:16). An even more striking alteration of this kind is reflected in the flat contradiction between the Christology of Philippians, where Paul says that when Christ came into the world he "emptied himself" (Phil. 2:7), and that of Colossians, where he writes, "For in him all the fulness was pleased to dwell, and through him to reconcile to himself all things" (Col. 1:19-20).

Paul acted on the principle that the Spirit, which "searches everything, even the depths of God," had been given "that we might understand the gifts bestowed on us by God" (I Cor. 2:10,12), and he never ceased to re-examine his understanding of God's purpose in the light of his own experience; nor did he hesitate, as a result of this constant critical process, to revise his teaching when new experiences dictated. The same principle applied to his interpretation of Scripture and of history. He did not consider himself bound to a particular interpretation of Scripture which he had adopted in the past. In II Corinthians he takes Jeremiah's prophecy of the new covenant as having been fulfilled in the Christian dispensation of grace, which gives life (II Cor. 3:6). In Romans, however, he adopts a new explanation: the law "written on their hearts" is the intuitive moral knowledge on the basis of which the Gentiles' conscience operates, proving them to be under the power of sin (Rom. 2:15). He could be just as free in his reinterpretation of history. In I Thessalonians he treats the opposition of the Jews to the gospel as the final act of wickedness on their part that will "fill up the measure of their sins" (I Thess. 2:16). In Romans, on the other hand, he explains the failure of the Jews to accept Christianity as a consequence of the deliberate act of God, who "gave them a spirit of stupor," so that they should not be converted "until the full number of the Gentiles come in" (Rom. 11:8,25).

But even if it be granted that Paul sometimes revised his thinking on specific points, the question remains whether the occasional changes in doctrine which the letters exhibit reflect a traceable development in Paul's theology. This question may certainly be answered in the affirmative with reference to his eschatology. If the letters are taken in their generally accepted chronological order (omitting Galatians, which displays little interest in eschatology, and about which there has been more serious disagreement with regard to date than the others), they fall into three groups: an early group consisting of I and II Thessalonians; a middle group consisting of I and II Corinthians and Romans; and a late group consisting of Philippians, Colossians, Philemon, and Ephesians.

The eschatological outlook of the Thessalonian letters centers on the hope of an immediate parousia. The two main problems with which they deal are the delay in the fulfillment of this hope and the death of some of the members of the church before it has taken place. Paul's answers to these questions are familiar: the parousia will not take place until the "present restrainer" is out of the way (II Thess. 2:7), and the Christian dead will be raised in time to meet the Lord as he comes in the air (I Thess. 4:16–17). The eschatological thought of these letters is not only extremely simple, it is also completely consistent with current Jewish apocalyptic, and it can be paralleled in almost every detail in such works as the Book of Jubilees, the Testaments of the Twelve Patriarchs, the Apocalypse of Baruch, and IV Esdras. Paul departed further and further from this position as the years passed.

I Corinthians, the earliest of the letters of the middle period, is not chiefly interested in eschatology but in problems of ethics and order—the wrangling of factions in the church, sexual promiscuity, the eating of meat offered to idols, excesses in the exercise of the gift of tongues, the profanation of the Lord's Supper. It enlarges, however, on the eschatological teaching of I Thessalonians by explaining that "we have received . . . the Spirit which is from God" (I Cor. 2:12), and that the dead will be raised at the parousia with completely spiritual bodies, while the living will be simultaneously changed from flesh to spirit "in a moment, in the twinkling of an eye, at the last trumpet" (I Cor. 15:51–52).

In II Corinthians 1–9 this aspect of the eschatological teaching of the letters of the middle period is developed still further. The emphasis, however, shifts from the original idea that the transformation from flesh to spirit will be accomplished in a brief moment at the parousia to the idea that this transformation is a long-term process which is even now in progress in the believer: "We all, with unveiled face, reflecting the glory of the Lord, are being changed into his likeness from one degree of glory to another. . . . So we do not lose heart. Though our outer nature is wasting away, our inner nature is being renewed every day" (II Cor. 3:18; 4:16). This shift in emphasis is reflected in the shift in the tense of the verb. In I Corinthians, Paul writes, "We shall all be changed" (I Cor. 15:51); in II Corinthians 1–9 he writes, "We all . . . are being changed" (II Cor. 3:18).

A similar shift in emphasis is detectable in the teaching of the letters of the middle period with regard to the death of the believer. Both I Corinthians and II Corinthians 1–9 frequently speak of death in the literal sense, with an occasional extension of this sense into the realm of the figurative: "That is why some of you are weak and ill, and some have died" (I Cor. 11:30); "I protest . . . I die every day!" (I Cor. 15:31); "We shall not all sleep" (I Cor. 15:51); "We felt that we had received the sentence of death" (II Cor. 1:9); "For while we live we are always being given up to death for Jesus' sake, so that the life of Jesus may be manifested in our mortal flesh" (II Cor. 4:11). But II Corinthians 1-9 also introduces the idea of a symbolic death that has already taken place in every believer as a result of his being "in Christ" and therefore sharing in Christ's death: "We are convinced that one has died for all; therefore all have died" (II Cor. 5:14). In Romans this new idea is paramount: "Do you not know that all of us who have been baptized into Christ Jesus were baptized into his death? . . . But if we have died with Christ we believe that we shall also live with him. . . . So you also must consider yourselves dead to sin and alive to God in Christ Jesus" (Rom. 6:3,8,11). The extent of the shift in emphasis is well illustrated in the contrast between the language of I Corinthians, with its concern about death in the future: "We shall not all sleep. . . . Then shall come to pass the saying that is written: 'Death is swallowed up in victory' " (I Cor. 15:51,54), and that of Romans, which is no longer concerned with physical death at all, since the only death that really matters in the case of the Christian has already taken place: "We have died with Christ" (Rom. 6:3).

When we turn from the middle letters to those of the last period, we detect a still further modification in Paul's eschatological teaching. In the middle letters, whether or not the believer's death is regarded as having already occurred, his resurrection is always regarded as future: "The trumpet will sound and the dead will be raised" (I Cor. 15:52); "He who raised the Lord Jesus will raise us also with Jesus" (II Cor. 4:14); "We shall certainly be united with him in a resurrection like his" (Rom. 6:5). In this respect these letters all agree. Colossians, on the other hand, which reflects the eschatology of the last period of Paul's life, contains a different teaching about the resurrection. According to that letter the Christian is no longer waiting for the resurrection but has already been raised: "If then you have been raised with Christ, seek the things that are above, where Christ is, seated at the right hand of God. . . . For you have died, and your life is hid with Christ in God. When Christ who is our life appears, then you also will appear with him in glory" (Col. 3:1,3-4).

Thus the shift in Paul's eschatological outlook can easily be followed as we move from the early to the late letters. According to the early letters the believer will be changed, according to the middle letters he is being changed, and according to the last letters he has been changed. The progress of this development is gradual, and the steps by which it proceeds from one letter to the next are often small. The movement is steady, however, and it is always in the same direction, with the result that the differences between the extremes are very great. One example will serve as an illustration. In the early teaching the believer who has died spends the time between his death and the parousia in the grave; in the late teaching he spends this interval in heaven. These two ideas cannot be accommodated to each other as partial statements of a larger doctrine that embraces both. They represent the beginning and the end of an extended development in Paul's eschatological thought, a development which it is possible to follow step by step from the earliest to the latest letters.

The main outlines of this development have been traced before, notably by R. H. Charles.[8] More recently C. H. Dodd has pointed out the real significance of II Corinthians 1-9 in this connection.[9] In spite of older assertions to the contrary the recognition that such a development did take place has been steadily gaining. It has now reached the point where it can no longer be left out of account.

A similar development can be traced in Paul's Christology and in his legal theory. As we shall see, it followed an orderly course from the earliest to the latest letters. We shall also see that the changes in the three lines of development are closely related. Again a single example will serve as an illustration. II Corinthians 1-9, as we have noted, develops the doctrine of the simultaneous possession by the believer of an earthly body of flesh, which is wasting away, and the down payment of a heavenly body of spirit, which is being renewed every day. This is eschatological, and it represents a modification of the doctrine of I Corinthians, according to which the body of the believer will be changed from flesh to spirit in a moment at the parousia. But the new approach is not limited to the eschatology of II Corinthians 1-9; it also affects the Christology and the legal theory of the letter. In I Corinthians Paul had argued that the believer could hope to be transformed from flesh into spirit in a moment at the resurrection,

[8] *Eschatology* (2nd ed.; London, 1913).
[9] *New Testament Studies* (Manchester, 1953).

since Christ had undergone a similar change: "The last Adam became a life-giving spirit" (I Cor. 15:45). In II Corinthians 1–9 he announces that he has arrived at a new way of knowing Christ, and he has now been enabled to see that "God was in Christ reconciling the world to himself" (II Cor. 5:16,19); that is to say, the "life-giving" aspect of Christ's work had not begun with his assumption of a body of spirit at his resurrection but had been going on in his earthly life as well. The law too had once possessed an earthly and a spiritual nature: It was "carved in letters on stone," but it also "came with glory" (II Cor. 3:7); when the glory, the visible sign of its spiritual nature, departed, the law became of no effect. Thus the Christology and the legal theory of II Corinthians 1–9 are subtly but significantly affected by the new eschatology of the letter, which is based on the idea of simultaneous possession.

Everywhere we look in the letters we discover that the phenomena are similar. The letters are internally consistent; we seldom find a substantial modification in one line of teaching that is not reflected, to some extent at least, in the others. Sometimes all the implications of a particular change are not completely worked out in one letter but must wait to be developed in the next. This is particularly true of much of the doctrine of Galatians, which only achieves its final form in Romans. But nowhere are such modifications introduced at random. In the fabric of each letter the threads always make a complete pattern. There are no floating strands, and no loose ends.

The recognition that Paul's thought developed during the period in which the letters were written has implications for the question of authenticity. The four great letters, Romans, I and II Corinthians, and Galatians, are, in a sense, self-authenticating. But two of the other letters, II Thessalonians and Ephesians, have often been suspected of being spurious, and two more, I Thessalonians and Colossians, have somewhat less frequently fallen under the same condemnation. The principal grounds for this judgment, where it is made, are always the same: the letters in question do not conform closely to the doctrine and language of the great letters and therefore cannot be considered to be Pauline. More than a hundred years ago, for example, DeWette rejected Ephesians because, although it repeats many of the leading ideas of Colossians (which he took to be genuine) and of the other letters as well, it differs markedly from them in thought and style. DeWette therefore concluded that Ephesians was a compendium of quotations and paraphrases from the genuine letters, put together by a later Paulinist. Shortly after the time of DeWette, F. C. Baur rejected the two Thessalonian letters on the ground that their eschatological teaching is inconsistent with that of I Corinthians. The assumption of both men was that Paul always held to the same ideas on a given subject.

This belief has a long history. Unquestioned in antiquity and the Middle Ages, it was taken over by the early Protestant theologians, who based their theology to a large extent on Galatians and Romans and accommodated the other letters, including the Pastorals, to the doctrine of these two. The belief was inherited in turn by the historical critics, who took over the study of Paul where the theologians had left off. But the critics were to put it to a new use. Where the theologians had sought to fit all the pieces of the Pauline correspondence into a single system, the critics, whose main interest was history rather than doctrine, were intent on discovering the pieces that would not fit the system at all. Schleiermacher really started the critical movement as it affected the epistles by noticing that the synthesis of the theologians contained too much. His suspicions were first directed at I Timothy; it was not long before the other two Pastorals were recognized as post-Pauline as well. Once started, the movement rapidly gained momentum, with one letter after another being examined critically for signs of post-Pauline authorship.

In the earliest stages of the investigation the ground rules seem to have been flexible. A letter was tested by being compared with whatever other letters the critic believed to be genuine. But it was not long before the four great letters, Romans, I and II Corinthians, and Galatians, had been settled on as the standard with which all other writings must be compared. If one of the other letters conformed to these, it was pronounced genuine; if it differed from them, it was condemned. The extent of divergence which was allowable was left to the judgment of the individual scholar, hence there was much disagreement among the various verdicts rendered. But there was no significant disagreement regarding the basic assumption on which the whole enterprise rested. No one doubted that there was a more or less fixed body of doctrine that could be labeled as Pauline, and that this body of doctrine was adequately represented in the four great letters.

The assumption being what it was, the results it produced were inevitable. Of the remaining six letters of the original corpus, only two could confidently hope for a verdict of acquittal in almost any court. These were Philemon, which was too short to be amenable to the usual tests, and too appealing to be suspect anyway; and Philippians, which not only matched the great letters very closely in style and thought, but also contained a violent anti-Judaistic passage which made it practically as self-authenticating as Galatians itself. Two others were sometimes condemned but more often acquitted. These were I Thessalonians, which was both like and unlike I Corinthians, and Colossians, which was quite unlike the great letters in some ways, but not sufficiently so to persuade most critics of its spuriousness. The remaining two, II Thessalonians and Ephesians, resembled the great letters least of all; they were most frequently condemned.

But this, leaving out Philemon, which, as we noted, is too brief to have been indicted, is a chronological list. The Thessalonian epistles are almost certainly the earliest of the letters, and it can scarcely be questioned that Colossians and Ephesians date after Romans. In other words, in the case of the doubtful letters it seems to have been the date of composition that really determined whether a particular letter was to be regarded as genuine or spurious, and when we consider that three of the four great letters, I and II Corinthians and Romans, were produced in a relatively short period in the middle of Paul's literary career (and the fourth, Galatians, was also very probably produced at the same time), we begin to see that the unsuspected critical factor in the rejection of a disputed letter may well have been simply the distance that separated its composition from the letters of the middle period. Development and genuineness, in short, would seem to be opposite sides of the same coin. If the possibility of development is denied, the early and late letters do not look genuine; if development is admitted, there is less difficulty in recognizing them as the work of Paul.

But even the great letters show signs of development. We have already noticed such a change in their eschatological viewpoint. A similar change can be detected in connection with the antithesis between faith and works, usually taken as a hallmark of Paul's style and thought. This antithesis nowhere occurs in the Corinthian correspondence, but is fundamental to the thought of Galatians and Romans. No sober critic would conclude from this that the Corinthian correspondence is spurious; all would say that a change of situation and of subject had dictated a change of thought and style. Lightfoot himself, whose contribution to Pauline scholarship probably bulks larger than that of any other single critic, clearly saw such signs of change, and did not hesitate to use them as criteria for determining the order in which the letters were written. His dating of Galatians, for example, rests entirely on such arguments. Since Lightfoot's day more and more evidence of this kind has been amassed, until it is now possible to follow the progress of these changes through the whole correspondence.

We have begun, therefore, with the assumption that the lines of development which are traceable in the three longest letters, I Corinthians, II Corinthians 1–9, and Romans, probably extend into the others. Since these three letters can be shown to have been written in that order on grounds that have nothing to do with the development of ideas, they provide an objective determination of the direction in which the development was moving. Once this direction has been determined, it is relatively easy to arrange the other letters in the proper order. That done, it is possible to reconstruct the order of the principal events in Paul's missionary career. And finally it is possible, by comparing this reconstruction with the order of events in Acts, to discover where the Acts chronology has gone wrong, and to correct the error in a simple but completely satisfactory way.

PART I:

 THE EVIDENCE OF
THE LETTERS

1

I CORINTHIANS, II CORINTHIANS 1–9, AND ROMANS

The principal problem that faces us as we attempt to trace the development of Paul's thought is not merely to identify the various forms of a particular doctrine which the separate letters exhibit, but to determine the order in which these forms arose. We dare not assume at the outset that the changing forms represent an orderly development and then arrange the letters along the line which this development presumably followed. That would be to reason in a circle. In order to be sure that the changing forms represent a development at all, and are not just random variations in Paul's language, we must know first of all the order of at least some of the letters in which they occur, and this order must be determined on grounds that have nothing to do with the development of ideas.

Fortunately, it can be shown that the three longest letters, I Corinthians, II Corinthians 1–9, and Romans, were written in that order. The determination of this order does not depend on arguments from development but on the references which all three letters contain to an external event, the collection for the saints. Those in I Corinthians were written when the collection was just beginning, those in II Corinthians 1–9 while it was in mid-course, and those in Romans as it neared its end.

The earliest mention of the collection is found in I Corinthians.

> Now concerning the contribution for the saints: as I directed the churches of Galatia, so you also are to do. On the first day of every week, each of you is to put something aside and store it up, as he may prosper, so that contributions need not be made when I come. And when I arrive, I will send those whom you accredit by letter to carry your gift to Jerusalem. If it seems advisable that I should go also, they will accompany me.
>
> I will visit you after passing through Macedonia, for I intend to pass through Macedonia, and perhaps I will stay with you or even spend the winter, so that you may speed me on my journey, wherever I go. For I do not want to see you now just in passing; I hope to spend some time with you, if the Lord permits. But I will stay in Ephesus until Pentecost, for a wide door for effective work has opened to me, and there are many adversaries.
>
> When Timothy comes, see that you put him at ease among you, for he is doing the work of the Lord, as I am. So let no one despise him. Speed him on his way in peace, that he may return to me; for I am expecting him with the brethren (I Cor. 16:1–11).

I Corinthians did not contain Paul's first intimation to the members of the church in Corinth of the forthcoming collection. It assumes that they already knew the use to which the money was to be put (it was to provide relief for the poor among the Christians in Jerusalem), and it also assumes that they knew of Paul's intention to visit them in the near future. Presumably they had gained this information from a letter, now lost, which Paul had written to Corinth not long before I Corinthians. This Previous Letter to the Corinthians, as it is commonly called, is mentioned in I Corinthians: "I wrote to you in my letter not to associate with immoral men" (I Cor. 5:9). It is only natural to suppose that it had also contained the first news of the collection and of Paul's plan to visit Corinth before the money was forwarded to Jerusalem.

The details of Paul's plan, according to I Corinthians, were as follows: He would remain in Ephesus until Pentecost, after which he would set out for Corinth by way of Macedonia. Before his departure, however, he expected the return of Timothy and the brethren, who had already started to travel this route ahead of him, as advance agents, to prepare for the gathering of the collection. His plans for the remote future were less definite. He had not decided whether he would accompany the brethren when they went to Jerusalem to deliver the money, or remain in Corinth over the winter.

II Corinthians 1–9 takes up the story of the collection after Paul had left Ephesus and proceeded to Macedonia.

> We want you to know, brethren, about the grace of God which has been shown in the churches of Macedonia, for in a severe test of affliction, their abundance of joy and their extreme poverty have overflowed in a wealth of liberality on their part. For they gave according to their means, as I can testify, and beyond their means, of their own free will, begging us earnestly for the favor of taking part in the relief of the saints—and this, not as we expected, but first they gave themselves to the Lord and to us by the will of God. Accordingly we have urged Titus that as he had already made a beginning, he should also complete among you this gracious work . . . .
>
> Now it is superfluous for me to write to you about the offering for the saints, for I know your readiness, of which I boast about you to the people of Macedonia, saying that Achaia has been ready since last year; and your zeal has stirred up most of them. But I am sending the brethren so that our boasting about you may not prove vain in this case, so that you may be ready, as I said you would be, lest if some Macedonians come with me and find that you are not ready, we be humiliated—to say nothing of you—for being so confident. So I thought it necessary to urge the brethren to go on to you before me, and arrange in advance for this gift you have promised, so that it may be ready not as an exaction but as a willing gift (II Cor. 8:1–7; 9:1–5).

II Corinthians 1–9 was written not many weeks after I Corinthians. It is not easy to reconstruct the complete sequence of events that occurred in the interval between the two letters, but a partial outline of what took place can be worked out without difficulty.[1] To begin with,

1 A number of disputed points in connection with the course of events that intervened between the writing of I Corinthians and II Corinthians 1–9, notably the possibility of an "intermediate visit" to Corinth and the identification of the Severe Letter, will be discussed in the chapter on II Corinthians 10–13. All we are concerned with at present is to establish the order in which I Corinthians, II Corinthians 1–9, and Romans were written, and that in no way depends on the solution of these problems.

while he was still in Ephesus, Paul had discovered—how, we do not know, though possibly the news was brought to him by Timothy and the brethren on their return from Corinth—that I Corinthians had not been well received by those to whom it was addressed. Instead of persuading the Corinthian Christians to resolve their disputes, it had apparently made at least some of them turn against Paul. Paul had therefore dispatched Titus to Corinth with instructions to return by way of Macedonia and Troas, where he planned to meet him and learn whether his mission had succeeded. Paul describes this meeting, which took place in Macedonia, at some length in II Corinthians 1-9.

When I came to Troas to preach the gospel of Christ, a door was opened for me in the Lord; but my mind could not rest because I did not find my brother Titus there. So I took leave of them and went on to Macedonia. . . .

For even when we came into Macedonia, our bodies had no rest but we were afflicted at every turn—fighting without and fear within. But God, who comforts the downcast, comforted us by the coming of Titus, and not only by his coming but also by the comfort with which he was comforted in you, as he told us of your longing, your mourning, your zeal for me, so that I rejoiced still more. For even if I made you sorry with my letter, I do not regret it (though I did regret it), for I see that that letter grieved you, though only for a while. As it is, I rejoice, not because you were grieved, but because you were grieved into repenting; for you felt a godly grief, so that you suffered no loss through us. For godly grief produces a repentance that leads to salvation and brings no regret, but worldly grief produces death. For see what earnestness this godly grief has produced in you, what eagerness to clear yourselves, what indignation, what alarm, what longing, what zeal, what punishment! At every point you have proved yourselves guiltless in the matter. So although I wrote to you, it was not on account of the one who did the wrong, nor on account of the one who suffered the wrong, but in order that your zeal for us might be revealed to you in the sight of God. Therefore we are comforted.

And besides our own comfort we rejoiced still more at the joy of Titus, because his mind had been set at rest by you all. For if I have expressed to him some pride in you, I was not put to shame; but just as everything we said to you was true, so our boasting before Titus has proved true. And his heart goes out all the more to you, as he remembers the obedience of you all, and the fear and trembling with which you received him. I rejoice, because I have perfect confidence in you (II Cor. 2:12–13; 7:5–16).

Titus' mission, in short, had been an unqualified success. But the Macedonian Christians, meanwhile, had begged earnestly "for the favor of taking part in the relief of the saints" (II Cor. 8:14). Paul therefore decided to remain with them for a while longer and to send Titus back to Corinth, "that as he had already made a beginning, he should also complete . . . this gracious work" among the Corinthians (II Cor. 8:6). So much is clear from II Corinthians 1–9, which Titus took with him on his return to Corinth.

Romans was clearly written as the collection neared its end.

> I hope to see you in passing as I go to Spain, and to be sped on my journey there by you, once I have enjoyed your company for a little. At present, however, I am going to Jerusalem with aid for the saints. For Macedonia and Achaia have been pleased to make some contribution for the poor among the saints at Jerusalem; they were pleased to do it, and indeed they are in debt to them, for if the Gentiles have come to share in their spiritual blessings, they ought also to be of service to them in material blessings. When therefore I have completed this, and have delivered to them what has been raised, I shall go on by way of you to Spain; and I know that when I come to you I shall come in the fulness of the blessing of Christ (Rom. 15:24–29).

This can only have been written as the collection drew to a close, for it reveals that Macedonia, which had first offered to participate in the collection only a short time before, "begging us earnestly for the favor of taking part in the relief of the saints" (II Cor. 8:4), had now, along with Achaia, "been pleased to make some contribution for the poor among the saints at Jerusalem" (Rom. 15:26), and Paul is apparently on the point of setting out for Judea with the money. He has given up the idea of wintering in Corinth; instead, as soon as the delivery of the collection has been accomplished, he plans to proceed to Italy and then to Spain.

If, as we have seen, it is relatively easy to determine the order in which I Corinthians, II Corinthians 1–9, and Romans were written, it is scarcely less easy to discover that they were written within a period of a few months of each other, between the early spring and the late fall of the same year.

That I Corinthians was written in the spring of the year is evident from the line, "I will stay in Ephesus until Pentecost" (I Cor. 16:8). Strictly speaking, this line might have been written at any time within the year previous to the Pentecost mentioned, but when Paul speaks of his half-formed plan of spending the winter in Corinth, it is natural to assume that he means the winter immediately succeeding and not two winters hence. This inference is borne out by two indications in I Corinthians that it was penned around the time of Passover. "Christ, our paschal lamb," Paul writes, "has been sacrificed. Let us therefore celebrate the festival, not with the old leaven, the leaven of malice and evil, but with the unleavened bread of sincerity and truth" (I Cor. 5:7f.). The festival to which this refers can only be Passover. Again, in citing examples from the Old Testament, he writes as follows:

> I want you to know, brethren, that our fathers were all under the cloud, and all passed through the sea, and all were baptized into Moses in the cloud and in the sea, and all ate the same supernatural food and all drank the same supernatural drink. For they drank from the supernatural Rock which followed them, and the Rock was Christ. Nevertheless with most of them God was not pleased; for they were overthrown in the wilderness.
>
> Now these things are warnings for us, not to desire evil as they did. Do not be idolaters as some of them were; as it is written, "The people sat down to eat and drink and rose up to dance." We must not indulge in immorality as some of them did, and twenty-three thousand fell in a single day. We must not put the Lord to the test, as some of them did and were destroyed by serpents; nor grumble, as some of them did and were destroyed by the Destroyer. Now these things happened to them as a warning, but they were written down for our instruction, upon whom the end of the ages has come (I Cor. 10:1–11).

These examples were chosen, not merely because they were apt, but because they occur in the part of the history of Israel that follows immediately after the Passover, and Paul wished his readers to reflect, as they pondered them in the Passover season, that they applied to the situation in Corinth.[2] It is undoubtedly safe to conclude, therefore, that the letter was written in the early spring.

Evidence of a similar nature connects II Corinthians 1–9 with Pentecost, seven weeks later. The part of Exodus that underlies the long argument of the third chapter of that letter—the giving of the law to Moses (Exod. 20:1ff.)—is precisely the portion of Scripture suitable to be read at Pentecost, and it is only natural to assume that Paul chose to refer to it for the same reason that he chose to refer to the Passover when writing I Corinthians, namely, that he knew it would be in the minds of the Corinthians at the time when his letter was received.[3] The interval of seven weeks between the two festivals would allow ample time for the mission of Titus to Corinth before his meeting with Paul in Macedonia, and Paul's anxiety to hear Titus' report would account for his not having remained in Ephesus until Pentecost had actually arrived.[4]

Just how long afterward Romans was written it is impossible to say, but if the collection was completed before the beginning of winter, as Paul had planned all along that it should be, the month of October, after which the seas were closed to navigation, would seem to be the latest point at which it can be placed.

We have thus established—on grounds that have nothing to do with the development of ideas—the relative dates of I Corinthians, II Corinthians 1–9, and Romans, the three longest letters of Paul. As we

[2] "It was a custom common to both the Jews and Samaritans to date the events during the wandering through the wilderness, which their calendar placed between the Passover and the Feast of Weeks." J. van Goudoever, *Biblical Calendars* (Leyden, 1961), p. 130.

[3] Although the connection of the giving of the law with the celebration of the Feast of Weeks did not become a part of the official tradition until the middle of the second century (Seder Olam, A.D. 150), it is certainly as early as the Book of Jubilees, fragments of which have been found in the Qumran caves, and probably much older than that. See van Goudoever, *op. cit.*, pp. 139ff.

[4] The argument, sometimes put forward, that II Corinthians 8–9 must have been written a year later than I Corinthians, since it says that the Corinthians had begun to participate in the collection "a year ago" (II Cor. 8:10), and that they had "been ready since last year" (II Cor. 9:2), is based on the assumption that they had not offered to contribute to the collection until after the receipt of I Corinthians. What these passages really tell us, of course, is that the Corinthians had agreed to contribute to the collection and had started to set aside money for this purpose on the receipt of the Previous Letter, which may well have been dispatched during the previous calendar year.

have seen, they were written in a very short period of time, say between March at the earliest for I Corinthians and October at the latest for Romans, a period of eight months at the longest. They contain no clear indication of the year in which they were written, but although it is perfectly possible to determine the year, the question of absolute dates is best postponed until all the letters have been arranged in sequence. Our task now is to enlarge and extend the list which we have begun to construct.

2

THE PREVIOUS LETTER, THE
CORINTHIAN REPLY, AND
I CORINTHIANS

I Corinthians was preceded by an earlier letter of Paul to the Corinthians, now lost, which is conveniently designated as the Previous Letter to Corinth.[1] This letter is referred to in I Corinthians: "I wrote to you in my letter . . ." (I Cor. 5:9). Its answer, which may be called the Corinthian Reply, is also referred to in I Corinthians: "Now concerning the matters about which you wrote . . ." (I Cor. 7:1). These words introduce a series of discussions: on marriage, the eating of meat offered to idols, spiritual gifts, the resurrection, and the collection, each of which had been the subject of a question that the Corinthians had put to Paul in the Corinthian

---

[1] The following reconstruction of the contents of the Previous Letter and the Corinthian Reply was first proposed some years ago in a series of lectures to students, one of whom, J. C. Hurd, Jr., has since subjected it to rigorous scrutiny in his *The Origin of I Corinthians* (New York, 1965). The present chapter, therefore, need not be more than a summary of the original arguments and conclusions, which are fully developed and discussed on pp. 216–239 of Hurd's book.

Reply. We have only to study the answers, therefore, in order to discover what the questions were.[2]

It is usual to assume that the questions had arisen quite naturally out of the situations which had developed in Corinth during Paul's absence. Indeed, it is very possible to imagine that the leaders of the Corinthian church had found themselves unable to deal with new problems of doctrine and discipline in the growing community and submitted to Paul a list of topics on which they desired further instructions. Close examination of the answers themselves, however, reveals that this hypothesis is inadequate, for the questions are too specific to have arisen out of general situations. This is immediately apparent with regard to the question concerning the collection, which had been a request for detailed instructions for the gathering of the money. The Corinthians had written in effect, "We agree to contribute to the fund for the Jerusalem church as you requested. But how and when is the money to be gathered, what arrangements are to be made for its safe-keeping, and by whom is it to be delivered to Jerusalem?" These are the specific questions which Paul answers:

> On the first day of every week each of you is to put something aside and save, as he may prosper, so that contributions need not be made when I come. And when I arrive I will send those whom you accredit by letter to carry your gift to Jerusalem. If it seems advisable that I should go also, they will accompany me (I Cor. 16:2–4).

In other words, Paul's response is so specific as to reveal precisely what questions the Corinthians had put to him. And from the questions we may infer in turn how much information about the collection had been contained in the Previous Letter. In that letter Paul had informed the Corinthians that a collection was about to begin, or was under way, for the purpose of ministering to the need of the Jerusalem church. He had described the situation in Jerusalem and urged the Corinthians to participate in the offering. He had also mentioned that the churches of

---

[2] All but one of Paul's answers, that on the resurrection, are introduced by the formula $περὶ δέ$, but the discussion there clearly deals with an issue raised by the Corinthians and even cites the position taken by them: "How do some of you say that there is no resurrection of the dead?" (I Cor. 15:12).

Galatia were taking part in the effort, for this knowledge on the part of the Corinthians is assumed. But he had given no specific instructions for the gathering of the money or its being forwarded to Jerusalem. These matters remained to be dealt with, and the Corinthians had asked about them.

If it is relatively easy to see the relationship between the three letters with reference to the collection, it is equally easy to see a similar relationship reflected in the discussion of marriage, the eating of meat sacrificed to idols, spiritual gifts, and the resurrection. But although the relationship is similar, it is not precisely the same. For the Corinthian Reply, in dealing with these subjects, had not contained merely a series of questions about each of these topics, but a series of sharp objections to certain things that Paul had said in the Previous Letter. To take the letters in the order in which they were written, Paul, in speaking of marriage in the Previous Letter, had said, in effect, "Normal monogamous marriage in which both partners are Christians must be the rule for all the churches. Therefore let every Christian man take a wife who is a Christian, and every Christian woman take a Christian husband." To this the Corinthians, who had attempted, without much success it would seem, to adopt a rule of celibacy, replied, "We hold to the standard that it is well for a man not to touch a woman, which is a higher standard than yours; and we have no intention of abandoning our position in favor of your new rule, which would mean that the unmarried and widows would have to marry, that Christians already married to pagans would have to divorce their present spouses in order to marry Christians, and that our 'spiritual couples,' who have vowed to remain permanently betrothed, would have to break their vows in order to marry."

It is these objections that Paul meets in I Corinthians. He concedes at the outset that it is, as the Corinthians have maintained, well for a man not to touch a woman. But because their inability to live up to this standard has led to promiscuity, the Corinthian Christians should marry. The unmarried and widows, if they can remain continent, he excepts from the rule, but only if they can control themselves. Christians married to pagans are not to divorce their spouses, and if a pagan husband should divorce his Christian wife, she may not remarry during his lifetime. "Spiritual couples" should marry if they cannot live up to their vows of celibacy. Marriage in such cases is not a sin. The seventh chapter of I Corinthians, in other words, does not answer questions; it meets the Corinthians' objections to the position which Paul had taken in the Previous Letter.

A similar exchange lies behind the discussion of the eating of meat sacrificed to idols (I Cor. 8:1–11:1). In the Previous Letter, Paul had said, in effect, "Christians must not eat meat that has been sacrificed to idols." The Corinthians had replied, "As Christians we all possess knowledge that an idol has no real existence, since there is no God but one. Therefore we cannot be injured by eating meat that has been offered to a so-called 'god' that is only an idol. Furthermore, to apply your rule would mean that we would have to shun the public market, since much of the meat sold there comes from sacrificial animals. And even then we would not be safe; when we were invited to dinner by an unbeliever, we would have to ask the host whether the meat he was serving had come from the temple or not. At this rate we would not be able to eat meat at all."

It is these objections that Paul meets in I Corinthians. All Christians, he concedes, have knowledge, and all agree that an idol has no real existence, since there is only one God. But the basic motive of Christian conduct is not knowledge, but love. And love dictates that the Christian must sometimes refrain from exercising his liberty if by the exercise of that liberty he may cause the downfall of a weaker brother who has not yet fully grasped the knowledge that all Christians are supposed to possess.

Further, as regards idols themselves, while it is undoubtedly true that they have no real existence, their worship is inspired by demons, whose existence is very real indeed, and the man who eats food offered to an idol is actually partaking of the table of demons. Christians cannot partake of the table of the Lord and the table of demons. To the Corinthians' captious objections about the difficulties attendant upon buying meat in the public market and eating meat at dinner parties Paul replies, somewhat drily, that unless someone makes a point of identifying a particular piece of meat as having been offered in sacrifice, it may safely be eaten. In eating and drinking, as in everything else, Christians must do all things to the glory of God. Once again, I Corinthians is not answering questions; it is meeting the Corinthians' objections to a position which Paul had taken in the Previous Letter.

Still another exchange of the same kind can be seen to lie behind the discussion of spiritual gifts (I Cor. 12:1–14:40). Paul in the Previous Letter had counseled the Corinthians not to encourage speaking in tongues, since the practice had led to excesses in their worship, but, rather, to encourage the form of reasoned utterance known as prophecy. The Corinthians, with some justice it would seem, had replied that Paul himself spoke in tongues, and that they had had his word for it in the beginning that their speaking in tongues was the outward and visible sign of the gift of the Spirit; if Paul had changed his mind on this point, they had not. In I Corinthians, Paul replied to the Corinthians' objections by arguing that although speaking in tongues was undoubtedly a gift of the Spirit, it was not the only such gift. In fact, of the many gifts of the Spirit, it was the least important, except for the gift that depended on it, that of interpreting what was said in a tongue. Paul's argument is long and detailed, and it rises to sublime heights in the famous passage beginning, "If I speak in the tongues of men and of angels, but have not love, I am a noisy gong or a clanging cymbal" (I Cor. 13:1). But, once again, every line of it is designed to meet the Corinthians' objections to the position he had taken in the Previous Letter. Even the thirteenth chapter, so easily excerpted and treated as an independent rhapsody, is shot through with irony as it details the characteristics of those Christians who have the gift of tongues, the understanding of all mysteries and all knowledge, and faith that can remove mountains, and yet lack love; they are impatient, unkind, jealous, boastful, arrogant, rude, insisting on their own way, irritable, resentful, rejoicing at wrong—in short, grown men who have not yet given up childish ways. It is all part and parcel of the same argument, designed to meet the objections which the Corinthians had raised.

Before proceeding to a consideration of the discussion of resurrection in the fifteenth chapter, it will be helpful to notice what the three preceding exchanges have had in common. In each case Paul has tried to correct an abuse which he has discovered to exist in the Corinthian church. He has done this by attempting to lay down rules of conduct which the Corinthians are to follow. They are to contract normal marriages between members of the church, they are to refrain from eating meat that has been offered in pagan sacrifices, and they are to discourage speaking in tongues in worship and to encourage reasoned utterance instead.

In each instance the Corinthians have objected to the rules which Paul has laid down. And in each instance their objections would seem to have been based on the same grounds: first, that the new rules ran counter to the accepted principles on which they had been operating from the beginning; and second, that these rules advocated a departure from the standard of conduct which Paul had previously taught them not only by precept but also by example. For Paul, on his first visit to Corinth, had not only discouraged the Christians from marrying by reason of the supposed shortness of the time; he had also pointed to himself as an example of the celibate life. He had not only told the Corinthians that they need not observe the laws regarding clean and unclean foods; he had also openly broken these laws himself by eating with Gentiles. He had not only taught his new converts that their ability to speak in tongues was the outward and visible sign of the reception of the Spirit, and hence of their acceptance by God; he had also spoken with tongues, perhaps more than anyone else. In I Corinthians we find him having to defend himself against these charges.

> To the unmarried and the widows I say that it is well for them to remain single as I do. But if they cannot exercise self-control, they should marry (I Cor. 7:8–9).
> For though I am free from all men, I have made myself a slave to all, that I might win the more. To the Jews I became as a Jew, in order to win Jews; to those under the law I became as one under the law—though not being myself under the law—that I might win those under the law. To those outside the law I became as one outside the law—not being without law toward God but under the law of Christ—that I might win those outside the law (I Cor. 9:19–22).
> I thank God that I speak in tongues more than you all; nevertheless, in church I would rather speak five words with my

> mind, in order to instruct others, than ten thousand words in a
> tongue (I Cor. 14:18–19).

The Corinthians, in other words, had a point when they objected
to the Previous Letter. The new rules of conduct which it laid down
not only represented a modification of the teaching they had previously received from Paul but also a departure from the example
which he himself had set.

Why then had the new rules been necessary? The reason is
obvious to even the casual reader of I Corinthians. The situation in
Corinth had changed. The attempt to make celibacy the ideal for
all Christians had failed, and its failure had opened the door to
promiscuity. The attempt to apply the rule that all meat is clean
meat to all situations had led some Corinthian Christians, who had
learned from Paul that idols had no real existence, to think they were
free even to participate in banquets in pagan temples. And the belief
that speaking in tongues was the principal manifestation of the Spirit
had resulted in its being encouraged in worship to the point where
an outsider or an unbeliever, if he should enter, could only conclude
that the Corinthian Christians were mad.

A large measure of responsibility for these developments, needless to say, rests with the Corinthians themselves. Had they been
wiser, more experienced, and more reflective, they would have fore-
seen the dangers into which they were running and taken steps to
avoid them. But unfortunately they appear to have been singularly
ill-equipped by nature and education to deal with their own situation,
and the low esteem in which they seem to have held sober utterance
and reasoned argument served to make it unlikely that they would
discover for themselves the principles of conduct that applied in their
present circumstances.

But if the Corinthians were poorly equipped to solve their own
problems, it must also be admitted that they had been poorly prepared to meet them, for Paul had limited his teaching in Corinth
to the barest essentials of the faith: "But I, brethren," he writes, "could
not address you as spiritual men, but as men of the flesh, as babes
in Christ. I fed you with milk, not solid food; for you were not ready

for it" (I Cor. 3:1–2). Of the Corinthians' limitations there can be no doubt, and these had unquestionably left Paul no choice but to adapt his instruction to their capacity to learn. But the content of that instruction was also influenced by another factor, namely, Paul's belief, at the time of his first visit to Corinth, that the parousia was imminent. The Corinthians, together with the rest of mankind, he believed, were living in the last days of the present age. They had no need, therefore, of an elaborate system of ethics designed to cover every situational problem that might arise over a long period of years.

This is perfectly clear from I Corinthians. Not only had the Corinthians been discouraged from contracting new marriages and founding families because of the shortness of the time, but they had also apparently been left with no definite instructions as to the degree to which they might continue to participate in the pagan culture from which they had come, and they had certainly not been sufficiently warned against the dangers of laxity in church organization and discipline or of out-and-out disorderliness in the conduct of worship. Paul's original ethical instructions to the Corinthians may have been perfectly adequate for the very brief period that he then expected to elapse before the parousia; they were totally unsuited to serve for an indefinite time, since they failed to take cognizance of the changes that time was bound to work in the situation in Corinth and in the Corinthians themselves.

It was precisely this failure to take the future into account that gave rise to the problem with which the fifteenth chapter of I Corinthians deals. The problem had originally arisen when, with the passage of time, natural deaths began to occur among the members of the Corinthian church. Paul had not previously prepared the Corinthians for this eventuality. On the contrary, he had assured them that they would all see the day of the Lord and share in the joys of the kingdom. Now, however, it was apparent that this very simple teaching was in need of expansion and elaboration. How did he go about this?

Here we are not forced to rely on a hypothesis. It is not a question of what Paul would, or should, or must have said to a church in which such a problem had arisen. The identical problem had arisen in the church in Thessalonica after Paul's first visit there, and since we possess the letter in which he dealt with it, we know exactly what he did in fact say. To the Thessalonians he wrote:

> But we would not have you ignorant, brethren, concerning those who are asleep, that you may not grieve as others do who have no hope. For since we believe that Jesus died and rose again, even so through Jesus, God will bring with him those who have fallen asleep. For this we declare to you by the word of the Lord, that we who are alive, who are left until the coming of the Lord, shall not precede those who have fallen asleep. For the Lord himself will descend from heaven with a cry of command, with the archangel's call, and with the sound of the trumpet of God. And the dead in Christ will rise first; then we who are alive, who are left, shall be caught up together with them in the clouds to meet the Lord in the air; and so we shall always be with the Lord (I Thess. 4:13–18).

In this passage Paul is telling the Thessalonians that there is one aspect of the Christian hope of which he does not wish them to be ignorant (implying that they have in fact been ignorant of it until now). Although the normal expectation of Christians is that they will live until the parousia, they will not have an advantage over those Christians who have died. For when the Lord descends from heaven on the last day, the Christian dead will be raised first, in a special resurrection (not to be confused with the general resurrection at the end of the Messianic age), and so all Christians will be together with the Lord.

It is precisely this modification in the original teaching, which Paul must have communicated to the Corinthians as well as to the Thessalonians, that the Corinthians had objected to in their reply to the Previous Letter. They had written, in effect, "You told us nothing about a special resurrection of Christians at the parousia on your first visit. On the contrary you told us that all Christians would live until the day of the Lord. We cannot believe in such a resurrection as you now tell us will take place. If the dead are to be raised for life in the Messianic kingdom on earth, with what kind of body will they come? Will they not be far gone in decay?"

I Corinthians meets these objections one by one. Paul cannot deny that on his first visit he had made no mention of the special resurrection of Christians. But he reminds his readers that the gospel he had preached was based on the fact of the resurrection of Christ.

> Now I would remind you, brethren, in what terms I preached to you the gospel, which you received, in which you stand, by which you are being saved, if you hold it fast—unless you believed in vain. For I delivered to you as of first importance what I also received, that Christ died for our sins in accordance with the scriptures, that he was buried, that he was raised on the third day in accordance with the scriptures, and that he appeared to Cephas, then to the twelve. Then he appeared to more than five hundred brethren at one time, most of whom are still alive, though some have fallen asleep. Then he appeared to James, then to all the apostles. Last of all, as to one untimely born, he appeared also to me. . . . Now if Christ is preached as raised from the dead, how can some of you say that there is no resurrection of the dead? (I Cor. 15:1–8,12).

A Christian, in other words, cannot deny the possibility of resurrection without denying the very gospel by which he was converted.

Further, Christ in his resurrection was "the first fruits of those who have fallen asleep" (I Cor. 15:20). This means that all will eventually be raised, but there is an order in which they will come; Christ has been the "first fruits," then will follow "those who belong to Christ," and not until the end of the Messianic reign, "when he delivers the kingdom to God the Father after destroying every rule and every authority and power," will the process be complete. "For he must reign until he has put all his enemies under his feet. The last enemy to be destroyed is death" (I Cor. 15:23–26).

The Corinthians, Paul argues, cannot be completely ignorant of this promise of resurrection, else why should they practice baptism on behalf of the dead? "If the dead are not raised at all, why are people baptized on their behalf?" (I Cor. 15:29).

"But some one will ask," he continues, " 'How are the dead raised? With what kind of body do they come?' " (I Cor. 15:35). This question, which the Corinthians undoubtedly had raised either explicitly or by implication, Paul proceeds to answer in terms of popular philosophy. He begins with an example. "What you sow," he writes, "does not come to life unless it dies" (I Cor. 15:36). The process to which he refers is one in which a whole plant—roots, stem, leaves, and flowers—wastes away, leaving only a seed from which a new plant comes into being, and it clearly involves the discarding of the old matter of which the parent plant was composed and the taking up of new matter for the elaboration of the new plant, for the seed does not contain enough matter to constitute the full-grown plant to which it gives rise: "What you sow is not the body which is to be, but a bare kernel, perhaps of wheat or of some other grain" (I Cor. 15:37). Where then does "the body which is to be" come from? It comes from God, who has ordained the processes of nature; and it is always a body of the proper species: "But God gives it a body as he has chosen, and to each kind of seed its own body" (I Cor. 15:38). In other words, although the matter that made up the old plant is not preserved in the new plant, the form of the old plant does survive in the new.

Having thus introduced the distinction between form and matter, Paul now proceeds to point out that there are gradations to be observed within both material and formal classifications. Flesh, for example, is a material classification, but not all flesh is alike. Human flesh, animal flesh, bird flesh, and fish flesh are different, depending on the kinds of bodies in which they occur. Similarly body is a formal classification, but not all bodies are alike; celestial bodies differ from terrestrial bodies. Even within the subclass of celestial bodies there are gradations depending on the matter of which the various bodies are composed. The sun has more "glory" (always in Paul thought of as the visible aspect of a material substance) than the moon; the moon more than the stars; and one star more than another star.

The purpose of this argument is to allow Paul to draw a distinction between resurrection of the flesh, which his opponents had understood him to mean, and resurrection of the body, which he actually had meant. He proceeds, "So it is with the resurrection of the dead. What is sown is perishable, what is raised is imperishable. . . . It is sown a physical body, it is raised a spiritual body" (I Cor. 15:42,44). The resurrection body, in other words, will not be made of flesh, it will be made of spirit.

But if the dead are to be raised with bodies composed of spirit, what of the Christians who have not died at all before the parousia? Will they still be required to wear their old bodies of flesh? Not at all.

> Lo! I tell you a mystery. We shall not all sleep, but we shall all be changed, in a moment, in the twinkling of an eye, at the last trumpet. For the trumpet will sound, and the dead will be raised imperishable, and we shall be changed. For this perishable nature must put on the imperishable, and this mortal nature must put on immortality. When the perishable puts on the imperishable, and the mortal puts on immortality, then shall come to pass the saying that is written: "Death is swallowed up in victory" (I Cor. 15:51–55).

Here Paul has carried the expansion of his teaching one step further than he had taken in I Thessalonians. Those who live until the parousia, he says, will not remain in the flesh, but at the very moment when the dead are being raised with new bodies made of spirit, the living will be similarly transformed. Their bodies of flesh will suddenly cease to exist, having been replaced by bodies of spirit like those of the resurrected dead. Thus all Christians will possess bodies of the same kind, and death will have been "swallowed up in victory." It is a masterful exposition of a difficult doctrine, but once again it is clear that it was undertaken, not to answer questions, but to meet the Corinthians' objections to what Paul had written in the Previous Letter.

Thus far we have limited our examination to the series of discussions which is introduced in I Corinthians with the words: "Now concerning the matters about which you wrote" (I Cor. 7:1). Another topic with which the Previous Letter dealt, however, is mentioned earlier in I Corinthians.

> I wrote to you in my letter not to associate with immoral men; not at all meaning the immoral of this world, or the greedy and robbers, or idolaters, since then you would need to go out of the world. But rather I wrote to you not to associate with any one who bears the name of brother if he is guilty of immorality or greed, or is an idolater, reviler, drunkard, or robber—not even to eat with such a one. For what have I to do with judging out-

siders? Is it not those inside the church whom you are to judge? (I Cor. 5:9–13).

By an odd chance, a fragment of the part of the Previous Letter to which this refers seems to have been accidentally preserved by being copied into II Corinthians by mistake. It reads as follows:

> Do not be mismated with unbelievers. For what partnership have righteousness and iniquity? Or what fellowship has light with darkness? What accord has Christ with Belial? Or what has a believer in common with an unbeliever? What agreement has the temple of God with idols? For we are the temple of the living God; as God said, "I will live in them and move among them, and I will be their God, and they shall be my people. Therefore come out from them, and be separate from them, says the Lord, and touch nothing unclean; then I will welcome you, and I will be a father to you, and you shall be my sons and daughters, says the Lord Almighty."

> Since we have these promises, beloved, let us cleanse ourselves from every defilement of body and spirit, and make holiness perfect in the fear of God (II Cor. 6:14–7:1).

This passage does not belong where it occurs in II Corinthians, and it is all but universally identified as having come from the Previous Letter. If this is correct—and there seems to be every reason for believing that it is—then the exchange can be reconstructed with ease. Paul, in the Previous Letter, had forbidden the Corinthians to have dealings with immoral men and idolaters. The Corinthians had objected that to comply with this ruling they "would need to go out of the world," since such men were everywhere. Paul then explained in I Corinthians that he had not been referring to pagans but to nominal Christians who were immoral and idolatrous. Once again the relationship between I Corinthians and the Previous Letter is seen to be the same. Paul had taken a position in the Previous Letter, the Corinthians had objected to it in the Corinthian Reply, and Paul had met the objection in I Corinthians.

We are now in a position to summarize the foregoing reconstruction. The Previous Letter had said at least the following things:

1. Have nothing to do with immoral men and idolaters.
2. Let every Christian man have a Christian wife, and every Christian woman a Christian husband.
3. Do not eat meat offered to idols.
4. Do not permit unlimited speaking in tongues but, rather, encourage prophesying.
5. Do not mourn for the Christian dead; they will be resurrected at the parousia.
6. There will be a collection for the poor in the church in Jerusalem; it is hoped that Corinth will contribute.

The Corinthians had objected to all except the last of these. Their replies had come under the following headings:

1. If we are to avoid immoral men and idolaters we shall have to go out of the world.
2. We hold to the principle that it is well for a man not to touch a woman.
3. We know that an idol has no real existence, since there is only one God.
4. Speaking in tongues is the sign of the gift of the Spirit.
5. We have never previously heard of a special resurrection of Christians at the parousia, and we cannot believe in such a resurrection. With what kind of body will they come?
6. We agree to contribute to the collection. How are we to proceed?

Paul's answers to each of these points are found in I Corinthians.

This exchange of letters cannot have occupied more than a few months at most. Its references to the collection alone indicate that. On the other hand, it took place during the winter, when travel was difficult and the delivery of letters was slow. As we have seen, II Corinthians 1–9 looks back on the collection as having been in progress since "a year ago," and while it would certainly be wrong to insist that that expression must be interpreted with literal exactness, it may well indicate that the Previous Letter was written as early as the previous fall.

For our present purpose, which is to establish the order in which the letters were written, the most important consequence of the reconstruction of the outline of the Previous Letter and the Corinthian Reply is that it enables us to see the relationship between the Previous Letter and I Thessalonians, and thus to assign a date to the latter.

3

I THESSALONIANS

I Thessalonians is invariably treated as an easy letter to date, since the book of Acts seems to provide a completely satisfactory occasion for its composition shortly after Paul's arrival in Corinth on his first visit. It is the purpose of the present chapter to show that the letter cannot have been written on that occasion but must have been written between Paul's departure from Corinth and the writing of I Corinthians, at about the same time as the writing of the Previous Letter.

We have already seen that the eschatological teaching of I Corinthians was developed to meet the Corinthians' objections to the teaching of the Previous Letter. This teaching had contained a modification of the older and simpler teaching that Paul had imparted to his converts on his first visit to Corinth. The old teaching had been that all Christians would live until the parousia. The modification, introduced in the Previous Letter because some Christians had meanwhile died, was that these would be raised at the parousia. The same modification, as we have also seen, was communicated to the church in Thessalonica in I Thessalonians, and for the same reason. Indeed the eschatological teaching of I Thessalonians was the same in every detail as that of the Previous Letter.

This fact is fatal to the theory that I Thessalonians was written before Paul left Corinth at the end of his first visit, for it is inconceivable that he should have communicated such a modification to the Thessalonians, while continuing to impart to the Corinthians the older eschatological teaching, to which he no longer subscribed. It hardly seems possible to escape from this conclusion. It cannot be argued, for example, that Paul may well have imparted the newer teaching to the Corinthians during his first visit to Corinth, since it is quite clear that their first objection to the modification, when they did hear about it in the Previous Letter, had been that Paul had *not* told them of it originally. Nor can it be argued that the two churches were in different stages of development and therefore were in need of different levels of instruction, for what is reflected here is not merely a local problem that could be dealt with in isolation; it is a general problem that affected all parts of the church equally. The solution which Paul gives, moreover, represents not merely an adaptation of the teaching to the peculiar needs of a particular place, but a considerable change in his own thinking. In plain words, when I Thessalonians was written, Paul no longer believed that all Christians would live until the parousia. Therefore it is out of the question to suppose that the letter could have been written while he was still pretending to the Corinthian church, no matter what its stage of development, that he still did believe this. I Thessalonians, in short, cannot have been written before Paul left Corinth at the end of his first visit.

Nor can it have been written after I Corinthians, for as we have seen, I Corinthians contains a further expansion of the modification in question, and it is inconceivable that Paul, having discovered the necessity for this expansion, should subsequently have omitted it from I Thessalonians. I Thessalonians, therefore, can only have been written after Paul's departure from Corinth and before the writing of I Corinthians. It thus falls in the same period as the Previous Letter.

That it was actually contemporaneous with the Previous Letter becomes even clearer as we examine another of its important sections. In the Previous Letter Paul had told the Corinthians that normal monogamous marriage between Christians was to be the rule of the church. One of the Corinthians' objections to this rule was that it marked a departure from their former rule of celibacy, which they considered a higher standard of Christian conduct, and Paul had answered this objection in I Corinthians. It is important to note that Paul in the Previous Letter was not merely recommending the maintenance of existing marriages but the contracting of new marriages. His reason was clear. The attempt to adopt the rule of celibacy had failed, and the failure had given rise to promiscuity.

This is precisely the counsel which Paul gives to the Thessalonians, and for the same reason:

> For this is the will of God, your consecration: that you abstain from immorality; that each one of you know how to take a wife for himself in consecration and honor, not in the passion of lust like heathen who do not know God; that no man transgress, and wrong his brother in this matter, because the Lord is an avenger in all these things, as we solemnly forewarned you. For God has not called us for uncleanness, but in consecration. Therefore whoever disregards this, disregards not men but God, who gives his Holy Spirit to you (I Thess. 4:3–8).

Once again the recognition of this fact makes it clear that I Thessalonians cannot have been written before Paul left Corinth at the end of his first visit, for it is unthinkable that he should have continued to encourage the Corinthians to remain unmarried after he had laid down the rule of monogamous marriage for the Thessalonians. As was the case in connection with the modification in Paul's eschatological teaching, this does not represent merely a limited solution to a local problem; it reflects a significant change in Paul's own thinking. When I Thessalonians was written, Paul no longer believed that Christians should refrain from marriage, and it is out of the question to suppose that the letter could have been written while he was still encouraging any local church to observe this rule. The letter cannot have been written, therefore, before he left Corinth.

A third objection to the traditional early date of I Thessalonians is that the letter does not sound as though it was being addressed to a church which had been founded only a very short time before. It seems to have been addressed to a maturing community. The problem of the death of Christians, for example, can hardly have assumed sufficient proportions to require a modification in Paul's eschatology in a church that had been in existence for only a few weeks, or even a few months. Similarly, Paul's admonition to watchfulness, since "the day of the Lord will come like a thief in the night" (I Thess. 5:2), is addressed in I Thessalonians to people who are saying, "There is peace and security" (I Thess. 5:3). This reflects a time after the first vivid expectation of the parousia had faded, and the Christian hope had lost something of its immediacy. Again, his advice, "Do not quench the Spirit, do not despise prophesying, but test everything" (I Thess. 5:19–21), is similar to his advice to the Corinthians that they should now give less prominence to speaking in tongues, the typical religious expression of the primitive convert, and more prominence to reasoned utterance. And to this is related Paul's concern for the stability of the internal organization of the church: "But we beseech you, brethren, to respect those who labor among you and admonish you, and to esteem them very highly in love because of their work" (I Thess. 5:12–13). The same concern is expressed in almost the same terms in I Corinthians: "Now, brethren, you know that the household of Stephanas were the first converts in Achaia, and they have devoted themselves to the service of the saints; I urge you to be subject to such men and to every fellow worker and laborer" (I Cor. 16:15–16).

Even more revealing is the following:

> But concerning love of the brethren you have no need to have any one write to you, for you yourselves have been taught by God to love one another; and indeed you do love all the brethren throughout Macedonia. But we exhort you, brethren, to do so more and more, to aspire to live quietly, to mind your own affairs, and to work with your hands, as we charged you; so that you may command the respect of outsiders, and be dependent on nobody (I Thess. 4:9–12).

The underlying theme of this whole section of I Thessalonians is that the Christian community should look upon itself as a stable social institution. Christians are to fulfill the normal obligations of members of society by being orderly, industrious, and self-supporting. The motives which Paul ascribes to this sort of behavior are worthy of remark. Christians, he says, are to be guided by practical conventions, not merely to avoid falling into poverty, but also to make a favorable impression on "those outside." Paul's concern for the institutional stability of the church, in other words, includes a consideration of its place in the larger social pattern. Christians cannot ignore the existence of the world around them, nor can they disregard the impression which their behavior makes on the unconverted.

In this respect I Thessalonians is very similar to I Corinthians, in that many of the practical discussions in that letter touch on the question of the relationship of the Christian community to the world outside. This consideration is prominent in the discussion of the problem of eating meat that has been offered to idols (I Cor. 8:1ff.), and even more striking is its place in Paul's discussion of speaking in tongues. He says, "If the whole church comes together and all speak in tongues, and uninstructed or unconverted men come in, will they not say that you are mad?" (I Cor. 14:23). The church, in other words, must have a concern for the impression it makes on the world. It cannot consider itself a community which can disregard its ties with the larger society of which it is a part.

All these attitudes reflect a concern for the stability of the church as a continuing institution in the world, and they belong, not to the very earliest days of Paul's ministry, when he clearly thought that the parousia could not be delayed, but to a later stage of his development, when he was beginning to realize that the end was probably not going to come as soon as he had once thought.

The indications, therefore, all point in the same direction. I Thessalonians cannot have been written before Paul's departure from Corinth, and it cannot have been written after I Corinthians. Moreover, its similarities with the Previous Letter are so close and so extensive as to make it virtually certain that the two writings were composed very close together in time.

But if I Thessalonians was not written before Paul's departure from Corinth, when was it written? There is evidence in the letter that bears on this question, and it supports the conclusion that has already been suggested, namely, that it was written after Paul's departure from Corinth. This evidence has to do with Paul's movements just prior to the writing of I Thessalonians. He writes:

> But since we were taken away from you, brethren, for a short time, in person not in heart, we endeavored the more eagerly and with great desire to see you face to face; because we wanted to come to you—I, Paul, again and again—but Satan hindered us. . . . Therefore when we could bear it no longer, we were willing to be left behind at Athens alone, and we sent Timothy, our brother and God's servant in the gospel of Christ, to establish you in your faith and to exhort you, that no one be moved by these afflictions. For when we were with you, we told you beforehand that we were to suffer affliction; just as it has come to pass, and as you know. For this reason, when I could bear it no longer, I sent that I might know your faith, for fear that somehow the tempter had tempted you and that our labor would be in vain. But now that Timothy has come to us from you, and has brought us the goods news of your faith and love and reported that you always remember us kindly and long to see us, as we long to see you—for this reason, brethren, in all our distress and affliction we have been comforted about you through your faith; for now we live, if you stand fast in the Lord (I Thess. 2:17–18; 3:1–8).

A great deal of information is contained in this passage. It tells us that since leaving Thessalonica Paul had wanted again and again to return, but he had always been prevented. Most recently the obstacle in the way of his coming had been a persecution, which apparently took place in Athens, and he was concerned that the Thessalonians should not lose confidence in him because of it. He had told them beforehand, he reminds them, that persecution was to be his lot, and what had happened to him had only borne out his earlier predictions. Since he could not come to Thessalonica himself, however, he had sent Timothy in his place, while he had remained behind in Athens, probably with Silvanus. When Timothy rejoined him, bringing a comforting report of the Thessalonians' steadfast faith and love, he had written I Thessalonians.

The implication of the passage as regards Paul's movements is plain. He was not, as is usually inferred from Acts, moving away from

Thessalonica but attempting to move toward it. He had, in fact, made repeated attempts to return to it since his departure. And it was only when he realized that he was not going to succeed in returning that he had sent Timothy. This can only mean that the stay in Athens to which I Thessalonians refers did not occur at the beginning of Paul's missionary activity in Achaia, before his first visit to Corinth, but at the end of it, as he was attempting to retrace his steps from Achaia to Macedonia and eventually to Antioch.

I Thessalonians, then, was written before I Corinthians. It was not written as early as it is usually dated on the evidence of Acts, but it is still clearly earlier than the three great letters of the middle period. In this position it gives us a fourth point in the series which we are endeavoring to establish, and our list of letters in the order in which they were written now reads: I Thessalonians, I Corinthians, II Corinthians 1–9, and Romans.

4

ESCHATOLOGY, CHRISTOLOGY, AND THE LAW IN I CORINTHIANS AND II CORINTHIANS 1–9

I Thessalonians, the Previous Letter to Corinth, and I Corinthians reveal that in the period of Paul's life when these letters were written his eschatological thought was undergoing a significant development. Three stages of this development can be traced. In the earliest stage, before the writing of I Thessalonians and the Previous Letter, he had taught that the parousia of Christ was imminent, and he had given his converts to understand that they could expect to live until it occurred. In the second stage, represented by I Thessalonians and the Previous Letter, he had had to deal with the problem raised by the failure of the parousia to take place as soon as he had expected, and by the occurrence of natural deaths among the members of the church. He had met this problem by explaining that the Christian dead would not be deprived of the fulfillment of their hope of witnessing the parousia and sharing in the Messianic reign, but would be raised from the dead in a special resurrection of Christians at the sound of the trumpet that would herald the coming of the

Lord. In the third stage, represented by I Corinthians, he had explained further that in this resurrection the dead would be raised with bodies made of spirit, and that the bodies of the living would be changed from flesh to spirit at the same moment. Thus all would possess bodies of the same kind.

When we turn from I Corinthians to II Corinthians 1–9 we discover that Paul's eschatological thought had continued to develop in the interval between the two letters.

The most readily observable difference between the eschatology of I Corinthians and that of II Corinthians 1–9 is that whereas in the first letter the change from the body of flesh to the body of spirit, both in the resurrection of the dead and in the transformation of the living, is thought of as instantaneous, happening "in a moment, in the twinkling of an eye, at the last trumpet" (I Cor. 15:52), in the second letter it is thought of as a gradual process, which begins in the believer at his conversion, when he "turns to the Lord" (II Cor. 3:16) and receives "the down payment of the Spirit" (II Cor. 5:5), and continues throughout his whole earthly life, as he progresses "from one degree of glory to another" (II Cor. 3:18). As we have already remarked, the shift in Paul's viewpoint in this regard is precisely reflected in the shift in the tense of the verb with which he describes the transformation. In I Corinthians he writes, "We shall all be changed" (I Cor. 15:51); in II Corinthians 1–9 he writes, "We all . . . are being changed" (II Cor. 3:38).

Paul describes the process in detail. It begins, as we have said, with conversion. Thereafter it progresses steadily:

> Now the Lord is the Spirit, and where the Spirit of the Lord is, there is freedom. And we all, with unveiled face, reflecting the glory of the Lord, are being changed into his likeness from one degree of glory to another; for this comes from the Lord who is the Spirit (II Cor. 3:17–18).

The ever-increasing measure of spirit which the Christian receives in this way is not visible to the observer, since the body of flesh covers and hides it. "We have this treasure in earthen vessels," Paul explains, "to show that the transcendent power belongs to God and not to us" (II Cor. 4:7). But the body of flesh is in process of wasting away, and when at last it is completely done away with, it will be entirely replaced by spirit:

> So we do not lose heart. Though our outer nature is wasting away, our inner nature is being renewed every day. For this slight momentary affliction is preparing for us an eternal weight of glory beyond all comparison, because we look not to the things that are seen but to the things that are unseen; for the things that are seen are transient, but the things that are unseen are eternal (II Cor. 4:16–18).

The final portion of the body of spirit to be received, the new outer covering with which the inner portion which has already been received will ultimately be clothed, is even now in heaven, waiting to be put on:

> For we know that if the earthly tent we live in is destroyed, we have a building from God, a house not made with hands, eternal in the heavens. Here indeed we groan, and long to put on our heavenly dwelling, so that by putting it on we may not be found naked. For while we are still in this tent, we sigh with anxiety; not that we would be unclothed, but that we would be further clothed, so that what is mortal may be swallowed up by life (II Cor. 5:1–4).

The death of the body of flesh, therefore, is not something to be feared or avoided; on the contrary, it is something to be eagerly awaited, for it marks the last step in the process by which the believer attains to the resurrection.

The substantial difference between this eschatological teaching and that of I Corinthians can be seen at a glance. Less readily observable, however, is another difference between the eschatology of I Corinthians and that of II Corinthians 1–9. This has to do with the resurrection of the Christian dead.

Those who believe that Paul's thought did not develop during the period of the letters, and therefore that it is permissible to read the details of the eschatology of I Corinthians into the apparent gaps in the eschatology of II Corinthians 1–9, invariably assume that when Paul speaks of the resurrection in the second letter his reference is still to the resurrection of all the Christian dead at the same moment at the parousia. But Paul does not actually connect the resurrection with the parousia in II Corinthians 1–9. He does speak of "the day of the Lord" (II Cor. 1:14), and he also declares that "he who raised the Lord Jesus will raise us also with Jesus" (II Cor. 4:14), but he does not say that the day of the Lord will be the occasion of this resurrection. On the contrary he seems to think of it as an individual resurrection which will follow immediately after death. He writes: "While we are at home in the body we are away from the Lord . . . and we would rather be away from the body and at home with the Lord" (II Cor. 5:6,8). The verbs ἐνδημέω and ἐκδημέω, which are contrasted in this passage, mean rather more than merely "to be at home" and "to be away." They denote place of residence, in the strict sense, and translated literally, with the proper force of the tenses taken into account, Paul's words mean, "While we maintain our residence in the body we maintain our residence away from the Lord . . . and we would rather go away from our residence in the body and take up our residence with the Lord." This does not contemplate that the believer will spend the interval between his death and the parousia in the grave; instead, it reflects a form of the Christian hope in which the believer, having left the body of flesh behind, will go immediately to be with Christ, in the "house not made with hands, eternal in the heavens."

The new eschatology is in large measure an extension of the old. There is nothing new, of course, in the idea that the Christian receives the Spirit at his conversion. The ability to speak in tongues, which was regarded apparently from the first as the mark of God's acceptance of the believer, was also interpreted as an outward and visible sign that God's Spirit had entered into him. The Spirit which had been given to the believer was also understood to be indestructible. In I Corinthians, Paul condemns the incestuous man to "be removed" from the Christian community and delivered to Satan "for the destruction of the flesh, that his spirit may be saved in the day of the Lord Jesus" (I Cor. 5:2,5). The principal function of the Spirit in the early teaching, however, is to serve as the vehicle of revelation, and consequently as the means of sanctification. The Spirit's role in revelation is described in I Corinthians: "Now we have received not the spirit of the world, but the Spirit which is from God, that we might understand the gifts bestowed on us by God. And we impart this in words not taught by human wisdom but taught by the Spirit, interpreting spiritual truths to those who possess the Spirit" (I Cor. 2:12–13). The Spirit's role in sanctification is repeatedly mentioned in the early letters also. In giving instructions to the Thessalonians about marriage, Paul writes: "This is the will of God, your sanctification: that you abstain from immorality. . . . Whoever disregards this, disregards not man but God, who gives his Holy Spirit to you" (I Thess. 4:3,8); and he justifies his right to give similar instructions to the Corinthians by saying, "I think that I have the Spirit of God" (I Cor. 7:40). The concept of the Spirit in these passages is primarily epistemological, the Spirit being the means by which the believer is enabled to come to know the will of God, and it was apparently by way of extension of this original concept that Paul developed the eschatological doctrine of I Corinthians, in which for the first time spirit is treated as the substance of which the resurrection body will be composed.

But although it may not be a new idea that the believer already possesses some measure of the substance of the body that is to be, it is a new idea that the final transformation to the body of spirit necessarily involves his physical death. In I Corinthians the death of the believer is still regarded as exceptional; it is a judgment for having done wrong (I Cor. 5:3; 11:29,31,32). The incestuous man will die because he has been delivered to Satan "for the destruction of the flesh" (I Cor. 5:5), and some of the Corinthian Christians have already died because they were "guilty of profaning the body and blood of the Lord" (I Cor. 11:27,30). But the normal expectation of the Christian who has done nothing to deserve such a judgment is that he will live to be changed from flesh to spirit in a moment at the parousia. This is not true of II Corinthians 1–9. There the death of the believer is not a judgment; it is the climax of the process by which he has been transformed from flesh to spirit. It is even possible for Paul to think of the Christian who is in the midst of this process as having died already, since that which follows death, namely, the reception of the body of spirit, has already begun in him, just as it has been completed in Christ:

> Because we are convinced that one has died for all: therefore all have died. And he died for all, that those who live might live

no longer for themselves but for him who for their sake died and
was raised (II Cor. 5:14–15).

The point at which the believer ceases to belong to the old creation and
begins to belong to the new, in other words, is no longer viewed as
lying in the future, as it had been in I Corinthians; it is now viewed
as having been reached already:

> From now on, therefore, we regard no one from a human
> point of view. . . . If anyone is in Christ, he is a new creation;
> the old has passed away, behold, the new has come (II Cor. 5:16–
> 17).

Needless to say, this represents a significant modification in Paul's
thinking. Moreover, if we are correct in dating the writing of I Corinthians at Passover and II Corinthians 1–9 at Pentecost, seven weeks
later, it took place within a remarkably short period of time. What can
have brought it about?

Paul answers this question explicitly in II Corinthians 1–9. Since
the Corinthians had last heard from him, he tells them, he had been the
victim of a persecution so violent that he despaired of his life.

> For we do not want you to be ignorant, brethren, of the
> affliction we experienced in Asia; for we were so utterly, un-
> bearably crushed that we despaired of life itself. Why, we felt
> that we had received the sentence of death; but that was to make
> us rely not on ourselves but on God who raises the dead; he de-
> livered us from such a deadly peril, and he will deliver us; on him
> we have set our hope that he will deliver us again (II Cor. 1:8–10).

The experience had had a profound effect on this thinking. Hitherto he
had always assumed that he would live until the parousia. In I Thessalonians he had written:

> For the Lord himself will descend from heaven with a cry
> of command, with the archangel's call, and with the sound of the
> trumpet of God. And the dead in Christ will rise first; then we
> who are alive, who are left, shall be caught up together with
> them in the clouds to meet the Lord in the air; and so we shall
> always be with the Lord (I Thess. 4:16–17).

Again in I Corinthians he had included himself among those who would be alive at the parousia.

> Lo! I tell you a mystery. We shall not all sleep, but we shall all be changed, in a moment, in the twinkling of an eye, at the last trumpet. For the trumpet will sound, and the dead will be raised imperishable, and we shall be changed (I Cor. 15:51–52).

As we have seen, even as recently as the writing of I Corinthians Paul had formed no adequate explanation of the natural death of Christians, and in that letter he had even gone so far as to tell the Corinthians that the reason for the death of at least some of their number was that they had partaken of the Lord's Supper in an unworthy manner.

> Let a man examine himself, and so eat of the bread and drink of the cup. For any one who eats and drinks without discerning the body eats and drinks judgment upon himself. That is why many of you are weak and ill, and some have died (I Cor. 11:28–30).

The implication is that those who partook of the Lord's Supper in a worthy manner could be confident of living until the parousia.[1] Paul still counted himself as one of those.

But shortly after the writing of I Corinthians, Paul had been brought face to face with death. The sentence of death, he thought, had been passed upon him. This meant, if he was to cling to the eschatological teaching of I Corinthians, that he must sleep in the grave until the parousia and only be restored to life in the resurrection on that day. At once the inadequacy of this teaching became apparent. And as quickly, it seems, he realized where the inadequacy lay. The doctrine of the ultimate resurrection of Christians at the parousia, which he had taught to the Thessalonians and the Corinthians, had not really been based on the pattern given in the resurrection of Christ, for Christ had not slept in the earth until the end of the present age but had been

---

[1] This implication is borne out by the obvious meaning of Paul's instructions in I Cor. 5:1–5, according to which the incestuous man is to be excommunicated and delivered to Satan "for the destruction of the flesh, that his spirit may be saved in the day of the Lord Jesus," i.e. in the resurrection.

raised from the dead immediately.[2] This could only mean, Paul reasoned, that his teaching had been wrong in positing a longer interval before the resurrection of the Christian dead.

It cannot have been easy for a man of Paul's temperament to acknowledge that he had been mistaken on a cardinal point of Christian teaching. His fault, he confesses, had been to assume that, no matter what happened to other people, he himself would live until the parousia, and God had had to bring him into the danger through which he had just passed in order, as he puts it, "to make us rely not on ourselves but on God who raises the dead" (II Cor. 1:9). It is so simply and directly stated that its full significance is easy to overlook. Also easy to overlook is its bearing on the eschatological teaching of the remainder of the letter, which is a thoroughgoing revision of his earlier teaching about the Christian hope. For as a result of the experience he had had, he now realized that he could no longer assume that he, or any other Christian, was assured of escaping death. The likelihood, in fact, seemed to be that he might be called upon to suffer a death like that of Jesus at the hands of violent men. But he now believed that in the event of his death he would be "at home with the Lord" (II Cor. 5:8).

In this new understanding of the Christian hope, then, there are two salient features which have not appeared in Paul's earlier eschatological teaching: the belief in the immediate resurrection of Christians who have died, and the belief in the simultaneous possession by the believer of the body of flesh, which is wasting away, and the down payment of the body of spirit, which is being renewed every day. The second of these beliefs, which can be described more simply as the doctrine of the simultaneous possession of two natures, plays an important part not only in the explicitly eschatological sections of II Corinthians 1–9 but also in the letter's treatment of the relation between law and grace and its teaching about the person and work of Christ.

No feature of II Corinthians 1–9 is more readily remarked than the sharpness of the antithesis which it draws between law and grace.

---

[2] That is, on the third day. The belief seems to have been common in antiquity that death was not final until three days had passed. Cf. John 11:17, where the point is made that Lazarus had been in the tomb for four days when he was raised.

The law of Moses is described as "the dispensation of death, carved in letters on stone" (II Cor. 3:7), as "the dispensation of condemnation" (II Cor. 3:9), and as "the written code" that "kills" (II Cor. 3:6). It is contrasted with "the dispensation of righteousness" (II Cor. 3:9), or "the dispensation of the Spirit" (II Cor. 3:6). The attitude of these passages is too clearly stated to require elucidation or comment.

In the letters which were written before II Corinthians 1-9 this antithesis is not so sharply drawn. I Thessalonians does not mention the law at all, and as far as we can tell, the Previous Letter was also silent on this score. I Corinthians, on the other hand, deals both implicitly and explicitly with the observance of the law by Jewish and Gentile Christians, and we can discover without difficulty on the basis of the evidence of that letter what Paul's attitude toward the law was at the time when it was written. Stated briefly, it was that "in the name of the Lord Jesus Christ and in the Spirit of our God" the Christian has been "washed . . . sanctified . . . justified" (I Cor. 6:11). He has escaped the penalty of the law forever.

The law is not necessarily bad, however. Paul can still say, "For it is written in the law of Moses, 'You shall not muzzle an ox when it is treading out the grain'" (I Cor. 9:9; cf. Deut. 25:4), and argue that the injunction does not apply to oxen but to Christian ministers, who should not be prevented from receiving material rewards for their labors. He can even say, "As in all the churches of the saints, the women should keep silence in the churches. For they are not permitted to speak, but should be subordinate, as even the law says" (I Cor. 14:33-34; cf. Gen. 3:16). He does not hesitate, in short, to use the law on occasion as the source of a supporting argument even when he is dealing with principles of Christian conduct. But he does not derive the principles themselves from the law. These he derives either from the teaching and example of Jesus or from his own judgment, guided by the Spirit. Thus in treating the question of divorce he writes, "To the married I give charge, not I but the Lord, that the wife should not separate from her husband (but if she does let her remain single or else be reconciled to her husband)—and that the husband should not divorce his wife" (I Cor. 7:10-11). Later he adds, "A wife is bound to her husband as long as he lives. If the husband dies, she is free to be married to whom she wishes, only in the Lord. But in my judgment she is happier if she remains as she is. And I think that I have the Spirit of God" (I Cor. 7:39–40). The basic motive underlying all Christian conduct, he maintains, is love. Thus, in treating the question of the eating of meat offered to idols he begins by reminding his readers that "knowledge puffs up, but love builds up" (I Cor. 8:1), and he ends the famous thirteenth chapter with the words, "So faith, hope, love abide, these three; but the greatest of these is love" (I Cor. 13:13).

By far the most important legal question with which I Corinthians deals, however, has to do with dietary regulations. Here Paul makes his position perfectly clear. Since the dietary laws are not binding on Christians, Gentile Christians need not regard them at all; Jewish Christians, however, may continue to observe them if they wish, though they must not think that they gain by the observance. "Food will not commend us to God. We are no worse off if we do not eat, and no better off if we do" (I Cor. 8:8). On more than one occasion, apparently, Paul had told the Corinthians that "all things are lawful" (I Cor. 6:12; 10:23), and he had not hesitated to eat with Gentiles himself. At the same time, when he was with Jews he had also continued to observe the dietary regulations:

> For though I am free from all men, I have made myself a slave to all, that I might win the more. To the Jews I became as a Jew in order to win Jews; to those under the law I became as one under the law—that I might win those under the law. To those outside the law I became as one outside the law—not being without law toward God but under the law of Christ—that I might win those outside the law. To the weak I became weak, that I might win the weak. I have become all things to all men, that I might by all means save some. I do it all for the sake of the gospel, that I may share in its blessings" (I Cor. 9:19–23).

He concludes:

> So whether you eat or drink, or whatever you do, do all to the glory of God. Give no offense to Jews or to Greeks or to the church of God, just as I try to please all men in everything I do, not seeking my own advantage, but that of many, that they may

be saved. Be imitators of me, as I am of Christ (I Cor. 10:31–11:1).

It is thus abundantly clear that when he wrote I Corinthians, Paul had not yet taken the position of II Corinthians 1–9, where the law is treated as the dispensation of condemnation and death which kills those who continue to observe it.

In II Corinthians 1–9, Paul is not only intent on establishing that the law is no longer binding, he is also at pains to prove that its continued observance is against the will of God. He does this by means of one of the most unusual exegetical arguments ever contrived. The law, he says, once possessed two natures, an earthly nature, since it was "carved in letters on stone," and a heavenly nature, since it "came with such glory that the Israelites could not look at Moses' face because of its glory" (II Cor. 3:7). But the law was not by its nature capable of remaining in force forever; it was to be superseded by a new covenant in the spirit. The outward sign that the law had expired was to be "the end of the fading glory" (II Cor. 3:13) and the appearance of "the glory that surpasses it" (II Cor. 3:10). This event, Paul argues, had already occurred with the gift of "the Spirit of the living God," which he identifies with the fulfillment of Jeremiah's prophecy of the new covenant, written "not on tablets of stone but on tablets of hearts of flesh" (II Cor. 3:3). But if this is so, why do not the upholders of the law admit it? Because, Paul states, Moses deceived them. He "put a veil over his face so that the Israelites might not see the end of the fading glory" (II Cor. 3:13). And, Paul continues, "to this day, when they read the old covenant, that same veil remains unlifted, because only through Christ is it taken away" (II Cor. 3:14).

Needless to say, Paul's exegesis of the story of the veiling of Moses involves a totally unwarranted inference based on the line, "And when Moses had finished speaking with them, he put a veil on his face" (Exod. 34:33). Nothing like Paul's meaning is even remotely suggested by this line; it does not imply that Moses deceived the people. One is tempted to see in Paul's strange exegesis of it a deliberate display of virtuosity, as if to say, in answer to the exegetes on the other side of the controversy, "You are not the only ones who can play this game." It may not be too much to suggest that it is also deliberately designed to be offensive to Paul's opponents, whom he has already contemptuously labeled "peddlers of God's word" (II Cor. 2:17). If so, it must have succeeded.

But for our present purpose the important feature to be noted in Paul's argument is not that it employs a curious exegesis of a passage in the book of Exodus but that it reflects his recently developed eschatological doctrine of the simultaneous possession of two natures. Indeed, it is nothing more nor less than this doctrine in reverse. For whereas in the eschatological doctrine it is the flesh that is destined to pass away, leaving only the living spirit, in the legal doctrine which we are now examining it is the spirit which has departed from the law, leaving only the letters carved on stone. Paul's new eschatology, in short, has provided him with an argument with which to demonstrate that the law, although it once had a measure of glory, could remain in force for only a limited period, at the end of which its glory finally expired. To continue to observe the law now, therefore, can only lead to death. This is a far more radical position than he had taken before.

Like the legal theory, the Christology of II Corinthians 1–9 also reflects the new eschatology of the letter. The pertinent passage reads as follows:

> From now on, therefore, we regard no one from a human point of view; even though we once regarded Christ from a human point of view, we regard him thus no longer. Therefore, if any one is in Christ, he is a new creation; the old has passed away, behold, the new has come. All this is from God, who through Christ reconciled us to himself and gave us the ministry of reconciliation; that is, God was in Christ reconciling the world to himself, not counting their trespasses against them, and entrusting to us the message of reconciliation (II Cor. 5:16–19).

This passage marks a departure from the Christological doctrine of the letters which we know to have been written before II Corinthians 1–9. I Thessalonians, strictly speaking, contains no doctrine of the person of Christ at all. Its entire interest is in the work of Christ, "who died for us so that whether we wake or sleep we might live with him"

(I Thess. 5:10), who was "raised from the dead" (I Thess. 1:10), who makes the Christians "increase and abound in love to one another and to all men" (I Thess. 3:12), who will "descend from heaven" (I Thess. 4:16) "with all his saints" (I Thess. 3:13), and deliver us "from the wrath to come" (I Thess. 1:10). Here the work of Christ, of which the parousia is the climax, is conceived of as having begun with his death.

I Corinthians, on the other hand, does contain a doctrine of the person of Christ in the identification of Christ as the second Adam: "Thus it is written, 'the first man Adam became a living being'; the last Adam became a life-giving spirit" (I Cor. 15:45). A great deal of misdirected learning has been applied to the explanation of this line as a supposed reflection of the Philonic treatment of the two creation stories in Genesis, but Paul is not contrasting the "ideal" man, created first (Gen. 1:26f.), with the man of dust, created second (Gen. 2:7). He is contrasting Adam with Christ, and he goes out of his way to make this clear:

> The first man was from the earth, a man of dust; the second man is from heaven. As was the man of dust, so are those who are of the dust; and as is the man of heaven, so are those who are of heaven. Just as we have borne the image of the man of dust, we shall also bear the image of the man of heaven (I Cor. 15:47–49).

Nor is there any reason to doubt that he means his argument to prove exactly what he says it proves: "As by a man came death, by a man has come also the resurrection of the dead. For as in Adam all die, so also in Christ shall all be made alive" (I Cor. 15:21–22).

The purpose of Paul's argument is to show that there must be a life in the spirit subsequent to the present life in the flesh. The design of the argument is simple. Both Adam and Christ, Paul points out, had a two-stage existence. Adam, having begun as a man of dust, "became a living soul"; Christ, having begun as a man of flesh, "became a life-giving spirit." Adam's body, however, even in the second stage of his existence was still "of earth" (and therefore mortal), whereas Christ's body in the second stage of his existence was "of heaven" (and therefore immortal). The reason why "in Adam" all die is that they bear the image of the man of dust; if "in Christ" all are to be made alive, it must be because they will bear the image of the man of heaven. Therefore flesh and blood, the substance of earthly life, must be destined to be succeeded by spirit, the substance of heavenly life.

In this system Christ is viewed as the prototype of a new humanity which will share the two stages of his existence, the first in a body of flesh, which he put off in his death, and the second in a body of spirit, which he put on in his resurrection. While this is a doctrine of the person of Christ as well as a doctrine of the work of Christ, it is as yet dimly conceived and inadequately developed. It does not make clear the relationship of Christ to God (unless it means to suggest that Christ, like Adam, was created), and it does not make clear the relationship of Christ to man (unless it means to suggest that in his earthly life he was not essentially different from other men). All it establishes is that Christ was a man of flesh before his death and a man of spirit after it. Here too the work of Christ begins with his death.

II Corinthians 1–9 repudiates this system and substitutes for it a system in which the work of Christ is viewed as having begun before his death. Even though Paul once regarded Christ after the flesh, that is, with human eyes, he regards him thus no longer. God, he now perceives, was in Christ even during his earthly life, reconciling the world to himself. This is yet another form of the eschatological doctrine of the simultaneous possession of two natures, for if God was at work in Christ during his earthly life, then at that stage of his existence Christ was not a being of flesh and blood only. He had possessed a heavenly nature as well.[3]

Thus II Corinthians 1–9 presents not only a new eschatology as over against I Corinthians but also a new theory of the relation of law to grace and a new Christology. The starting point for this modification was the new doctrine of the simultaneous possession of two natures, which Paul developed for the first time after the "persecution in Asia." This being the case, if we should possess a writing of Paul that dates between the persecution in Asia and II Corinthians 1–9, that writing

[3] In I Corinthians Christ is described as "the power of God and the wisdom of God" (I Cor. 1:24), but this clearly means that the foolishness and weakness, which were all that men could see in Christ crucified, have been vindicated by the resurrection and thus proved to be "wiser than men" and "stronger than men" (I Cor. 1:25). It has nothing to do with Christ's possession of divine attributes during his earthly life.

should bear certain marks by which we could distinguish it from I Corinthians, on the one hand, and from II Corinthians 1-9, on the other. We should expect it to show a development beyond that of the earlier letter, especially in the matter of eschatology, but we should also expect its legal theory and its Christology to be less fully developed than the treatment of these subjects in II Corinthians 1-9. In fact, the lines along which Paul's thought was developing during this period are by now so clear that it should be quite impossible to misdate a writing which falls after the persecution in Asia and before II Corinthians 1-9.

Such a writing is the letter to the Philippians.

5

PHILIPPIANS

Conventional chronologies of Paul's letters all but universally date Philippians, Colossians, Philemon, and Ephesians late in Paul's life. The chief reason for this is that these letters were written from prison, and the story of Paul's life as it is told in Acts contains only two imprisonments long enough to have served as the occasion for their writing. These are the imprisonment at Caesarea (Acts 23:33ff.) and the house arrest in Rome (Acts 28:16ff.).

Discerning critics have often been disturbed by this solution to the problem of dating the prison epistles. Many have noted that Acts is unreliable as a guide to Paul's imprisonments, since the letters speak of more imprisonments than Acts seems to know about. In one famous passage Paul is explicit on this point: "Are they servants of Christ? I am a better one . . . with far greater labors, far more imprisonments, with countless beatings, and often near death. Five times I have received at the hands of the Jews the forty lashes less one. Three times

I have been beaten with rods" (II Cor. 11:23–25). A few critics have noticed a more serious difficulty, namely, that Philippians is so different from the other prison epistles that it seems most improbable that all four letters could have been written during the same period of Paul's life. The most penetrating study of this aspect of the problem is that of Lightfoot in his commentary on Philippians, in which he concludes that the letter must have been written in the period of Romans. What Lightfoot failed to discern was that Philippians was actually written before II Corinthians 1–9.

The first critic to see this seems to have been Albertz, but he did not succeed in persuading the majority of scholars of the rightness of his views, and by now they have been largely forgotten.[1] There is ample evidence, however, that Albertz was in fact correct.

We have already seen that the new eschatology of II Corinthians 1–9 grew out of Paul's experience during the persecution in Asia, when, as he puts it, "we felt that we had received the sentence of death" (II Cor. 1:9). Philippians is a description of the naked experience itself:

> I want you to know, brethren, that what has happened to me has really served to advance the gospel, so that it has become known throughout the whole praetorium and to all the rest that my imprisonment is for Christ; and most of the brethren have been made confident in the Lord because of my imprisonment, and are much more bold to speak the word of God without fear. . . . For I know that through your prayers and the help of the Spirit of Jesus Christ this will turn out for my deliverance, as it is my eager expectation and hope that I shall not be at all ashamed, but that with full courage now as always Christ will be honored in my body, whether by life or by death. For to me to live is Christ, and to die is gain. If it is to be life in the flesh, that means fruitful labor for me. Yet which I shall choose I cannot tell. I am hard pressed between the two. My desire is to depart and be with Christ, for that is far better. But to remain in the flesh is more necessary on your account (Phil. 1:12–14,19–24).

[1] For a discussion of Albertz's theory, see K. Lake in *Expositor*, 8th series, vii (1914), 492ff. Variations of the theory have been proposed by Deissmann, in *Light from the Ancient East* (Eng. trans., New York, 1910), and Duncan, in *St. Paul's Ephesian Ministry* (London, 1929).

It is evident from these words that Paul's old confidence that he would live until the parousia was now gone. He had come face to face with what seemed to be the certainty of his own death, and although he was still able to hope that he might be spared, he had prepared himself to meet death, if it should come, in such a way as to bring honor to Christ. More significantly he had given up his former belief that those Christians who died before the parousia would have to wait until the parousia to be resurrected. His desire, he writes, is "to depart and be with Christ" (Phil. 1:23). In other words, he now believed, in his own case at least, that death would be followed by an immediate resurrection. That this belief marked a departure from his former eschatological thinking is borne out in a later passage in the letter in which Paul speaks of a new hope:

> . . . that I may know him and the power of his resurrection, and may share his sufferings, becoming like him in his death, that if possible I may attain the resurrection from the dead. Not that I have already obtained this or am already perfect; but I press on to make it my own, because Christ Jesus has made me his own. Brethren, I do not consider that I have made it my own; but one thing I do, forgetting what lies behind and straining forward to what lies ahead, I press on toward the goal for the prize of the upward call of God in Christ Jesus. Let those of us who are mature be thus minded; and if in anything you are otherwise minded, God will reveal this also to you (Phil. 3:10–15).

But what is this new understanding? Again Paul has been quite explicit. It is that the Christian is to share the sufferings of Christ, even to the extent of becoming like him in his death, in the hope that he may also attain to the resurrection of the dead. This, of course, differs sharply from the doctrine of the early letters. Even as late as I Corinthians Paul believed that the Christian might reasonably hope to remain alive until the parousia, at which time he would be changed from flesh into spirit without experiencing death. Death would be "swallowed up" in victory. The difference between this doctrine and the doctrine of Philippians is at once apparent. Suffering and death, for which Paul had previously had no positive explanation, have now become the Christian's supreme way of knowing Christ.

It is apparent from Paul's words that he himself had attained only recently to this new understanding. Much of it he expresses in tentative terms. Thus he writes, "That *if possible* I may attain the resurrection of the dead"; and even having stated this with caution he hastens to add, "Not that I have already obtained this or am already perfect." His earlier words, "to depart and be with Christ," however, clearly underlie his imagery when he speaks of pressing on "toward the goal for the prize of the upward call of God in Christ Jesus." He faces a martyr's death and he is confident that he will receive a martyr's reward in the form of immediate resurrection. As regards those who have not died before the parousia, however, the older system of I Corinthians remains unchanged. Paul writes, "But our commonwealth is in heaven, and from it we await a Savior, the Lord Jesus Christ, who will change our lowly body to be like his glorious body, by the power which enables him even to subject all things to himself" (Phil. 3:20-21). The eschatological thought of Philippians, in short, is transitional between that of I Corinthians and that of II Corinthians 1-9, and totally unlike that of Colossians, in which the Christian is said to have died and been raised already (Col. 3:1-3).

Its Christology is also unlike that of the later letters. The key passage reads as follows:

> Have this mind among yourselves, which you have in Christ Jesus, who, though he was in the form of God, did not count equality with God a thing to be grasped, but emptied himself, taking the form of a servant, being born in the likeness of men. And being found in human form he humbled himself and became obedient unto death, even death on a cross. Therefore God has highly exalted him and bestowed on him the name which is above every name, that at the name of Jesus every knee should bow, in heaven and on earth and under the earth, and every tongue confess that Jesus Christ is Lord, to the glory of God the Father (Phil. 2:5-11).

This passage is a carefully developed exposition, in expanded form, of the Christology of I Corinthians, in which Christ is identified as the second Adam. Both Adam and Christ, as divinely originated prototypes, were "in the form of God." Unlike Adam, however, Christ "did not consider equality with God a thing to be grasped." [2] Instead, he "emptied himself," when he was "born in the likeness of men," by "taking the form of a slave." Here the form of the earthly Christ, that is, his coming in a body indistinguishable from that of a descendant of Adam, is explained as the consequence of a deliberate choice on his part. Having assumed this form, moreover, Christ deliberately "humbled himself," unlike Adam who had attempted to exalt himself, and accepted an undeserved and shameful death. What Christ did, in other words, was to reverse the fall of Adam. Therefore, Paul concludes, God highly exalted him.

The entire passage is thus an expansion of the earlier statement, "As by a man came death, by a man has come also the resurrection of the dead" (I Cor. 15:21). It is more than that, however, for it succeeds in relating the developing doctrine of the person of Christ as the prototype of the new humanity to the older doctrine of the work of Christ as the one who "died for our sins." This Paul had not really done in I Corinthians.

In that letter Paul had been chiefly interested in establishing that since Christ had first possessed a body of flesh and then gained a body of spirit, those "in Christ," who now possessed bodies of flesh, could also expect to gain bodies of spirit. The means by which the one body was to be exchanged for the other he did not attempt to explain. The transformation would be effected by God, miraculously and automatically. But by the time Paul wrote Philippians, he had been forced to find a place in this system for his own death, which he believed was imminent. Since it was clear to him that if he should be put to death it would not be because of sin but because of his obedience to God, it was natural that he should reflect that this was what had also happened to Christ. From that point on it was only a short step to the realization that the connection between the new doctrine of the person of Christ

[2] Critics who deny that Paul could have been referring here to the picking and eating of the forbidden fruit leave out of account his habit of seizing on just such circumstantial details of the Scripture narrative. Nor does he by any means consider it necessary to mention these details explicitly, but frequently contents himself with the bare identification of the passage in which they occur. Cf. II Cor. 3:13, where he quotes only the words "Moses put a veil over his face," although his whole argument depends on the circumstance that, according to Exod. 34:33, Moses only put the veil over his face *after he had finished speaking to the people,* a fact which Paul does not bother to state.

as the second Adam and the older doctrine of the work of Christ as the one who "died for our sins" lay in the contrast between Adam's disobedience and Christ's obedience unto death. The Christology of Philippians was the result.

If it is clear that this new doctrine can have been arrived at only after the writing of I Corinthians, it is equally clear that it is prior to II Corinthians 1–9. There are two reasons why this must be so. The first is, as we have already noted in connection with the eschatology, that there is as yet no sign of the doctrine of the simultaneous possession of two natures in Philippians. Christ is wholly human before his death and only acquires the new nature in the resurrection. There is no suggestion in Philippians that "God was in Christ" during his earthly life. On the contrary, the point is stressed that when Christ "was born in the likeness of men" he had "emptied himself" of every attribute of the divine nature.

The second has to do with an aspect of Paul's doctrine of salvation which we have not had occasion to mention until now, namely, the place where Paul conceives of the immediate initiative in the work of Christ as having resided. In the earlier system the death of Christ, although it is within the providence of God, is at his own initiative. He "died for us so that whether we wake or sleep we might live with him" (I Thess. 5:10). He "died for our sins in accordance with the scriptures" (I Cor. 15:3). This is still the case in Philippians. Christ deliberately chooses to "empty himself" and to "humble himself." And it is only after he has completed his work that God rewards him: "Therefore God has highly exalted him and bestowed on him the name which is above every name" (Phil. 2:9).

In II Corinthians 1–9, however, all this is changed. Not only is it made clear that God took an active part in the earthly life of Christ, but Paul even goes so far as to say that God "made him to be sin who knew no sin" (II Cor. 5:21), meaning, as he was to explain later, that God had sent Christ "in the likeness of sinful flesh" (Rom. 8:3). Here the immediate initiative in the work of Christ lies with God, and this is to be Paul's position from now on. The Christology of Philippians, therefore, like its eschatology, is clearly prior to II Corinthians 1–9. Needless to say, it is also prior to that of Colossians, which states that "in him all the fulness was pleased to dwell" (Col. 1:19).

Like the eschatology and Christology of Philippians, which can only be placed after I Corinthians and before II Corinthians 1–9, the legal theory of Philippians also belongs between these two longer letters. It represents a departure from the legal theory of I Corinthians in that it draws a sharp distinction between the righteousness that comes from law and the righteousness that comes from God through the faith of Christ, but it does not relate this distinction to the doctrine of the two natures that makes its first appearance in II Corinthians 1–9.

The occasion for the change in Philippians was the activity of the Judaizers. Paul writes, "Some indeed preach Christ from envy and rivalry, but others from good will. The latter do it out of love, knowing that I am put here for the defense of the gospel; the former proclaim Christ out of partisanship, not sincerely but thinking to afflict me in my imprisonment" (Phil. 1:15–17). These opponents of Paul were preaching a Christianity which involved the keeping of the law.

> To write the same things to you is not irksome to me, and is safe for you. Look out for the dogs, look out for the evil-workers, look out for those who mutilate the flesh. For we are the true circumcision, who worship God in spirit, and glory in Christ Jesus, and put no confidence in the flesh. Though I myself have reason for confidence in the flesh also. If any other man thinks he has reason for confidence in the flesh, I have more: circumcised on the eighth day, of the people of Israel, of the tribe of Benjamin, a Hebrew born of Hebrews: as to the law a Pharisee, as to zeal a persecutor of the church, as to righteousness under the law blameless (Phil. 3:1–6).

What follows shows that Paul knows the arguments which the Judaizers are using.

> But whatever gain I had, I counted as loss for the sake of Christ. Indeed I count everything as loss because of the surpassing worth of knowing Christ Jesus my Lord. For his sake I have suffered the loss of all things, and count them as refuse, in order that I may gain Christ and be found in him, not having a righteousness of my own that comes from law, but that which is through the faith of Christ, the righteousness that comes from God, that depends on faith; that I may know him and the power

of his resurrection, and may share his sufferings, becoming like
him in his death, that if possible I may attain the resurrection
from the dead (Phil. 3:7–11).

This passage, in which righteousness that comes from law is contrasted with righteousness that comes from God, expresses Paul's antilegal attitude in close connection with his new Christology. Just as
Christ gave up the form of God, which was properly his own, so Paul
has given up his own righteousness, which came from law. And just
as Christ, having deigned to be born in the form of a descendant of
Adam, accepted a human death in the faith that God would raise him
from the dead, so Paul has relinquished his former hope of avoiding
death and has now made up his mind to become like Christ in his
death in order to be worthy of a resurrection like his. It is important
to note that in this system faith means trust in God. Christ has faith
in God that he will raise him from the dead, and Paul has a similar
faith. (There is no mention of "faith *in* Christ," as RSV and NEB un-
accountably mistranslate the phrase.) Similarly the righteousness on
the basis of which Christ is accepted as worthy to be raised from the
dead does not come from the law but is a gift from God, and this is
no less true of the righteousness on the basis of which Paul expects to
be found worthy of resurrection.

Here Paul is plainly moving in the direction of the later doctrine
of righteousness through trust as opposed to righteousness through
works of the law, but just as plainly he has not yet reached it. Indeed,
Christ is still pictured in Philippians as having effected salvation by
performing a work, namely, reversing the fall of Adam, and the
Christian is still required to "work out" his own salvation with fear
and trembling (Phil. 2:12). The legal theory of Philippians, in short,
has evolved beyond that of I Corinthians, but Paul has not yet developed any historical argument to prove that the law is a dispensation
of death. That argument is to make its first appearance in II Corinthians 1–9.

The three lines of reasoning thus lead to a single conclusion. The
eschatology of Philippians is developed beyond that of I Corinthians
but has not yet reached the stage which is exhibited in the doctrine of
the simultaneous possession of two natures in II Corinthians 1–9. The

Christology of Philippians is a modification of the doctrine of the two Adams of I Corinthians, but this modification has not reached the stage of the doctrine of II Corinthians 1–9, where God is seen to have been at work in Christ during his earthly life.[3] And the legal theory of Philippians exhibits a sharpening of Paul's hostility to the law as over against the attitude of I Corinthians, but it does not yet say that the continued keeping of the law leads to death. These facts in themselves are significant. Even more significant is the fact that in II Corinthians 1–9 the eschatology, Christology, and legal theory have all been systematized under the single large doctrine of the simultaneous possession of two natures. Neither the doctrine nor the systematization appears in Philippians. Therefore, Philippians must fall between I Corinthians and II Corinthians 1–9.

This conclusion depends to a certain extent on the assumption, which has been made throughout the foregoing discussion, that Philippians is a single letter rather than a collection of fragments. Philippians as a whole maintains a consistent position relative to both I Corinthians and II Corinthians 1–9, and this fact speaks in favor of the supposition that the letter is a unity. The very close connection which we have seen to exist between the Christology of the second chapter and the legal theory of the third is in itself a strong positive argument in favor of the supposition that the two were written at the same time.

The principal argument against the integrity of Philippians is based on the extremely awkward transition from the mention of Epaphroditus in the end of the second chapter to the anti-Judaistic passage in the beginning of the third. It lies in the following sentences:

> . . . for he nearly died for the work of Christ, risking his life to complete your service to me.
> Finally, my brethren, rejoice in the Lord. To write the same things to you is not irksome to me, and is safe for you.

[3] Philippians comes very close to this idea in the line, "for God is at work in you, both to will and to work for his good pleasure" (Phil. 2:13), but here the reference is to the Christians, in whom God is at work. There is no reference to God's having been at work in Christ. By the time he came to write II Corinthians 1–9, however, Paul had seen the Christological implications of the idea and was ready to employ it in connection with his new doctrine of the work of Christ, according to which God was at work in Christ during his earthly life,

Look out for the dogs, look out for the evil-workers, look out for those who mutilate the flesh . . . (Phil. 2:30–3:2).

For a moment it has seemed as though Paul is about to enter the closing section of the letter; then suddenly he launches forth on a new subject, which is apparently unrelated to what has gone before, and adopts a noticeably sharper tone. The whole change is so abrupt and unexpected as to have given rise to the theory that the section beginning, "Look out for the dogs," is a separate fragment and not part of the letter which contained the first two chapters. But an examination of the awkward transition to discover at precisely what point in it the break occurs yields interesting results.

At first glance there seem to be three possible points at which there might be a sufficient break in the sense. The first of these lies between the end of the second chapter and the beginning of the third, indicated by the first paragraph break above. But this has nothing to recommend it, since the line, "Finally, my brethren, rejoice in the Lord," has no closer connection in sense or tone with the following anti-Judaistic passage than it has with what has gone before. More popular with critics is a division between the first two verses of the third chapter, indicated by the second paragraph break above. This allows the line, "Look out for the dogs," to be the opening of the second fragment. A break at this point, however, ignores the fact that the preceding sentence, "To write the same things to you is not irksome to me, and is safe for you," is eminently suitable as an introduction to a set of warnings and leads naturally into "Look out for the dogs." The third possible point for the break is after the sentence, "Finally, my brethren, rejoice in the Lord," and before the sentence, "To write the same things . . . ." It is at this point that the letter seems to be embarking on one course and then suddenly jibes over onto another tack.

This impression is due to the fact that "Finally, my brethren, rejoice in the Lord" sounds as though the letter is drawing to a close. But instead of entering a closing section it introduces the subject of the Judaizers and Paul's new insight into the resurrection, a topic which consumes the whole of the following chapter. The actual closing section of the letter does not begin until the fourth chapter. After a refer-

ence to a personal disagreement between two women in the church
(Phil. 4:2–3), Paul writes, "Rejoice in the Lord always; again I will
say, Rejoice" (Phil. 4:4), and the letter enters upon its final paragraphs.
In other words, the letter contains the start of its closing section twice.
But only the latter of these starts actually leads into the closing section;
the former is a false start. Commentators who would partition Philippians see in this false start the work of a bungling editor. The resultant
text of the letter, however, contains persuasive evidence that the person
responsible for this awkward spot was not an editor but was Paul
himself.

This evidence lies in the manner in which the two critical transi-
tions are made. It is universally recognized, of course, that Paul's letters
were for the most part dictated. A scribe, Tertius, identifies himself
on one occasion (Rom. 16:22), and Paul occasionally calls attention to
the fact that he himself rather than the scribe has written the closing
greeting (I Cor. 16:21; Gal. 6:11; Col. 4:18; II Thess. 3:17; cf. also
Philem. 19). There is good reason to believe, moreover, that the scribe
did not first make a rough copy, which was later corrected and tran-
scribed in a fair hand to be sent, but made the final copy directly from
Paul's original dictation. Proof that this was at least sometimes the
case may be found in I Corinthians, where the final text at one point
reads as follows:

> Or were you baptized in the name of Paul? I am thankful
> that I baptized none of you except Crispus and Gaius; lest anyone
> should say that you were baptized in my name. (I did baptize also
> the household of Stephanas. Beyond that, I do not know whether
> I baptized anyone else.) For Christ did not send me to baptize
> but to preach the gospel (I Cor. 1:13–17).

This text is clearly the result of a familiar slip in dictation. In dictating
the second quoted sentence Paul momentarily forgot the baptism of
the household of Stephanas. By the time he did remember it the second
sentence had already been written in a form which could not be allowed to stand without qualification. He did not, however, have this
offending sentence stricken out or corrected. He allowed it to stand and
repaired the difficulty by inserting the necessary correction as he proceeded. It is psychologically most interesting to note, moreover, that

the slip made him suddenly self-conscious, for his next words are an admission that his memory may still be faulty.

Now precisely the same signs of a slip in dictation are present in Philippians. Paul says, "Finally, brethren, rejoice in the Lord. To write the same things to you is not irksome to me, and is safe for you. Look out for the dogs . . . ." We have noted already that the first of these sentences is a false start. But it is not stricken out. Instead it is followed by a sentence which is nothing more nor less than an admission on Paul's part that what is to follow is an apparent digression. Again it is psychologically interesting to note the appearance of the verb "to write." The slip which Paul has just made in dictation has focused his attention on himself in the act of writing a letter. Without realizing what has happened he finds himself saying that he is writing.

When we now turn to the second occurrence of "Rejoice in the Lord" the evidence that the slip was Paul's reappears. He writes, "Rejoice in the Lord always; again I will say, Rejoice." Long familiarity with this sentence is apt to blind the reader to the fact that it is unique in all of Paul's writing. Nowhere else does he repeat a word or phrase and introduce the repetition with the words, "Again I will say." This trick of style occurs not infrequently in oratory, where it is employed to guard against the possibility that a key word or phrase may have gone unheard. But Philippians is not oratory. The explanation of the phenomenon here is to be found once again in the psychology of dictation. It has already been noted that when signs of a slip in dictation occur, they are accompanied by signs that Paul became self-conscious. In one instance he alluded to his memory, in another he quite unnecessarily called attention to the fact that he was writing. And here again he is conscious of himself in the act of repeating what he has already said: "Again I will say." He knows that he has already used the line, "Rejoice in the Lord," out of place. When he now comes to the proper place for this sentence he debates momentarily whether to use it again. If he merely repeats it in its original form it will sound flat and ineffective. But if he purposely gives it a new emphasis, the effect of anticlimax can be overcome. This is exactly what he has done. And his manner of doing it betrays him in the act.

Once it is seen that the awkward transition into the anti-Judaistic passage is the work of Paul and not of a redactor, the only serious argument against the integrity of Philippians vanishes. What remains is an overwhelming mass of evidence that the underlying doctrine of the letter is homogeneous throughout and represents a theological position which Paul held for a single brief period in his life. Against this the arguments based on mere surface phenomena must give way.

Such surface data as are important agree admirably with a date of writing during the persecution in Asia. The persecution provides the necessary prison situation. The location of the persecution is suitable for the exchange of information and of visits which is required to explain the letter's references to Epaphroditus. It is plain that someone had taken to Philippi news of Paul's imprisonment; that the Philippians had sent Epaphroditus with a gift; that Epaphroditus, after his arrival, had fallen sick, and someone had carried news of his illness back to Philippi; that the Philippians had become alarmed and had sent inquiries concerning him; and that on his recovery Epaphroditus returned to Philippi taking Paul's letter with him. But perhaps the strongest evidence which Philippians offers to the effect that it was written before II Corinthians 1–9 is its silence concerning the collection for the Jerusalem church. Arguments from silence are usually considered weak. But this particular silence clamors for explanation. Philippians is a letter of thanks for a gift. It makes a point of recalling the former occasions on which the church at Philippi had given generously to support Paul's missionary work. But it says nothing of any Philippian gift at the time of the great collection. This omission is strange in view of the fact that it is all but certain that the Philippians contributed to the collection. Paul had not planned originally to receive contributions in Macedonia, but when he arrived there the churches begged him earnestly "for the favor of taking part in the relief of the saints" (II Cor. 8:4) and gave "beyond their means" (II Cor. 8:3). It is hardly conceivable in view of these words the Philippi contributed nothing, for it was apparently the most substantial of the Macedonian churches and had a long history of generous giving. But in Philippians Paul says nothing of any contribution from Philippi to the great collection, though he is recalling the past generosity of his readers. If Philippians was written after the collection Paul's silence is inexplicable. If, on the other hand, the letter was written before the Macedonian churches offered to contribute, no problem exists.

Philippians, therefore, was written from Asia, by which Paul undoubtedly means Ephesus, during the persecution which he suffered there during the collection trip. It was written not long after I Corinthians and not long before II Corinthians 1–9, and when correctly interpreted reveals clearly the starting point from which arose the great theological modification that makes its first systematic appearance in the latter work. In this position it gives us a fifth point in the list of the letters in the order of their composition, which now reads: I Thessalonians, I Corinthians, Philippians, II Corinthians 1–9, and Romans.

6

GALATIANS

Just as it is possible to date Philippians between I Corinthians and II Corinthians 1–9 by showing that its eschatology, Christology, and legal theory represent a stage in the development of Paul's thought that took place between the dates of these two letters, it is also possible to show that Galatians represents a stage in the development that falls between II Corinthians 1–9 and Romans.[1] The historical limits within which Galatians must be dated can be determined on the basis of the evidence of the first two chapters of the letter, from which we derive the following information: (1) It was written after Paul's second visit to Jerusalem, which took place at least fourteen years after his conversion (Gal. 1:18;2:1). (2) It was written after Paul had acceded to the request of James, Cephas, and

[1] Portions of the following arguments have appeared in two articles: (1) Buck, "The Date of Galatians," *Journal of Biblical Literature*, LXX (1951), 113–122; and (2) Taylor, "The Function of ΠΙΣΤΙΣΟΥΧΡΙΣΤ in Galatians," *Journal of Biblical Literature* LXXXV (1966), 58–76. References to the passages in Gaius' *Institutes* which bear on the Roman law of inheritance are given in the latter.

John that he and Barnabas should "remember the poor," which very thing, he says, he "made haste to do" (Gal. 2:10). (3) It was written during the controversy with the Judaizers over the keeping of the law by Gentile Christians, which arose in Antioch after the second visit to Jerusalem (Gal. 2:11ff.). These data suggest that Paul's response to the request that he should remember the poor was the collection mentioned in the Corinthian correspondence and Romans, and that the controversy with the Judaizers that began in Antioch was the same as that reflected in Philippians, II Corinthians 1–9, and Romans. The alternative supposition, that these letters reflect a different effort on behalf of the poor of Jerusalem which coincided in time with a different controversy over the keeping of the law, seems most unlikely. The letters give the impression that there was only one collection and only one controversy with the Judaizers.

The literary evidence for the date of the letter points to the same period in Paul's life, for the literary affinities of Galatians are principally with Romans and II Corinthians 1–9. Lightfoot, after an exhaustive study of Galatians and Romans, declared that "the Epistle to the Galatians stands in relation to the Roman letter as the rough model to the finished statue," [2] and this conclusion has not been successfully challenged in the century that has elapsed since Lightfoot reached it. It is universally recognized that Galatians was written before Romans.

A second conclusion by Lightfoot, that Galatians was written after II Corinthians, has not fared so well in critical estimation. His own arguments for this position were admittedly weaker than those for the former hypothesis, since he could not claim that II Corinthians was in any sense a model for Galatians. The similarity which he detected between these two letters was, in his own phrase, "not so much in words and arguments as in tone and feeling." Nor could he support his hypothesis with any very good objective evidence. Yet in spite of the subjectivity of the argument, and in spite of the seriousness of the chronological disagreement with Acts which his conclusions involved, he still maintained that one could not interpose any part of the Corinthian correspondence between Galatians and Romans without experiencing a feeling of dislocation.

[2] *St. Paul's Epistle to the Galatians* (London, 1865), p. 49.

The specific weakness of this argument is in its assumption of the integrity of II Corinthians. The similarity in tone and feeling which Lightfoot detected was between Galatians and II Corinthians 10–13. Indeed, the cited passage from II Corinthians by which he sought to demonstrate this similarity was drawn from the twelfth chapter. Modern critics, however, are practically unanimous in the opinion that the last four chapters of II Corinthians were not written at the same time as the first nine, and once these last four chapters are separated from the remainder of the letter, Lightfoot's argument is seriously weakened. In modern writing on the subject it seems largely to be ignored.

No successor followed Lightfoot's lead by investigating fully the evidence of chronological relationship that lies in the literary and logical structure of the three letters concerned. That such evidence exists, however, and in ample measure to prove Lightfoot's hypothesis, may be demonstrated by the following synoptic arrangement of parallel passages from II Corinthians 1–9, Galatians, and Romans. The passages are abridged, only those verses being printed for which there is a definite parallel. The order throughout is that of Romans.

II CORINTHIANS 1–9	GALATIANS	ROMANS
3:17 Now the Lord is the Spirit, and where the Spirit of the Lord is, there is freedom.	5:13 For you were called to freedom, brethren . . .	8:2 For the law of the Spirit of life in Christ Jesus has set me free . . .
	14 For the whole law is fulfilled in one word . . .	4 . . . that the just requirement of the law might be fulfilled in us,
	16 But I say, walk by the Spirit, and do not gratify the desires of the flesh.	who walk not according to the flesh but according to the Spirit.
	17 For the desires of the flesh are against the Spirit, and the desires	5 For those who live according to the flesh set their minds on

II CORINTHIANS 1–9	GALATIANS	ROMANS
	of the Spirit are against the flesh . . .	the things of the flesh, but those who live according to the Spirit set their minds on the things of the Spirit.
	19 Now the works of the flesh are plain: immorality . . .	6 To set the mind on the flesh is death,
	22 But the fruit of the Spirit is love, joy, peace . . .	but to set the mind on the Spirit is life and peace.
	21 . . . those who do such things shall not inherit the kingdom of God.	8 . . . those who are in the flesh cannot please God.
	24 And those who belong to Christ Jesus have crucified the flesh with its passions and desires.	10 But if Christ is in you, although your bodies are dead because of sin,
	25 If we live by the Spirit, let us also walk by the Spirit . . .	your spirits are alive because of righteousness.
		14 For all who are led by the Spirit of God are sons of God.
	4:1 . . . the heir . . . is no better than a slave 2 . . . until the date set by the father.	15 For you did not receive the spirit of slavery to fall back into fear,
	5 . . . that we might receive adoption as sons.	but you have received the spirit of sonship.

II CORINTHIANS 1–9	GALATIANS	ROMANS
	6 And because you are sons, God has sent the Spirit of his Son into our hearts, crying, "Abba! Father!"	When we cry, "Abba! Father!" it is the Spirit himself bearing witness with our spirit, that we are children of God,
	7 So through God you are no longer a slave but a son, and if a son then an heir.	17 and if children, then heirs, heirs of God and fellow heirs with Christ,
4:10 . . . always carrying in the body the death of Jesus, so that the life of Jesus may also be manifested in our bodies.		provided that we suffer with him in order that we may also be glorified with him.
17 For this slight momentary affliction is preparing for us an eternal weight of glory beyond all comparison . . .		18 I consider that the sufferings of this present time are not worth comparing with the glory that is to be revealed in us.
5:2 Here indeed we groan and long to put on our heavenly dwelling . . .		22 . . . the whole creation has been groaning in travail . . .
5 He who has prepared us for this very thing is God, who has given us the down payment of the Spirit.		23 And not only the creation, but we ourselves, who have the first fruits of the Spirit, groan inwardly as we wait for adoption as sons, the redemption of our bodies.
4:18 . . . we look not to the things that are		24 . . . hope that is seen is not hope . . .

II CORINTHIANS 1–9	GALATIANS	ROMANS
seen but to the things that are unseen; for the things that are seen are transient, but the things that are unseen are eternal.		25 But if we hope for what we do not see, we wait for it with patience.

It is at once apparent that the Romans passage reproduces with remarkable fidelity the logical outlines of arguments which also appear in II Corinthians 1–9 and Galatians. Romans has drawn both words and arguments from the two shorter letters and its method of adapting them in each case has been exactly the same. But it has not only drawn arguments from the two other letters, it has also combined them. In the passage under discussion it has combined arguments which were originally separate and which, when they are read separately, have no obvious common elements. Once they are combined, however, it is apparent that their underlying thought and application are the same. This weaving together has been accomplished by a process of conflation, in which key words and ideas, upon which the separate arguments turn, have been brought together in order to provide connecting links.

The process may be seen most clearly at work in two places. The first is where Romans, which up to now has been reproducing the legal doctrine of Galatians about inheritance by adoption, suddenly makes a transition to the eschatological doctrine of II Corinthians 1–9 about suffering and death on earth as a necessary prelude to the manifestation of the heavenly glory. It does this by the simple expedient of following the conclusion of the legal argument of Galatians ("if children, then heirs, heirs of God") with a new phrase showing the relation of these heirs to Christ ("and fellow heirs with Christ") which is immediately modified by a conditional clause derived from the eschatological argument of II Corinthians 1–9 ("provided that we suffer with him, in order that we may also be glorified with him"). The second is at the end of this eschatological section, where Romans directly connects the conclusion of the argument from II Corinthians 1–9 about the simultaneous possession of two natures ("we ourselves, who have the first fruits of the Spirit, groan inwardly") with the central argument from the legal doctrine of Galatians ("as we wait for adoption as sons"). II Corinthians 1–9, in other words, has served as a model for Romans in exactly the same way as has Galatians.

But Lightfoot's hypothesis cannot be said to have been completely proved unless it be demonstrated that Galatians was written after II Corinthians 1–9. Here again, however, there is ample evidence, the full significance of which seems to have gone unnoticed.

No feature of Paul's style is more readily detected, even by the casual reader, than his love of antithesis. Not only does he repeatedly stress in speaking of his own life and the lives of his converts the radical change that has taken place in them; he expresses ideas in general in terms of vivid contrast. Flesh is opposed to spirit, law to grace, works to faith. Between the members of each of these pairs of terms, moreover, there is in Paul's developed thought a radical opposition. Spirit does not improve flesh; the two war against one another. Grace does not supplement law; it annuls it. Faith does not add to the merit of works; it stands alone, to the complete exclusion of works, as the sole ground for justification. There is no middle ground on which these terms may be said to overlap. They are contradictory and mutually exclusive.

The most frequently used of these pairs in all of Paul's writing are spirit-flesh and faith-work. In I Corinthians, II Corinthians 1–9, Galatians, and Romans, the frequency of occurrence of the four words that make up these pairs is as follows: spirit (105), flesh (57), faith (73), and work (32). More significant than their frequency of occurrence, however, is their distribution. The spirit-flesh antithesis is found in all four of these letters. But the faith-work antithesis occurs only in Galatians and Romans. Nowhere in I Corinthians or II Corinthians 1–9 is it either expressed or implied.[3] The separate words of the pair do occur with reasonable frequency, but they are never placed in opposition to one another. In I Corinthians faith is employed quite casually to mean one of the many gifts of the Spirit. It is at best equal in importance to

[3] The basis of comparison with regard to length is almost exact, since I Corinthians and II Corinthians 1–9 together occupy just one more WH page than do Galatians and Romans.

wisdom and knowledge (I Cor. 12:8,9). It is explicitly said to be inferior to love (I Cor. 13:2,13). In its other four occurrences in the letter it seems to mean hardly more than the belief and trust which are characteristic of the Christian. Nor is any broader meaning involved in the use of the term in II Corinthians 1–9. In short, nowhere in these two writings is the word used in the technical "Pauline" sense, familiar from Galatians and Romans, in which it means the sole ground, as opposed to works, upon which God accepts the believer.

A corresponding change may be observed in connection with work. In only one of its eight occurrences in I Corinthians does it mean an evil deed (I Cor. 5:2), and there it is the context—the passage is about the incestuous man—that supplies this meaning. In four cases (I Cor. 3:13–15) it is used of the work which each believer contributes to the building up of the Christian edifice on the foundation laid by Paul. In one case (I Cor. 9:1) the Corinthians are spoken of as Paul's "work in the Lord." And in the remaining two (I Cor. 15:58;16:10) the word occurs in the phrase, "the work of the Lord." Its single occurrence in II Corinthians 1–9 is in the phrase, "for every good work" (II Cor. 9:8). In no case in either letter is it used in the plural, in no case is it used in connection with law, in no case is it used in opposition to faith. In short, the technical "Pauline" sense of the word is not encountered in I Corinthians and II Corinthians 1–9 at all. Detailed examination of the usage of these words in Galatians and Romans is unnecessary. It is well known that they are used repeatedly in those letters in dialectical opposition to each other, and with a definite change of technical meaning as over against the meanings illustrated above.

It seems impossible to avoid the conclusion that what we are witnessing in the phenomena just described is the emergence in Paul's theological vocabulary of the antithesis between faith and work. Examination of the use of these terms in Galatians, moreover, reveals that in that letter they have been combined with the older antithesis between flesh and spirit in much the same way as sequences of ideas from II Corinthians 1–9 and Galatians were subsequently to be combined in Romans. Thus Paul writes in Galatians, "Did you receive the Spirit by works of the law, or by hearing with faith? . . . Having begun with the Spirit, are you now ending with the flesh? . . . Does he who supplies the Spirit to you and works miracles among you do so by works of the law, or by hearing with faith?" (Gal. 3:2-5). Here the two pairs of terms are used in intimate association, faith being connected with spirit and works with flesh. The same association occurs repeatedly in Romans. We may now ask whether it is likely that Paul, having once made this identification between the two pairs, and having used them in such intimate connection, should have failed to make the same identification, and ignored this connection, in a later discussion of the identical problem. That is, if he had already written Galatians when he came to write II Corinthians 1-9, with its developed doctrine of the simultaneous possession of two natures and its vehement antilegal position, is it conceivable that he should have omitted to connect spirit with faith and flesh with works of the law in II Corinthians 1-9? In view of the fact that Romans, which we know to have followed II Corinthians 1-9, again takes up the connection between the two antitheses and develops it at length, we should have to argue that having made the connection in Galatians, Paul then decided to abandon this line of argument in II Corinthians 1-9, only to change his mind again and revive it in Romans. This explanation of the phenomena seems unlikely to recommend itself.

Both the historical and the literary evidence, then, point to the same conclusion with regard to the date of Galatians, the historical evidence placing it after the beginning of the collection for the saints and the controversy with the Judaizers, and the literary evidence fixing it between II Corinthians 1-9 and Romans. That this is indeed the correct position of Galatians is amply proved as we trace the development of the eschatology, legal theory, and Christology through the three letters.

The eschatology of Galatians reflects an enlargement of one element of the new eschatology of II Corinthians 1-9 rather than a modification of the system as a whole. In the former letter Paul had not only systematized the idea of the simultaneous possession of two natures for the first time; he had also introduced a related idea which was to play an increasingly important part in the thinking of the later letters. This was the idea that although the believer might still inhabit a body of flesh, that body could be looked upon as having already died. He writes, "We are convinced that one has died for all; therefore all have died" (II Cor. 5:14). This is a new note, and in II Corinthians 1–9 it is sounded briefly and alone.

In Galatians it not only achieves a fuller statement but also begins to be associated with other ideas. Paul writes, "For I through the law died to the law, that I might live to God. I have been crucified with Christ; it is no longer I who live, but Christ who lives in me; and the life I now live in the flesh I live by the faith of the Son of God, who loved me and gave himself for me" (Gal. 2:20). And again, "But far be it from me to glory except in the cross of our Lord Jesus Christ, by which the world has been crucified to me, and I to the world" (Gal. 6:14).

In Romans the statement is fuller still. There it is associated first with sin:

> How can we who died to sin still live in it? Do you not know that all of us who have been baptized into Christ Jesus were baptized into his death? We were buried therefore with him by baptism into death, so that as Christ was raised from the dead by the glory of the Father, we too might walk in newness of life. For if we have been united with him in a death like his, we shall certainly be united with him in a resurrection like his. We know that our old self was crucified with him so that the sinful body might be destroyed, and we might no longer be enslaved to sin. For he who has died is freed from sin. But if we have died with Christ, we believe that we shall also live with him. For we know that Christ being raised from the dead will never die again; death no longer has dominion over him. The death he died he died to sin, once for all, but the life he lives he lives to God. So you also must consider yourselves dead to sin and alive to God in Christ Jesus (Rom. 6:2–11).

Later the association with law is developed at greater length:

> Likewise, my brethren, you have died to the law through the body of Christ, so that you may belong to another, to him who has been raised from the dead in order that we may bear fruit for God. While we were living in the flesh, our sinful passions, aroused by the law, were at work in our members to bear fruit for death. But now we are discharged from the law, dead to that which held us captive, so that we serve not under the old written code but in the new life of the Spirit (Rom. 7:4–6).

And finally the association with the simultaneous possession of two natures is made explicit:

> But you are not in the flesh, you are in the Spirit, if the Spirit of God really dwells in you. Any one who does not have the Spirit of Christ does not belong to him. But if Christ is in you, although your bodies are dead because of sin, your spirits are alive because of righteousness. If the Spirit of him who raised Jesus from the dead dwells in you, he who raised Christ Jesus from the dead will give life to your mortal bodies also through his Spirit which dwells in you. So then, brethren, we are debtors, not to the flesh, to live according to the flesh—for if you live according to the flesh you will die, but if by the Spirit you put to death the deeds of the body you will live (Rom. 8:9–13).

In these passages Paul has now completely committed himself to the idea that the believer must regard himself as having already died. But the believer has not yet been delivered "from this body of death" (Rom. 7:24). He still inhabits it, and he still possesses only "the first fruits of the Spirit" (Rom. 8:23). Resurrection still lies in the future.

Galatians refers to the resurrection in general terms: "For through the Spirit, by faith, we wait for the hope of righteousness" (Gal. 5:5). And again, "He who sows to the Spirit will from the Spirit reap eternal life" (Gal. 6:8). Romans, however, is specific: "For if we have been united with him in a death like his, we shall certainly be united with him in a resurrection like his" (Rom. 6:5). The "death like his" of which Paul speaks is the martyr's death which has been uppermost in his mind since the persecution in Asia, when he believed that the sentence of death had been passed on him (II Cor. 1:8–9), and the "resurrection like his" is the immediate resurrection of which he had spoken in Philippians: "My desire is to depart and be with Christ" (Phil. 1:23). He had continued to think of the resurrection in these terms in II Corinthians 1–9: "We know that while we are at home in the body we are away from the Lord . . . and we would rather be away from the body and at home with the Lord" (II Cor. 5:6,8). As in those letters, it is still regarded as a future event.

But Romans also introduces a new eschatological term, "the manifestation of the sons of God," for which "the creation waits with eager longing" (Rom. 8:19). This disclosure of "the glory that is to be revealed in us" (Rom. 8:18) is equated with "the redemption of our bodies" (Rom. 8:23) and corresponds to the transformation of the living at the last day (I Cor. 15:51–52; Phil. 3:21) and the final "putting on" of the heavenly dwelling (II Cor. 5:1–4). It too is a future event, but it can no longer be thought of as taking place simultaneously with the resurrection of those individuals who will have died, for they will already have been raised immediately after death; it belongs in a more distant future. Resurrection and manifestation, in other words, are treated in Romans as separate events, occurring at different points in future time. With the formal incorporation into the system of this distinction, which is foreshadowed as early as Philippians, we are within one step of the final modification in Paul's eschatology, in which the two are completely separated, the former no longer being treated as a future event at all but being regarded as having already occurred, and only the latter still being looked upon as an event that will take place at the parousia (Col. 3:1–4).

The legal theory of Galatians, unlike its eschatology, exhibits a marked departure from that of II Corinthians 1–9. In the earlier letter Paul had set out to demonstrate with scriptural arguments that the law of Moses was no longer binding. He did this, it will be recalled, by arguing that the law was capable of applying for a limited time only. When its glory, the visible sign of its heavenly nature, had completely faded, it had become a dead letter, and it had been superseded by the new covenant "in the Spirit" (II Cor. 3:4–18). This argument is based entirely on the nature of the law. In Galatians we find a completely new set of arguments stated in purely legal terms. The reason for the change is to be found in the special circumstances which gave rise to Galatians.

It will be recalled that just as the collection trip was about to begin Paul had engaged in a conflict in Antioch with a group of conservative Jewish Christians who had insisted that Gentile converts should keep the whole law of Moses. Later Paul learned that these men, or others who took the same position, had visited the churches of Galatia and persuaded at least some of the Galatian Christians to submit to circumcision. They had apparently employed two effective arguments: first, that righteousness was defined in such a way in the Bible as to make clear that it required the keeping of the whole law; and second, that Paul himself upheld the keeping of the whole law when he was with Jews; he had simply not taught the Galatians about this requirement because he felt they were not ready for it.

It is very possible that Paul had given his opponents some grounds for these arguments. He had admitted to the Corinthians, "To the Jews I became as a Jew, in order to win Jews; to those under the law I became as one under the law—though not being myself under the law—that I might win those under the law" (I Cor. 9:20), and he had also admitted to them that he had not been able to address them "as spiritual men, but as men of the flesh, as babes in Christ." He had fed them "with milk, not solid food," for they were "not ready" for solid food (I Cor. 3:1–2). These practices may well have lent credibility to the charge that he preached a different gospel in different places, but the charge, he insists, is false: "If any one is preaching to you a gospel contrary to that which you received, let him be accursed" (Gal. 1:9). He denies that he is a man-pleaser; if he were, he would still be a Jew: "Am I trying to please men? If I were still pleasing men, I should not be a servant of Christ" (Gal. 1:10). Nor does he preach circumcision: "If I, brethren, still preach circumcision, why am I still persecuted?" (Gal. 5:11).

The legal argument could not be disposed of so readily. Paul did preach that "the unrighteous (ἄδικοι) shall not inherit the kingdom of God" (I Cor. 6:9). He had also written, "You were washed, you were sanctified, you were justified (ἐδικαιώθητε) in the name of the Lord Jesus Christ and in the Spirit of our God" (I Cor. 6:11). Righteousness and its achievement, in other words, were an integral part of his message. His task, therefore, was to find a scriptural proof of his contention that righteousness is achieved apart from law. This he does in Galatians by demonstrating that righteousness in the Scripture is associated primarily with a system of testamentary inheritance. The demonstration depends in considerable measure on the ambiguity of the Pauline idea of faith, which comprehends four distinct meanings: (1) conviction or belief; (2) trust; (3) faith; and (4) faithfulness or fidelity. The second and fourth of these meanings have a place in the technical legal vocabulary, and it is to this technical use that Paul puts them in the argument of Galatians that the inheritance is by way of a trust and that the conditions of the trust have been fulfilled by the faithfulness of Christ the trustee.[4]

The background of the argument is not difficult to reconstruct. Paul had maintained apparently from the beginning that Gentiles who were converted were "washed . . . sanctified . . . justified in the name of the Lord Jesus Christ and in the Spirit of our God" (I Cor. 6:11). That is to say, they were cleansed of their former sins in baptism, dedicated to a life of holiness, and accepted by God as righteous. The Judaizers had quarreled with the last of these claims. Righteousness, they had maintained, was a legal concept, and therefore the only righteous man was the man who kept the law. Paul answered this contention in Galatians.

He begins with the facts as they relate to Jewish Christians: "We ourselves, who are Jews by birth and not Gentile sinners, yet who know that a man is not justified by works of the law but through the faith of Jesus Christ, even we have believed in Christ Jesus, in order to be justified by the faith of Christ and not by works of the law, because by works of the law shall no one be justified" (Gal. 2:15–16). In other words, even the Judaizers must know from experience that justification does not come from the law but from Christ; otherwise they would not have "believed in Christ Jesus." Indeed, if the law brought justification, nothing at all would have been accomplished by the work of Christ: "For if justification were through the law, then Christ died to no purpose" (Gal. 2:21).

He then turns to the facts as they relate to Gentile Christians. As Gentiles the Galatians certainly know from their own experience that their acceptance by God as righteous had not come through the keeping of the law: "Did you receive the Spirit by works of the law, or by hearing with faith?" (Gal. 3:2). Here again, as in the case of the Jews, the facts supported Paul's contention. In the case of the Gentiles also, justification had not come through law but through Christ. Since there could be no question as to its having come, however, the only question was, how had it been conveyed?

[4] See W. H. P. Hatch, *The Pauline Idea of Faith* (Cambridge: Harvard University Press, 1917).

Paul's answer to this question is that it had been conveyed by means of a trust, and that the conditions of the trust had been fulfilled by the faithfulness of Christ the trustee. God had said to Abraham, "In you shall all the nations be blessed" (Gal. 3:8), and since blessing in this context is the scriptural term for the bestowal of an inheritance, what he had meant was that the "nations" were to inherit something from God himself by means of a testamentary disposition in which Abraham was somehow involved. The "something," Paul argues, is righteousness, since this is what God had "reckoned" to Abraham. And the proof that the conveyance had been effected through Christ is that the Gentiles had received the Spirit.

The blessing, however, had not been transmitted to the Gentiles through Abraham's descendants the Jews. They had not possessed it. It had been transmitted to the Gentiles by Christ alone. This, Paul points out, is precisely what the Scripture contemplates, for the promise had been confirmed in a testament in which God had said, "I will establish my covenant [testament] between me and you and your offspring" (Gen. 17:7). This verse is not quoted in full in Galatians, but it is clearly referred to in the line, "Now the promises were made to Abraham and his offspring" (Gal. 3:6). The word "offspring" in this verse, Paul points out, is singular; therefore the offspring must be an individual. God had also promised to bestow the blessing on "all the nations," a group of heirs clearly distinguishable from the individual offspring. This must mean, Paul concludes, that God, the testator, had willed the blessing first to Abraham in trust, then still in trust to his own son Jesus Christ, who was also Abraham's offspring, with the intention that Christ, the final trustee, should distribute it to the ultimate beneficiaries, "all the nations."

Running parallel to this argument is a second argument to the effect that in this whole system the blessing of righteousness is never based on law but always on faith, or trust. Paul begins this argument with the example of Abraham, who "believed [trusted] God and it was reckoned to him as righteousness" (Gen. 15:6; Gal. 3:6). The case of Abraham, in other words, is the precedent which is to be followed when the blessing is conveyed to the other beneficiaries. "So it is those of faith [trust] who are blessed with faithful [trusting] Abraham" (Gal. 3:9).

The law, on the other hand, does not convey a blessing but a curse: "For it is written, 'Cursed be every one who does not abide by all things written in this book, and do them'" (Deut. 27:26; Gal. 3:10). Moreover God has promised that "he who through faith [trust] is righteous shall live" (Hab. 2:4; Gal. 3:11), but the law knows only of performance: "He who does them shall live by them" (Lev. 18:5; Gal. 3:12). Therefore "it is evident that no man is accepted as righteous before God by the law" (Gal. 3:11).

Christ, however, "redeemed us from the curse of the law, having become a curse for us—for it is written, 'Cursed be every one who hangs on a tree'" (Deut. 21:23; Gal. 3:13). That is, Christ had taken on himself the curse of the law, although as the heir of the promised righteousness under the terms of God's testament he need not have, and thus redeemed those who had incurred the curse of the law, "that in Christ Jesus the blessing of Abraham might come upon the Gentiles, that we might receive the promise of the Spirit through faith [trust]" (Gal. 3:14).

Paul now gives still another reason why the inheritance cannot come by the law. God had given it to Abraham "by a promise" (Gal. 3:18), and this promise had been ratified in a testamentary bequest (Gal. 3:17). The law had not come until "four hundred and thirty years afterward" (Gal. 3:17). Therefore it cannot have annulled the testament, which had been already ratified by God, for "no one annuls even a man's testament, or adds to it, once it has been ratified" (Gal. 3:15).

In the final step of Paul's argument he explains how the inheritance has been conveyed from Christ the trustee to the ultimate heirs, "all the nations." At the time of the ratification of the testament God had said to Abraham, "You shall be the father of a multitude of nations" (Gen. 17:4). Since "nations" means Gentiles, and since the definition of a Gentile is one who is not a descendant of Abraham, God must have meant that the Gentiles were to become sons of Abraham by adoption, this being the only way in which Abraham could become their father. And this is what God had accomplished through Christ. Paul's proof of this is ingenious. All Christians, he points out, are sons of God, for they are "in Christ Jesus" and have "put on" Christ, who is himself the Son of God. By the same token, therefore, they are also sons of Abraham, for Christ is also the son of Abraham, the offspring to whom the promise was made. What Christ had effected, in short, was the adoption of the Gentiles as sons of both Abraham and God, and thus joint heirs of God with himself.

In order to fulfill the trust Christ had had to accomplish two things. First, he had, so to speak, to reintroduce trust into the world, so that the beneficiaries by appropriating it could be accepted by God as righteous on the ground of trust and thus qualify for the blessing of trusting Abraham. And second, he had to redeem the beneficiaries by satisfying their previous obligations and thus free them for adoption. The first he did by accepting the trust, the second by giving his life. This was the work of Christ.

But if this had been God's plan for salvation all along, "Why then the law?" Paul asks. What follows is a bold stroke. "It was added," he answers, "because of transgressions, till the offspring should come to whom the promise had been made; and it was imposed by angels through an intermediary. Now an intermediary is not 'of one,' but God is one" (Gal. 3:19–20). That is, the law of Moses was not given by a single being, God, but by a plurality of beings, the angels, the "elemental spirits of the universe" (Gal. 4:3).[5]

This is a far more radical and extreme position with regard to law than Paul had taken in II Corinthians 1–9. In that letter he had been content to show that the law, the "old covenant" (II Cor. 3:14), had expired and been replaced by the "new covenant" (II Cor. 3:6). There is nothing to suggest that the old covenant had not been enacted by God. In Galatians, however, the terms "old covenant" and "new covenant" disappear, since Paul has substituted the promise to Abraham for the new covenant of Jeremiah,[6] and the promise was made before

[5] The idea that the law was delivered to Moses by an angel, or angels, is not Paul's invention, but seems to have been current in his day. It is reflected in the Book of Jubilees as well as in Stephen's speech in Acts 7:53.

[6] In Romans, Paul identifies the covenant of Jeremiah with the intuitive moral knowledge of the Gentiles, who "show that the work of the law is written in their hearts" (Rom. 2:15).

the enactment of the law of Moses. (In the allegory of Hagar and Sarah in the fourth chapter, the two women are not said to represent the "old covenant" and the "new covenant" but merely "two covenants," since Sarah became Abraham's wife before Hagar became his concubine, even though Sarah's child was not born until after Hagar's.) The law in Galatians, therefore, is not only not God's law but it also, like the authority of a tutor, has a doubly limited jurisdiction. There was a time before its enactment when it was of no effect, and there is a time after its expiration when it is of no effect. The promise was made in the former of these times; the fulfillment of the promise has come about in the latter.

The brilliance and originality of this argument must not blind us to its defects, two of which are serious. First, it explicitly denies the direct sovereignty of God over men during the period in which the law was in force. And second, it implicitly denies that all the parts of the Old Testament are equally inspired. The relationship of Galatians to Romans becomes clear when we see the way in which these defects are repaired in the latter letter.

Romans modifies Galatians in the first instance by omitting any mention of angels or elemental spirits of the universe in connection with the giving and enforcing of the law. Where Galatians speaks of those under the law as slaves of the elemental spirits (Gal. 4:3,9), Romans speaks of them as slaves of sin (Rom. 6:16–17,20), and although Romans may speak of sin as "reigning," it only speaks of it as reigning "in your mortal bodies" (Rom. 6:12); the sole divine sovereign is God. Finally, Paul makes it clear that he is not attacking God's law. "Do we then overthrow the law by this faith? By no means! On the contrary, we uphold the law" (Rom. 3:31). "The law is holy, and the commandment is holy and righteous and good" (Rom. 7:12). It is "the law of God" (Rom. 7:22).

But there is another law, a "law of sin which dwells in my members" (Rom. 7:23). Although this law is a reflection of the law of God, it is the instrument of sin, the reigning sovereign of mortal bodies. And since it is the instrument of sin, it works in reverse. It says, "Thou shalt not covet," but its effect is to instruct the innocent how to covet and thus to awaken the desire to do what it forbids

(Rom. 7:7). The source of this desire, says Paul, is sin. "I was once alive apart from the law," he writes, "but when the commandment came, sin revived and I died; the very commandment which promised life proved to be death to me. For sin, finding opportunity in the commandment, deceived me and by it killed me" (Rom. 7:9–11). And he concludes, "So then, I of myself serve the law of God with my mind, but with my flesh I serve the law of sin" (Rom. 7:25).

But this is not the end of the matter, for "the law of the Spirit of life in Christ Jesus," Paul explains, "has set me free from the law of sin and death" (Rom. 8:2). The work of Christ, he continues, was performed in order that "the righteous requirement of the law might be fulfilled in us, who walk not according to the flesh but according to the Spirit" (Rom. 8:4). The explanation of how this operates is eschatological. The Christian's body of flesh is already dead, for he has died with Christ. He is therefore "dead to sin," the sovereignty of sin having been limited to his flesh (Rom. 6:6–11). He is also "alive to God," for he has received the spirit. He is thus "discharged from the law, dead to that which held us captive," and enabled to serve God "not under the old written code but in the new life of the Spirit" (Rom. 7:6).

This legal theory employs elements from both Galatians and II Corinthians 1–9. Its setting is in the Galatians framework of the promise to Abraham: "The promise to Abraham and his descendants, that they should inherit the world, did not come through the law but through the righteousness of trust" (Rom. 4:13). But the doctrine of the two natures, one of which is subject to the law of sin and the other to the law of God, is an adaptation of the eschatological teaching of II Corinthians 1–9. The effect of the modification is to preserve the doctrine of righteousness through trust while at the same time avoiding the suggestion that law is not the instrument of God and that the whole Bible is not divinely inspired.

The Christology of Galatians and that of Romans are so similar that the two may be treated together. As late as Philippians Paul had regarded the work of Christ as having been performed on his own initiative. Christ had emptied himself, assumed human form, humbled himself, and become obedient unto death. As a reward for his perfect obedience God had raised him from the dead (Phil. 2:5–11). In II Corinthians 1–9 Paul had disavowed this teaching and substituted for it the view that "God was in Christ reconciling the world to himself" (II Cor. 5:19). That is to say, the initiative in the work of Christ had been God's. In Galatians this view is made even more explicit. There Paul writes, "When the time had fully come, God sent forth his Son, born of woman, born under the law, to redeem those who were under the law" (Gal. 4:4–5). Romans also emphasizes the initiative of God. The redemption is in Christ Jesus, "whom God put forward as an expiation by his blood, to be received by faith" (Rom. 3:24–25).

This is but a part of a larger combination of ideas. Philippians and II Corinthians, like the earlier letters, had treated the work of Christ primarily in eschatological terms having to do with attainment to the resurrection. Galatians had treated it primarily in legal terms having to do with the fulfillment of the promise and the achievement of righteousness on the ground of trust. Romans combines the two treatments throughout. A single example will suffice to show how thoroughly this is accomplished:

> There is therefore now no condemnation for those who are in Christ Jesus. For the law of the Spirit of life in Christ Jesus has set me free from the law of sin and death. For God has done what the law, weakened by the flesh, could not do: sending his own Son in the likeness of sinful flesh and for sin, he condemned sin in the flesh, in order that the just requirement of the law might be fulfilled in us, who walk not according to the flesh but according to the Spirit. For those who live according to the flesh set their minds on the things of the flesh, but those who live according to the Spirit set their minds on the things of the Spirit. To set the mind on the flesh is death, but to set the mind on the Spirit is life and peace. For the mind that is set on the flesh is hostile to God; it does not submit to God's law, indeed it cannot; and those who are in the flesh cannot please God. But you are not in the flesh, you are in the Spirit, if the Spirit of God really dwells in you. Any one who does not have the Spirit of Christ does not belong to him. But if Christ is in you, although your bodies are dead because of sin, your spirits are alive because of righteousness. If the Spirit of him who raised Jesus from the dead dwells in you, he who raised Christ Jesus from the dead will give life to your mortal bodies also through his Spirit which dwells in you (Rom. 8:1–11).

Examples of such combinations of ideas could be multiplied. They all point to the same conclusion. Romans is a combination of a legal theory based on Galatians, but without its defects, with the eschatology and Christology introduced in II Corinthians 1-9. Nor can there be any question of the order in which the letters were written, for the legal theory of Galatians, which is substantially repeated in Romans, is clearly a substitute there for the legal theory of II Corinthians 1-9.

Once again we have found that a significant modification in Paul's thinking arose in response to a specific situation. In this case the Judaizers had contended that righteousness could be attained only through the law. In answer to that contention Paul wrote Galatians, in which he proved that righteousness could not be attained through the law at all, since God had arranged, by means of a testamentary bequest, that it should be conveyed solely in trust. Galatians is a strikingly original performance by a brilliant legal mind. It was written in haste and anger, however, and it shows the marks of both. Some of the positions it takes, notably the contention that the law was the instrument of the elemental spirits rather than of God, are untenable, and Paul modified these when he wrote Romans a short time later. Romans itself is a synthesis. It combines elements from all the letters that preceded it, modifying what it draws from them where necessary and adapting everything to its over-all system of thought. The foundation on which it rests, however, and from which it rises to the full stature of its greatness, is Galatians.

With the dating of Galatians, the chronological list of the letters now reads: I Thessalonians, I Corinthians, Philippians, II Corinthians 1-9, Galatians, and Romans.

7

II CORINTHIANS 10–13

The location of II Corinthians 10–13 in the sequence of the letters is in many ways the most tantalizing of all the problems connected with the Pauline chronology. The letter contains a substantial amount of factual information, and much of this information is clearly related to the historical data to be found in the other letters of the collection period. It is also a highly personal letter, revealing Paul's state of mind as he wrote it with perfect clarity and in great detail. But the factual information falls short of disclosing the precise date of the letter, and the personal passages deal almost entirely with Paul's thought about his ministry as such and make almost no reference to the eschatology, Christology, or legal theory on the basis of which it might be compared with the other letters of the same general period.

The relevant factual information contained in II Corinthians 10–13 concerns four points: (1) the time that has elapsed since Paul's conversion, (2) the dates of his two previous visits to Corinth, (3) the relationship of Titus to the Corinthian church, and (4) the nature of the opposition to Paul within the Corinthian congregation.

It is the time elapsed since Paul's conversion that enables us to fix the outer limits of the period within which the letter was written.[1] In speaking of his credentials as an apostle, he writes:

> I must boast; there is nothing to be gained by it, but I will go on to visions and revelations of the Lord. I know a man in Christ who fourteen years ago was caught up to the third heaven —whether in the body or out of the body I do not know, God knows. And I know that this man was caught up into Paradise —whether in the body or out of the body I do not know, God knows—and he heard things that cannot be told, which man may not utter (II Cor. 12:1–4).

The revelation to which this refers may have been one of many (II Cor. 12:7), but it cannot have taken place before Paul's conversion, and the letter therefore cannot be dated less than fourteen years after that event. A similar line of reasoning fixes the earliest possible date of Paul's second visit to Jerusalem, for although there is more than one possible way of interpreting the figures in the first two chapters of Galatians, the second visit to Jerusalem, which occurred before Galatians was written, cannot on any calculation have taken place less than fourteen years after the conversion (Gal. 1:16; 2:1). The same lower *terminus* therefore applies to the second visit to Jerusalem, the composition of II Corinthians 10–13, and the composition of Galatians; all three fall at least fourteen years after the conversion.

As regards Paul's previous visits to Corinth, II Corinthians 10–13 tells us not only that there had been two of these but also that on the second Paul had had to threaten some of the members of the Corinthian church with disciplinary action. He writes, "This is the third time I am coming to you. Any charge must be sustained by the evidence of two or three witnesses. I warned those who sinned before and all the others, and I warn them now while absent, as I did when present on my second visit, that if I come again I will not spare them" (II Cor.

---

[1] See John Knox, "Fourteen Years Later: A Note on the Pauline Chronology," *Journal of Religion*, XVIX (1936), 341–349. Knox has since given up the position which this article takes. He should not have. He was right the first time.

13:1-3). The first of these two visits, of course, was the occasion for the founding of the church in Corinth. The second would seem to be the "painful visit" alluded to in II Corinthians 1-9: "For I made up my mind not to make you another painful visit" (II Cor. 2:1). It thus occurred before the writing of that letter. But how long before? There are only two possibilities. Either it took place before the beginning of the collection trip or between the writing of I Corinthians and of II Corinthians 1-9. It cannot have taken place between the beginning of the collection trip and the writing of I Corinthians, for I Corinthians makes it clear that Paul had not been in Corinth since the writing of the Previous Letter, which coincided with the beginning of the collection trip. Nor can it have taken place after the writing of II Corinthians 1-9, for the evidence of that letter, corroborated by the evidence of Romans, reveals that Paul's difficulties with the Corinthians had been settled when he met Titus in Macedonia, and there is no evidence of the renewal of these difficulties at a later date. Most commentators believe that it took place after the writing of I Corinthians, but there are good reasons for believing that the earlier date may be correct. There is little available time in the collection trip, as we now understand it, to allow for such a visit. Only seven weeks seem to have elapsed between the writing of I Corinthians from Ephesus at Passover and the writing of II Corinthians 1-9 from Macedonia at Pentecost, and we now know that within that interval the following events took place: I Corinthians was delivered to Corinth, news of its reception was brought back to Paul in Ephesus, Titus was dispatched to Corinth as Paul's emissary, Paul was arrested and imprisoned for a long enough time to allow for an exchange of letters with Philippi, and finally Paul was released and made his way to Troas and from there to Macedonia. Biographers of Paul, even without taking into consideration the imprisonment which we now know to have occurred in Ephesus in this period, have been aware of the difficulty of fitting the second visit into the time available after the writing of I Corinthians, and they have stressed that it must have been of extremely short duration. Once the imprisonment is taken into account it is hard to see how such a visit could have occurred in this interval at all.

But if it did not take place after the writing of I Corinthians, then it must have taken place before the beginning of the collection trip, and while the letters tell us very little about that particular period, they do suggest one occasion for such a visit. That occasion is immediately before Paul left Achaia at the close of his first trip to Europe. We have seen that I Thessalonians was probably written at about that time. Shortly before writing I Thessalonians, however, he had been in Athens (I Thess. 3:1). He had hoped to revisit Thessalonica, but he had been prevented (I Thess. 2:18). This suggests that he was returning from Europe at the end of his first stay there, and that he planned to travel north from Athens and revisit the churches of Macedonia on the way. It seems unlikely that he would plan to revisit the Macedonian churches, however, without also revisiting Corinth, and it may very well be that when he arrived in Athens he had just come from his second visit to Corinth. Such a "painful visit" as we know the second visit to have been (II Cor. 2:1) would explain the very sharp tone of the Previous Letter, which was written at the same time as I Thessalonians, and which betrays an intimate knowledge of the conditions in the Corinthian church to which it addresses itself. The best that can be said for this solution to the problem of the second visit is that it accords with all the evidence at our disposal without involving us in the very real difficulty connected with a date for the second visit during the collection. It does not tell us any more than we already know about the date of II Corinthians 10–13, however.

The evidence concerning Titus' relations with Corinth is similarly inconclusive. We know that Titus went to Corinth as Paul's emissary after the writing of I Corinthians. Presumably he was sent because Paul had heard that I Corinthians had not been well received. We also know that Titus' mission was successful. When he met Paul in Macedonia, he reported that the Corinthians had repented and wished to be forgiven (II Cor. 7:6–16). Was this Titus' first visit to Corinth? At first glance II Corinthians 1–9, written on the occasion of his meeting with Paul in Macedonia, seems to imply that it was. Paul writes, "And besides our own comfort we rejoiced still more at the joy of Titus, because his spirit has been set at rest by you. For if I have expressed to him some pride in you, I was not put to shame; but just as everything we said to you was true, so our boasting before Titus has proved true" (II Cor. 7:13-14). This has been taken to mean that Titus had known the Corinthians previously only through Paul's boasting about them. But it does not necessarily mean that. It can just as well mean that Titus had been to Corinth previously, had formed an unfavorable impression of the Corinthians in spite of Paul's boasts about them, and had only discovered during a subsequent visit that Paul's boasting had been true after all. There may even be a reference to such a sequence of events in Paul's statement that Titus' spirit had been "set at rest" by the Corinthians. But again the evidence falls short of proof either way.

Connected with the problem of Titus' visits to Corinth is the problem of the Severe Letter. We know that Paul had sent a Severe Letter, written "out of much affliction and anguish of heart and with many tears," to Corinth before the writing of II Corinthians 1-9 (II Cor. 2:3-4,9; 7:8). Presumably Titus was the bearer of this letter. Attempts have been made to show that the Severe Letter was none other than II Corinthians 10-13,[2] but the arguments advanced depend on a series of references in II Corinthians 1-9 to a threatened visit that did not take place: "It was to spare you that I refrained from coming to Corinth" (II Cor. 1:23); "I wrote as I did, so that when I came I might not be pained by those who should have made me rejoice" (II Cor. 2:3); "This is why I wrote, that I might test you and know whether you are obedient in everything" (II Cor. 2:9). This visit is identified with the one threatened in II Corinthians 10-13: "If I come again I will not spare . . ." (II Cor. 13:2); "I write this while I am away from you, in order that when I come I may not have to be severe" (II Cor. 13:10); ". . . being ready to punish every disobedience, when your obedience is complete" (II Cor. 10:6). Unfortunately, the references to a threatened visit will fit just as well with certain passages in I Corinthians: "I do not write this to make you ashamed, but to admonish you as my beloved children" (I Cor. 4:14); "Some are arrogant, as though I were not coming to you. But I will come to you soon, if the Lord wills, and I will find out not the talk of these arrogant people but their power" (I Cor. 4:18-19); "What do you wish? Shall I come to you with a rod, or with love in a spirit of

[2] See K. Lake, *The Earlier Epistles of St. Paul* (London, 1911), pp. 154ff.

gentleness?" (I Cor. 4:21). The sentiments are such commonplaces that it is hard to see how they could be avoided in any writing that threatens a visit for punishment but expresses at the same time the hope that such punishment may not prove necessary.

As regards the nature of the opposition to Paul in the Corinthian congregation, there is a good deal of evidence in II Corinthians 10–13. The leaders of the opposition are Jews (II Cor. 11:22) who "claim that in their boasted mission they work on the same terms" as Paul (II Cor. 11:12). Paul calls them "false apostles, deceitful workmen, disguising themselves as apostles of Christ" (II Cor. 11:13). They are not members of the Corinthian church, but have come from outside, and "boast beyond limit in other men's labors" (II Cor. 10:15). Paul writes, "If some one comes and preaches another Jesus than the one we preached, or if you receive a different spirit from the one you received, or if you accept a different gospel from the one you accepted, you submit to it readily enough. I think that I am not in the least inferior to these superlative apostles" (II Cor. 11:4–5). One of their charges against Paul seems to have been that although he pretended not to accept money for his work he had taken advantage of the Corinthians through his agents. He counters, "Did I commit a sin in abasing myself so that you might be exalted, because I preached God's gospel without cost to you?" (II Cor. 11:7). And he continues, "But granting that I myself did not burden you, I was crafty, you say, and got the better of you by guile. Did I take advantage of you through any of those whom I sent to you? . . . Did Titus take advantage of you? Did we not take the same steps?" (II Cor. 12:17–18).

Who were these leaders of the opposition? They do not seem to have been Judaizers, for although they were clearly Jewish Christians, there is no indication in the letter that they had tried to persuade the Corinthians to accept circumcision and undertake the keeping of the whole law. Neither circumcision nor law is mentioned in the letter at all. There is some indication that they may have been the leaders of the so-called "Christ party" mentioned in I Corinthians: "It has been reported to me by Chloe's people that there is quarreling among you, my brethren. What I mean is that each one of you says, 'I belong to Paul,' or 'I belong to Apollos,' or 'I belong to Cephas,' or

'I belong to Christ' " (I Cor. 1:11–12).[3] But who the members of the Christ party were, or what their beliefs were, I Corinthians does not tell us. Nor do the references to those "of Christ" in II Corinthians 10–13. Paul merely says, "If any one is confident that he is Christ's let him remind himself that as he is Christ's, so are we" (II Cor. 10:7).

This identification, however, provides the closest link to be found between II Corinthians 10–13 and any of the other letters. II Corinthians 10–13 can be read and understood, in fact, as an intensification of the position which Paul had taken in the first four chapters of I Corinthians. Those chapters had dealt with divisions in the Corinthian church, and Paul had employed two principal lines of argument in his attempt to undermine the claims of the various factions. The first was that the gospel did not rest on "wisdom" or "power" of the sort that these factions were using to support their positions, but on "Christ the power of God and the wisdom of God" (I Cor. 1:25). The second was that there could be no distinction among Christians based on the relative merits of those persons through whose ministry they had been converted. These were merely "servants through whom you believed, as the Lord assigned to each" (I Cor. 3:5). II Corinthians 10–13 employs the same two arguments throughout. Paul writes, "The weapons of our warfare are not worldly but have divine power to destroy strongholds. We destroy arguments and every proud obstacle to the knowledge of God, and take every thought captive to obey Christ" (II Cor. 10:4–5). He is even more explicit with reference to the claim of his adversaries to possess a greater authority than his. He writes, "Not that we venture to class or compare ourselves with some of those who commend themselves. But when they measure themselves by one another, and compare themselves with one another, they are without understanding" (II Cor. 10:12). And he develops with the same irony the theme of his own weakness as the mark of the genuineness of his apostleship. He is "unskilled in speaking" (II Cor. 11:6), he "robbed other churches by accepting support from them" so that he might serve the Corinthians without cost (II Cor. 11:8), and he speaks "not with the Lord's authority but as a fool, in this boastful confidence"

[3] This assumes that Paul was referring to a "Christ party" and not saying of himself, "But I am of Christ."

(II Cor. 11:17)—surely a reference to criticism for having written, "To the rest I say, not the Lord," and "In my judgment she is happier if she remains as she is. And I think that I have the Spirit of God" (I Cor. 7:12,40). The climax is distilled bitterness: "For you gladly bear with fools, being wise yourselves! For you bear it if a man makes slaves of you, or preys upon you, or takes advantage of you, or puts on airs, or strikes you in the face. To my shame, I must say, we were too weak for that!" (II Cor. 11:19–21). If he must boast he will boast of his hardships—labors, imprisonments, beatings, shipwrecks, peril, and deprivations (II Cor. 11:23–27). He even had to flee from Damascus by being "let down in a basket through a window in the wall" (II Cor. 11:33). He can boast of "visions and revelations of the Lord" (II Cor. 12:1), but he has also been given "a thorn in the flesh, a messenger of Satan, to harass me, to keep me from being too elated" (II Cor. 12:7). He concludes, "I will all the more gladly boast of my weaknesses, that the power of Christ may rest upon me" (II Cor. 12:9). This whole long passage echoes themes from I Corinthians, particularly the contrast between folly and wisdom and between weakness and strength, and the emphasis on the apostle's role as servant rather than master. It foreshadows a significant theme of II Corinthians 1–9 in the emphasis on Paul's sufferings, but this theme is not yet developed to the point where Paul can say, "If we are afflicted, it is for your comfort and salvation" (II Cor. 1:6). Nor is there any trace in II Corinthians 10–13 of the idea of the simultaneous possession of two natures. He cannot yet speak of himself in his afflictions as "always carrying in the body the death of Jesus, so that the life of Jesus may also be manifested in our bodies" (II Cor. 4:10).

II Corinthians 1–9, however, is filled with references to II Corinthians 10–13. These are not only in the familiar commonplaces about a threatened visit that proved unnecessary (which, as we have seen, can refer just as well to the threatened visit of I Corinthians as to that of II Corinthians 10–13) but in a series of quite specific allusions to the special circumstances out of which II Corinthians 10–13 arose and to Paul's response to those circumstances in that letter. With reference to his opponents' claim that he had been dishonest, and his impassioned defense of himself against this charge in II Corinthians 10–13, he now writes, calmly and dispassionately, "We have behaved in the world, and still more toward you, with holiness and godly sincerity, not by earthly wisdom but by the grace of God" (II Cor. 1:12). He repeatedly, by allusion and implication, contrasts his own ministry with that of his opponents: "Not that we lord it over your faith; we work with you for your joy" (II Cor. 1:24). "For we are not, like so many, peddlers of God's word" (II Cor. 2:17). "Do we need, as some do, letters of recommendation to you, or from you?" (II Cor. 3:1). "We have renounced disgraceful, underhanded ways; we refuse to practice cunning or to tamper with God's word, but by the open statement of the truth we would commend ourselves to every man's conscience in the sight of God" (II Cor. 4:2). "For what we preach is not ourselves, but Jesus Christ as Lord, with ourselves as your slaves for Jesus' sake" (II Cor. 4:5). "Therefore, knowing the fear of the Lord, we persuade many; but what we are is known to God, and I hope it is also known to your conscience" (II Cor. 5:11).

Recalling the accusation of dishonesty, he now writes, with touching simplicity, "Open your hearts to us; we have wronged no one, we have corrupted no one, we have taken advantage of no one"; and reflecting that the Corinthians now know that they had accused him falsely, he adds, "I do not say this to condemn you" (II Cor. 7:2-3). And recalling the further accusation that he had taken advantage of the Corinthians through Titus and the brother whom he had sent to Corinth earlier (II Cor. 12:16-18), he now explains that he is not only sending Titus and the same brother back to Corinth, but he is also sending a third man, "the brother who is famous among all the churches for his preaching of the gospel; and not only that, but he has been appointed by the churches to travel with us in this gracious work which we are carrying on" (II Cor. 8:18-19). The reason for this is stated plainly: "We intend that no one should blame us about this liberal gift which we are administering, for we aim at what is honorable not only in the Lord's sight but also in the sight of men" (II Cor. 8:20-21).

Even more revealing are the references in II Corinthians 1-9 to the "boasting" of II Corinthians 10-13. In that letter Paul had written: "For even if I boast a little too much of our authority . . ." (II Cor.

10:18); "But we will not boast beyond limit" (II Cor. 10:13); "We do not boast beyond limit in other men's labors" (II Cor. 10:15); ". . . so that we may preach the gospel in lands beyond you, without boasting of work already done in another's field" (II Cor. 10:16); "Let him who boasts, boast in the Lord" (II Cor. 10:17); ". . . this boast of mine shall not be silenced in the regions of Achaia" (II Cor. 11:10); "And what I do I will continue to do, in order to undermine the claim of those who would like to claim that in their boasted mission they work on the same terms as we do" (II Cor. 11:12); "I too may boast a little" (II Cor. 11:16); "I say . . . in this boastful confidence; since many boast of worldly things, I too will boast" (II Cor. 11:17–18); "But whatever any one dares to boast of . . . I also dare to boast of that" (II Cor. 11:21); "If I must boast, I will boast of the things that show my weakness" (II Cor. 11:30); "I must boast . . . I will go on to visions and revelations of the Lord" (II Cor. 12:1); "On behalf of this man I will boast, but on my own behalf I will not boast, except of my weaknesses" (II Cor. 12:9). It is an astonishing display, quite unmatched elsewhere in the writing of Paul, and it is clearly referred to in II Corinthians 1–9, where "boasting" is again prominently mentioned. But only once in that letter does Paul boast of himself: "For our boast is this, the testimony of our conscience that we have behaved . . . with holiness and godly sincerity"; and he is quick to add that he has been able to do so, "not by earthly wisdom but by the grace of God" (II Cor. 1:12). Elsewhere his boasting is of the Corinthians. Describing his joy at the return of Titus, he says, "For if I have expressed to him some pride in you, I was not put to shame, but just as everything we said to you was true, so our boasting before Titus has proved true" (II Cor. 7:14). By way of encouraging the Corinthians to complete the gathering of the collection under the direction of Titus and the two brothers who accompanied him, he writes, "So give proof, before the churches, of your love and of our boasting about you to these men" (II Cor. 8:24). He continues, "I know your readiness, of which I boast about you to the people of Macedonia . . . . But I am sending the brethren so that our boasting about you may not prove vain" (II Cor. 9:2–3).

In II Corinthians 1–9 Paul refers to his boasting about himself, but he uses a milder word, which he had also used in the earlier letter. He had written, "For it is not the man who commends himself that is accepted, but the man whom the Lord commends" (II Cor. 10:18). Now, with clear reference to the boasting of the earlier writing, he says, "Are we beginning to commend ourselves again?" (II Cor. 3:1). And later, "We are not commending ourselves to you again but giving you cause to boast of us, so that you may be able to answer those who boast on the ground of a man's position and not of his heart" (II Cor. 5:12). These passages are so clear as to leave little room for doubt as to what they refer to.

Two further correspondences between II Corinthians 10–13 and II Corinthians 1–9 deserve mention. In the midst of one of the angriest outbursts of boasting in the former letter, Paul had interjected, "I am talking like one out of his mind!" (II Cor. 11:23). In the latter, in the course of denying that he is commending himself again, he suddenly remarks, "For if we were beside ourselves, it was for God: if we are in our right mind, it is for you" (II Cor. 5:13). It sounds very much like a reference to the earlier passage.

Finally, one of the explicit references in II Corinthians 1–9 to the Severe Letter reads as follows: "For I wrote you out of much affliction and anguish of heart and with many tears, not to cause you pain but to let you know the abundant love that I have for you" (II Cor. 2:4). Here, as we have remarked earlier, we are in the realm of the commonplace, but it may not be without significance that II Corinthians 10–13, notwithstanding its anger and irony, contains an open declaration of this love. Boasting of his having refused to accepted financial support from the Corinthians, and insisting that his boast "shall not be silenced in the regions of Achaia," Paul concludes, "And why? Because I do not love you? God knows I do!" (II Cor. 11:10–11).

All of the available evidence, then, seems to point to a single conclusion, that II Corinthians 10–13 is the Severe Letter that Paul sent to Corinth by the hand of Titus shortly after he had heard that I Corinthians had not succeeded in its purpose of restoring order in the Corinthian church. It was clearly written before Paul's imprisonment in

Ephesus, for it not only does not mention the imprisonment but implies that Paul was free to come to Corinth at any time he chose. Its place between I Corinthians and Philippians is thus plain, and the sequence of the letters now reads: I Thessalonians, I Corinthians, II Corinthians 10–13, Philippians, II Corinthians 1–9, Galatians, and Romans.

8

COLOSSIANS AND PHILEMON

Colossians is usually treated by scholars as a late letter. Two arguments are used to support this conclusion. The first is that the letter was written from prison, and Acts knows of only two imprisonments, one in Caesarea and one in Rome, that might have provided the occasion for its composition. The second is that the doctrine of the letter, particularly as it touches on eschatology and Christology, exhibits a development over the ideas of the earlier letters and achieves a richness of statement which is not to be found elsewhere in Paul's writing. The first of these arguments, since it treats Acts as a primary source, may be ruled out of consideration in the present stage of our discussion. The second, however, can be used to establish that Colossians must have been written after the letters which we have already placed within the period of the collection.

As we have seen, those letters reflect a development in Paul's eschatology, the lines of which are as follows: Before the writing of I Thessalonians Paul had believed that the parousia was imminent and that he and all other Christians would live to see it. By the time I Thessalonians was written, however, some Christians had died, and Paul had modified his original teaching by adding to it the promise of a special resurrection of Christians at the parousia. In I Corinthians he had further modified the teaching by adding the prophecy that the living would be transformed from flesh to spirit at the moment of the resurrection of the Christian dead. Shortly after the writing of I Corinthians, however, Paul had been brought face to face with what seemed to be certain death, and that experience had forced him to change his teaching again. He now believed that instead of having to sleep in the ground until the parousia, he could look forward to an immediate resurrection after death. This modification first appears in Philippians, where Paul applies it only to himself. In II Corinthians 1–9, however, the new eschatology is applied to all Christians (II Cor. 5:6–8). In the same letter Paul introduces the idea that all Christians have already died with Christ: "We are convinced that one has died for all; therefore all have died" (II Cor. 5:14). In Galatians he writes, "I have been crucified with Christ; it is no longer I who live, but Christ who lives in me; and the life I now live in the flesh I live in the faith of the Son of God, who loved me and gave himself for me" (Gal. 2:20). The same idea is expressed at greater length in Romans. "Do you not know that all of us who have been baptized into Christ Jesus were baptized into his death? We were buried therefore with him by baptism into death, so that as Christ was raised from the dead by the glory of the Father, we too might walk in newness of life. For if we have been united with him in a death like his, we shall certainly be united with him in a resurrection like his" (Rom. 6:3–5). Newness of life, in this system, begins before resurrection. And resurrection is no longer delayed until the parousia. It is "a resurrection like his," that is to say, a resurrection immediately after death. The parousia in this eschatological system has thus necessarily ceased to be the occasion for the resurrection of the Christian dead; it is still, however, the occasion for the manifestation of the living, and presumably for the reappearance of those who have died and been "with the Lord" (Phil. 1:23; II Cor. 5:6–8). The death of the Christian is regarded in the system as having already taken place, but the resurrection, although it is no longer attached to the parousia, is still treated as future.

When we turn to Colossians we discover that a significant further modification has been introduced. Two of the features of the earlier system, death and manifestation, remain unchanged. Paul writes, "For you have died, and your life is hid with Christ in God. When Christ who is our life appears, then you also will appear with him in glory" (Col. 3:3–4). But the resurrection of the Christian is no longer looked on as a future event; it has now already taken place: "If then you have been raised with Christ, seek the things that are above, where Christ is, seated at the right hand of God" (Col. 3:1).

The effect of this change is to be seen throughout the letter. One striking example may be observed in the line, "He has delivered us from the dominion of darkness and transferred us to the kingdom of his beloved Son" (Col. 1:13), where entrance into the kingdom is a present reality, as contrasted with the earlier line, "You know how, like a father with his children, we exhorted each one of you and encouraged you and charged you to lead a life worthy of God, who calls you into his own kingdom and glory" (I Thess. 2:11–12), where entrance into the kingdom is still a future hope. Another may be seen in the degree to which what was eschatological in the earlier letters has become ethical in Colossians. In II Corinthians 1–9 the death of the earthly body, which is to be followed by the putting on of the heavenly body, is treated as a literal concept. In Colossians it has a new application. "Put to death therefore what is earthly in you: immorality, impurity, passion, evil desire, and covetousness, which is idolatry. . . . Put on them, as God's chosen ones, holy and beloved, compassion, kindness, lowliness, meekness, and patience" (Col. 3:5,12). Finally, since death and resurrection have already taken place, and the Christian has already been transferred to the kingdom while he is still in this world, the future hope has taken on a larger meaning. It is no longer merely a share in the blessings of the new age on earth that will begin with the parousia. It is now also a "share in the inheritance of the saints in light" (Col. 1:12). The parousia, which was once looked on as imminent, has now receded into the indefinite future, and the Messianic kingdom, which was once looked on as a state that would come into being only after the parousia, has now come to be regarded as already present.

The lines of development of Paul's Christology are no less clear than those of his eschatology. I Thessalonians reflects an early stage in his thinking, when his interest was predominantly futuristic. The work of Christ, rather than the person of Christ, occupied Paul's thought, and while he conceived of this as having begun with Christ's death and resurrection, the principal part of Christ's work remained to be performed in the Messianic reign which was still to come. The Christology of I Corinthians is still heavily influenced by eschatological considerations. In that letter Christ is thought of as the second Adam, the prototype of a new humanity destined to succeed the present race of mankind, and his having possessed a body of flesh and having subsequently acquired a body of spirit is cited as proof that those "in Christ" will likewise acquire bodies of spirit. In Philippians this doctrine is developed in such a way as to relate it to the doctrine of Christ's work. Unlike the first Adam, who had eaten the forbidden fruit in disobedience to God's command, considering equality with God a thing that could be seized, the second Adam had emptied himself and become obedient to death, thus reversing the first Adam's fall. Therefore, God had raised him from the dead.

In Philippians the earthly life of Christ is still completely human, but in II Corinthians 1–9 a modification is introduced in which Christ is viewed as having possessed a divine nature even during his earthly life. God was in him, reconciling the world unto himself. In this passage it is made clear for the first time that the initiative in the work of Christ had been with God rather than with Christ, as seems to be assumed in the earlier letters, and Galatians and Romans emphasize the importance of this new idea. "But when the time had fully come, God sent forth his Son, born of woman, born under the law, to redeem those who were under the law, so that we might receive adoption as sons" (Gal. 4:5). "They are justified by his grace as a gift, through the redemption which is in Christ Jesus, whom God put forward as an expiation by his blood, to be received by faith" (Rom. 3:24–25).

In Colossians the Christology of Philippians is fully—and one is almost tempted to say deliberately—reversed. Christ is still "the image of the invisible God," but his existence before the creation of the world is now emphasized more than it was in the earlier letter. He is "the first-born of all creation; for in him all things were created, in heaven and on earth, visible and invisible, whether thrones or dominions or principalities or authorities—all things were created through him and for him. He is before all things, and in him all things hold together" (Col. 1:15–17). The Christ of Colossians, moreover, does not empty himself when he comes into the world; that could only be said before the development of the doctrine according to which "God was in Christ reconciling the world unto himself" (II Cor. 5:18). Colossians states that "in him all the fulness was pleased to dwell, and through him to reconcile to himself all things, whether on earth or in heaven, making peace by the blood of his cross" (Col. 1:19–20). A second statement of this idea is even more explicit than the first: "For in him the whole fulness of deity dwells bodily" (Col. 2:9). Everywhere in the letter the emphasis is on the complete divinity of Christ, in his existence before his birth, in his earthly life, and in his present life in heaven.

Just as striking is the development of the doctrine of the work of Christ. In the earliest letters, as we have seen, the focus of Paul's interest in this doctrine was largely futuristic. Although Christ had "died for our sins," this was only the beginning of his work; it would not be complete until the "day of salvation," which was to come with the parousia. In Colossians the work of Christ is looked upon as having been completed in the crucifixion and resurrection, having been going on all during his earthly life:

> You have come to fulness of life in him, who is the head of all rule and authority. In him also you were circumcised with a circumcision made without hands, by putting off the body of flesh in the circumcision of Christ; and you were buried with him in baptism, in which you were also raised with him through faith in the working of God, who raised him from the dead. And you, who were dead in trespasses and the uncircumcision of your flesh, God made alive together with him, having forgiven us all our trespasses, having cancelled the bond which stood

> against us with its legal demands; this he set aside, nailing it to
> the cross. He disarmed the principalities and powers and made a
> public example of them, triumphing over them in him (Col.
> 2:10–15).

Some of this doctrine, notably the part about the nailing of the bond
to the cross, is far from clear to the present-day reader, but one thing
about it is unmistakable, and that is that its focus is on the past. Its
interest is no longer chiefly in what Christ will do, it is in what Christ
has done.

The legal theory of the letter is simplicity itself:

> If with Christ you died to the elemental spirits of the uni-
> verse, why do you live as if you still belonged to the world?
> Why do you submit to regulations, Do not handle, Do not taste,
> Do not touch (referring to things which all perish as they are
> used), according to human precepts and doctrines? These have
> indeed an appearance of wisdom in promoting rigor of devotion
> and self-abasement and severity to the body, but they are of no
> value in checking the indulgence of the flesh (Col. 2:20–23).

Gone are the complications of Romans with its two laws, one for the
flesh and another for the spirit. Here, since the Christian has already
"put off the old nature with its practices and put on the new nature,
which is being renewed in knowledge after the image of its creator"
(Col. 3:9–10), there is no need of regulations, and Paul is satisfied
to state this position without bothering to argue it at any length. Some
of the Colossians, or perhaps it is only one of them, believe that questions of food and drink, or of festivals, new moons, and Sabbaths, are
important, and the attempt seems to have been made to impose regulations concerning these matters on the rest of the congregation. Paul's
attitude on this subject seems surprisingly mild, but he was writing
to a church which he had not founded, and which he had never
visited, and he may have felt that he could not take a more authoritative
tone without seeming to interfere in another man's field. He may also,
by this time, have discovered that the conflict with the Judaizers had
been less important than it had seemed when it was at its height. The
evidence of the letters makes it reasonably clear that the Judaizers did

not extend their activities beyond Antioch and Galatia, and the subsequent history of the Gentile mission demonstrates that their effort to Judaize Paul's churches was a failure. Colossians suggests by its tone that Paul had already discovered this. It takes the expected Pauline position, but it is not excited about it. The crisis, one suspects, is over. The consequence of this is that Paul no longer has to prove that the law is not binding. He can simply state it as a fact.

Therefore, the legal theory of Colossians is not a complete system, in that it fails to make clear how the believer is availed of the positive benefits of the work of Christ. It insists that the Christian, having died with Christ to the elemental spirits of the universe, no longer belongs to the world and need not submit to worldly regulations. But it does not incorporate the system of trust developed in Galatians and Romans to explain how the Christian is made an heir of the promise and adopted as a son of God. As we shall see when we come to discuss Ephesians, Paul was to notice the omission and supply what was lacking.

When and where was Colossians written? Traditional lives of Paul place it in Rome during the final imprisonment, or in Caesarea before Paul's departure for Rome, but that, as we have already seen, is because Acts provides no other occasion for its composition. Without Acts to influence the decision, however, it would undoubtedly be placed in Asia Minor, and probably in Ephesus itself. To begin with, it is addressed to Colossae, and it is also interested in Laodicea and Hierapolis. Tychicus, the bearer of the letter, and Onesimus, himself a Colossian, are with Paul and are about to travel to Colossae with news of him (Col. 4:7-9). Another of Paul's companions, Epaphras, is also a Colossian (Col. 4:12). Still others are apparently known to at least some of the Colossian Christians; among these are Aristarchus, Luke, and Demas (Col. 4:10,14). Mark, the cousin of Barnabas, is also with Paul and is expected to journey to Colossae in the near future (Col. 4:10). And although Paul has never been in either Colossae or Laodicea himself, he knows at least some of the Christians in both places, notably Nympha, in whose house the Laodicean church gathered (Col. 4:15), and Archippus, who seems to have resided in Colossae (Col. 4:17).

The indications would seem to be that Paul was writing from a place considerably closer to Colossae than Rome, and this supposition is strengthened by the evidence of the letter to Philemon.

Philemon has long been recognized as a companion letter to Colossians, the two having been written and sent at the same time. If Tychicus was the bearer of Colossians, Onesimus was the bearer of Philemon. No end of romance has been woven around this little letter—the theory being that the slave Onesimus had run away from his master, Philemon, and made his way to Paul, who had converted him and persuaded him to return, giving him a letter designed to appease his master's justifiable anger—but the letter itself tells us only that the slave had become a Christian while he was with Paul and that he was being sent back because he did not have his master's consent to remain away. There is no evidence that Onesimus had run away from home (he might just as plausibly have been sent on an errand of mercy to Paul), but there is every indication that Paul had detained him longer than his master had intended him to stay. Paul writes, "If he has done any wrong ($\dot{\eta}\delta\acute{\iota}\kappa\eta\sigma\epsilon\nu$) to you, or owes you anything, charge that to my account. I, Paul, write this with my own hand, I will repay it" (Philem. 18–19). In Colossians, Paul, commanding slaves to obey their masters, concludes, "For the wrongdoer will be paid back for the wrong he has done" (Col. 3:25), using the same Greek word, apparently in the sense of "disobey." Here, since Paul has caused Onesimus' disobedience, it is he rather than Onesimus who must be held responsible. Indeed, the letter nowhere suggests that Onesimus has been guilty of any serious crime, and it nowhere asks Philemon to forgive him, as it surely would have done if Onesimus had run away. Futhermore, while it is serious in tone when it speaks of Onesimus' conversion, it employs a light touch in its references to his absence from home "for an hour" (Philem. 15), playing on the meaning of his name ("useful"), and suggesting that Paul might have kept him longer had he not preferred to do nothing without Philemon's consent! It also contains a broad hint that Paul would like to have Onesimus back for the duration of his imprisonment, which he thinks will be over before long. It concludes, "At the same time, prepare a guest room for me, for I am hoping through your prayers to be granted to you" (Philem. 22).

That this exchange took place between Colossae and Rome is unlikely and unnecessary.[1] It seems far more likely to have taken place between Colossae and a city closer by. Wherever it was written, however, it clearly dates with Colossians, and the list of the letters in the order of their composition now reads: I Thessalonians, I Corinthians, II Corinthians 10–13, Philippians, II Corinthians 1–9, Galatians, Romans, Colossians, Philemon.

---

[1] The argument sometimes put forward that a runaway slave from Colossae would naturally have fled to Rome seems to be based on a more intimate knowledge of the psychology of runaway slaves than is vouchsafed to the general run of historians. It is a pity that those who possess such knowledge do not explain why the runaway, after he had gained the supposed safety of the great city, should have then revealed his whereabouts to a group of his master's friends.

9

EPHESIANS

With the dating of Colossians and Philemon after Romans, the establishment of the relative chronology of all the letters except II Thessalonians and Ephesians is complete. Up to this point in the argument we have not depended on either of these letters for evidence of Paul's development. The exclusion of their evidence was deliberate, for although the easiest way of showing that a development took place is to point to the contrast between its extremes, we could not ignore the doubts as to the genuineness of these letters. For that reason we began with the middle letters, where the question of genuineness does not arise. Proceeding from that starting place we have located nine letters, or parts of letters, at seven different points on the line of development that passes through I Corinthians, II Corinthians 1–9, and Romans. (Philemon does not occupy a point of its own, since it must be dated with Colossians, and development of ideas does not figure in the dating of II Corinthians 10–13.) That it is possible to do this is proof that the line of development is real, and not, as it has sometimes been called, a fantasy of the critical imagination. It may also be pointed out that it forestalls any possible objection on the part of those who question the genuineness of II Thessalonians and Ephesians, or either of them, that this development could only be shown by assuming that these letters are by Paul. Even if II Thessalonians and Ephesians are condemned as forgeries, the development still runs from I Thessalonians through Colossians in exactly the same way. As a matter of fact, even if I Thessalonians and Colossians are forgeries, as has been suggested from time to time, the development is just as real in I Corinthians, Philippians, II Corinthians 1–9, Galatians, and Romans. On the other hand, the fact that the line of development which runs through the unquestionably genuine letters connects directly with these others is in itself a strong argument that they are genuine also.

The supposition that Ephesians is a forgery demands that the supposed forger possessed not only Colossians, which served as his principal model, but also most or all of the other letters as well. This is the basis of DeWette's original argument, and it remains the basis of all the later versions of that argument which have appeared since his day. DeWette, however, was unaware of the development of Paul's thought in the earlier letters, and he therefore failed to notice the most remarkable feature of the relationship which Ephesians bears to them. That is that the author of Ephesians not only knew that such a development had taken place in Paul's thought but also knew the stages through which it had passed. Ephesians never mistakes the direction of this movement. It never quotes material from the early letters without editing it in such a way as to bring it into conformity with Paul's mature theological position, and it never borrows from these letters any of those elements of Paul's early doctrine that were discarded as his thought matured. It knows better, for example, than to use I Corinthians as a source for Paul's fully developed eschatology, or Philippians for his final Christology, or II Corinthians 1–9 for his completed legal theory. This is not because it is ignorant of these letters. It quotes or paraphrases from them repeatedly. But it also knows what parts of them to omit, what parts to correct, and what parts to retain unchanged. That an ancient Paulinist, even if he had been an intimate of the apostle, could have acquired sufficiently detailed knowledge of the development of his master's thought to accomplish this staggering feat without making a single slip is highly improbable. That this knowledge, if it ever was possessed in the church, should have perished without leaving so much as a trace in the Pauline tradition is beyond belief.

Like Romans, Ephesians is a synthesis. Just as Romans uses the outline of Galatians as a framework for the developed doctrine which had been emerging in the letters that preceded it, so Ephesians uses the outline of Colossians for the same purpose. And just as in Romans the doctrine of Galatians is enlarged and extended, while the ideas of the earlier letters are modified in such a way as to bring them into conformity with this later stage of Paul's thinking, so in Ephesians the doctrine of Colossians is extended, and the ideas of the earlier letters are modified in the same way.

The resemblance of Ephesians to Colossians is even closer and more striking than that of Romans to Galatians. Both follow the same structural pattern, and both take the same theological point of view. At a number of points they employ the same words and phrases, and even the same sentence outlines. The verbal correspondence between them, in fact, is so extensive as to suggest that Paul, in writing Ephesians, deliberately set out to produce a revised and enlarged version of Colossians. This suggestion is supported by what is surely the most curious feature of the style of Ephesians, its tendency to employ longer sentences of more elaborate structure than one finds in the other letters.[1]

This feature of Ephesians has been often noted and variously described. Its admirers have characterized it as elevated, lofty, and inspired; one has called it liturgical, another has compared it with a Eucharistic hymn. Its detractors have labeled it awkward, cumbrous, and even incoherent. Both judgments are intemperate. They are also

---

[1] There is a large literature on the style and language of Ephesians. The earlier portion of this literature, which tends to pronounce against the genuineness of the letter, is covered in Moffatt, *Introduction to the Literature of the New Testament* (3rd ed.; Edinburgh, 1918). The whole of it is reviewed in E. Percy, *Die Probleme der Kolosser- und Epheserbriefe* (Lund, 1946). Percy's verdict is that the style and language are Pauline.

inaccurate insofar as they give the impression that they apply to the whole letter, when as a matter of fact they apply only to the first three chapters, and in particular to two sentences of extraordinary length and complexity that occur very early in the work (Eph. 1:3–14; 2:1–7).[2] These two sentences contain material not found in Colossians, and their purpose in each case is to provide the necessary theological introduction to material from the two opening sections of the shorter letter. Their relation to the material derived from Colossians can easily be seen when the outlines of the doctrinal sections of both letters are placed side by side.

COLOSSIANS	EPHESIANS
Salutation (1:1–2)	*Salutation* (1:1–2)

1. THE NEW LIFE IN CHRIST

Theological introduction (1:3–14)

God's choice of us to be sons, our redemption through the blood of Christ, the seal of the Spirit for our inheritance

Thanksgiving (1:3–20)	*Thanksgiving* (1:15–23)
I give thanks for your faith and love, because of your hope, and pray that you may know the power of the resurrection	I give thanks for your faith and love, and pray that you may know the hope, and the power of the resurrection

2. RECONCILIATION IN CHRIST

Theological introduction (2:1–10)

God, by grace, made you alive, and made us alive, and raised us to the heavenly places.

[2] There are other long sentences in the first half of Ephesians, notably 1:15–23 and 3:1–7, but these are of the ordinary run-on kind that occur, for example, in Rom. 1:1–6 and II Cor. 6:1–10. There are no unusually long sentences in the second half of the letter at all.

COLOSSIANS	EPHESIANS
Reconciliation (1:21ff.)	*Reconciliation* (2:11–22)
You, once estranged, he has reconciled	You Gentiles, once aliens, have been reconciled with us to God

3. THE MINISTRY OF RECONCILIATION

The minister of reconciliation (1:24–2:5)	*The minister of reconciliation* (3:1–13)
Now I rejoice in my sufferings for your sake,	I, Paul, a prisoner on behalf of you Gentiles . . . a steward by God's grace of the mystery now revealed to his holy apostles and prophets by the Spirit
and for the church of which I became a minister	that the Gentiles are fellow heirs . . . was made a minister by God's grace
to make the word of God fully known to the Gentiles	to preach to the Gentiles . . . that through the church the wisdom of God might be made known to the principalities and powers I am suffering for your glory

4. GROWTH IN FAITH AND LOVE

Application (2:6–7)	*Application* (3:14–19)
Live in Christ, "rooted and built up" in him, and established in faith, abound in thanksgiving	May Christ dwell in your hearts by faith, and may you, being "rooted and grounded" in love, know the love of Christ and be filled with the fullness of God.

It is at once apparent from this comparison that the two sentences in question, like the expanded section on the minister of reconciliation, serve the purpose of introducing into the fabric of Ephesians certain theological themes which are either not treated in Colossians or not sufficiently explained there. Among these are God's grace, Christ's trust, the work of the Spirit, the unity of the church, and the function of the church (which has been exalted with Christ to the heavenly places) to complete the work of Christ by making known the manifold wisdom of God to the principalities and powers. All of these except the last are themes that Paul had fully worked out in the great letters of the middle period, and their absence from Colossians tells us only that Paul knew the Colossians to be familiar with them already. Ephesians, however, was written to a church to which Paul was a stranger. In it he must introduce not only himself but also the main themes of his teaching, and he did this by inserting into a revised and enlarged version of Colossians a highly compressed but quite complete outline of those parts of his basic theology which Colossians had not contained. It is precisely the method of Romans, which was also designed to serve the same double function of introducing both the writer and his theology to a church which he had not yet visited. Against this background a somewhat more detailed comparison between Colossians and Ephesians is instructive.

The distinctive mark of the eschatology of Colossians, as we have seen, is its teaching that the believer has already been raised with Christ: "If then you have been raised with Christ, seek the things that are above, where Christ is, seated at the right hand of God. Set your minds on things that are above, not on things that are on earth. For you have died, and your life is hid with Christ in God. When Christ who is our life appears, then you also will appear with him in glory" (Col. 3:1–4). Ephesians contains the same teaching, but in greater detail. It reads, "But God, who is rich in mercy, out of the great love with which he loved us, even when we were dead through our trespasses, made us alive together with Christ (by grace you have been saved), and raised us up with him, and made us sit with him in the heavenly places in Christ Jesus, that in the coming ages he might show the immeasurable riches of his grace in kindness toward us in Christ Jesus" (Eph. 2:4–7). The purpose of the added detail is not only to make clear that all this has happened through God's grace, but also to make explicit what is only implied in Colossians, that the believer as well as Christ has been made to "sit with him in the heavenly places."

Similarly Colossians teaches that the believer has already entered the kingdom: "He has delivered us from the dominion of darkness and transferred us to the kingdom of his beloved Son" (Col. 1:13). It also teaches that the believer has already exchanged his old nature for the new: "You have put off the old nature with its practices and have put on the new nature, which is being renewed in knowledge after the image of its creator" (Col. 3:9–10). Ephesians explains this idea more fully: "Put off your old nature which belongs to your former manner of life and is corrupt through deceitful lusts, and be renewed in the spirit of your minds, and put on the new nature, created after the likeness of God in true righteousness and holiness" (Eph. 4:22–24).

This form of Paul's teaching about the two natures is the final stage in a long development. In I Corinthians the two natures had been thought of as being possessed consecutively. The believer had the earthly nature to begin with; he would only acquire the heavenly nature at the parousia, when his flesh would be replaced by spirit. In II Corinthians 1–9 the two natures are thought of as being possessed simultaneously. Beneath the body of flesh the believer already possesses the down payment of the body of spirit; on the death of the body of flesh he will be "further clothed upon" with the remainder of the body of spirit. This form of the doctrine persists in Galatians: "The life I now live in the flesh I live by the trust of the Son of God" (Gal. 2:20), and Romans: "Who will deliver me from this body of death?" (Rom. 7:24). In Colossians and Ephesians the idea of simultaneous possession is finally given up, and the two natures are once again thought of as being possessed consecutively. Only now the change from one nature to the other is treated as having taken place already; the old nature has been put off and the new nature put on.[3]

When we turn to the Christology of the two letters the phenomena are exactly parallel. The distinctive feature of the Christology of Colossians is its emphasis on the pre-existence of Christ, his function as the agent of creation, and his possession during his earthly life of the whole fullness of deity: "He is the image of the invisible God, the first-born of all creation; for in him all things were created, in heaven

---

[3] It is worth remarking in this connection that the highly advanced ethical teaching of Colossians and Ephesians is a direct outgrowth of this final development in Paul's eschatological thought.

and on earth, visible and invisible, whether thrones or dominions or principalities or authorities—all things were created through him and for him. . . . For in him all the fulness was pleased to dwell" (Col. 1:15–16, 19). Ephesians adopts this Christology, supporting it with a scriptural argument: "Therefore it is said, 'When he ascended on high he led a host of captives, and he gave gifts to men.' In saying, 'He ascended,' what does it mean but that he had also descended into the lower parts of the earth?" (Eph. 4:8–9; Ps. 68:18). But Ephesians goes beyond Colossians in explaining that God's choice of the elect in Christ had also been made before the creation: "Even as he chose us in him before the foundation of the world" (Eph. 1:4). The doctrine of election, of course, appears repeatedly in Paul's writing, but the earlier letters never specifically date the election as early as this. Galatians implies that it took place at least as early as the promise to Abraham, and Romans reinforces this idea: "For those whom he foreknew he also predestined to be conformed to the image of his Son, in order that he might be the first-born among many brethren" (Rom. 8:29). Ephesians tells us that Paul continued to develop the implication of this doctrine to its logical conclusion.

Colossians introduces its doctrine of the work of Christ as follows: "In him all the fulness was pleased to dwell, and through him to reconcile to himself all things, whether on earth or in heaven, making peace by the blood of his cross" (Col. 1:19–20). This clearly echoes the thought of II Corinthians 1–9, where Paul had written, "God was in Christ reconciling the world to himself" (II Cor. 5:19). It also echoes Galatians and Romans in its emphasis on the cosmic dimensions of the effect of Christ's work. But Colossians nowhere explains how the positive benefits of this work are transmitted to the Christian. It discourses at length on his release from bondage to "the elemental spirits of the universe" (Col. 2:20) and his freedom from "human precepts and doctrines" (Col. 2:22), but it does not once mention either the Christian's adoption as a son of God or the means whereby the adoption is effected through Christ's trust. For example, Paul writes:

> And you, who were dead in trespasses and the uncircumcision of your flesh, God made alive together with him, having forgiven us all our trespasses, having canceled the bond which

stood against us with its legal demands; this he set aside, nailing it to the cross. He disarmed the principalities and powers and made a public example of them, triumphing over them in him (Col. 2:13–15).

The reader familiar with the legal theory of Galatians and Romans has no difficulty in supplying what is missing in this argument. That is, that Christ, the trustee through whom the inheritance was transmitted, had assumed the obligations of the heirs, and had discharged these with the sacrifice of his life, thus canceling the debt which stood against them and making them free to accept the adoption. The Colossians must have known this, otherwise the passage would have had very little meaning for them. But the recipients of Ephesians had not been taught this, and the letter to them systematically sets out to supply the omitted explanation. It begins:

> Blessed be the God and Father of our Lord Jesus Christ who has blessed us in Christ with every spiritual blessing in the heavenly places, even as he chose us in him before the foundation of the world, that we should be holy and blameless before him. He destined us in love to be his sons through Jesus Christ, according to the purpose of his will, to the praise of his glorious grace which he freely bestowed on us in the Beloved. In him we have redemption through his blood, the forgiveness of our trespasses, according to the riches of his grace which he lavished upon us (Eph. 1:3–8).

Here Paul makes it clear that the legal transaction in which Christ participated was an adoption: "He destined us in love to be his sons through Jesus Christ." He also makes it clear that the choice of the heirs by adoption was an act of grace freely bestowed, and that the redemption of the heirs through the death of Christ was a further act of grace, "which he lavished on us." This is the fully developed legal theory of Galatians and Romans, the framework of the adoption argument having been derived from the former and the emphasis on grace and predestination from the latter.

Similarly Colossians is deficient in any adequate doctrine of the Spirit, doubtless because the recipients of the letter had already been sufficiently instructed on this point. Ephesians is concerned to remedy the deficiency. It does this, again at the outset of the letter, in the following passage:

> In him, according to the purpose of him who accomplishes all things according to the counsel of his will, we who first hoped in Christ have been destined and appointed to live for the praise of his glory. In him you also, who have heard the word of truth, the gospel of your salvation, and have believed in him, were sealed with the promised Holy Spirit, which is the down payment of our inheritance, until we acquire possession of it, to the praise of his glory (Eph. 1:11–14).

This is the familiar doctrine, introduced in II Corinthians 1–9, of the down payment of the spirit, but here it is used to explain what the Colossians must already have known, that the down payment of the spirit is the seal which guarantees the inheritance. Ephesians is once again filling a gap in the teaching of Colossians, and once again the doctrinal element which it supplies turns out to have an intimate connection with the testamentary scheme of Galatians and Romans.

This use of ideas from the earlier letters in new connections is one of the most striking features of Ephesians, and it is nowhere more noticeable than in that letter's doctrine of the church. The idea of the church as the body of Christ and of the individual Christians as members of that body occurs as early as I Corinthians: "Now you are the body of Christ and individually members of it" (I Cor. 12:27). It is echoed in Romans: "We, though many, are one body in Christ, and individually members one of another" (Rom. 12:5). In Colossians it is restated: "He is the head of the body, the church" (Col. 1:18), and brought into connection with the doctrine of the atonement: "Now I rejoice in my sufferings for your sake, and in my flesh I complete what is lacking in Christ's afflictions for the sake of his body, that is, the church" (Col. 1:24). The mystery "hidden for ages and generations but now made manifest to his saints" is that Christ dwells in this body, and this constitutes its hope of glory (Col. 1:26–27). Ephesians makes this more explicit by defining the church as "his body, the fulness of him who fills all in all" (Eph. 1:23). It also explains that it is through the church that the manifold wisdom of God is to be made known to the principalities and powers in the heavenly places (Eph. 3:10). The church, in other words, is no longer merely the passive recipient of God's grace on earth but also, through the Christians who now "sit with" Christ "in the heavenly places" (Eph. 2:6), the active agent of the revelation of his purpose to the cosmos. Paul's prayer, therefore, can now be that as Christ dwells in the Christians' hearts by faith, they "may be filled with all the fulness of God" (Eph. 3:14–19). This is not merely exalted language. It exactly reflects the advanced eschatology and Christology toward which Paul has been steadily moving.

Earlier generations of scholars who were unaware of any development in Paul's thought frequently seized on this aspect of the doctrine of the church as evidence that Ephesians was not by Paul. They doubted that Paul, who had said earlier that the church could not be built on any other foundation than Jesus Christ (I Cor. 3:11), should have said in Ephesians that it was "built on the foundation of the apostles and prophets" (Eph. 2:20). But the elevation of Christ from the role of foundation to that of capstone is precisely what is required by Paul's new thought of Christ as the head (Col. 1:18; Eph. 4:15,16) and of the church as the body, growing and being built up, "until we all attain . . . to the measure of the stature of the fulness of Christ" (Eph. 4:13,16). These same scholars were particularly scornful of the idea that Paul could have written, "When you read this you can perceive my insight into the mystery of Christ, which was not made known to the sons of men in other generations as it has now been revealed to his holy apostles and prophets by the Spirit; that is, how the Gentiles are fellow heirs, members of the same body, and partakers of the promise in Christ Jesus through the gospel" (Eph. 3:4–6). This, however, merely states what we now know to be a fact, that Paul had himself originated the legal argument according to which Gentiles were recognized as fellow heirs by adoption. It also implies that other leaders of the church, guided by the Spirit, had now accepted this doctrine. This contention we have no reason to reject, since we know that Paul's position in the conflict with the Judaizers prevailed. History tells us that the Gentile churches were not Judaized. The theory that Paul would have been too modest to point out that he had been right from the beginning hardly does justice to the vehemence with which he had urged his cause in Galatians. And to argue that he would have been too vindictive to refer to the apostles who now agreed with him as "holy"—a term which he uses elsewhere of ordinary members of the church—is surely to forget the ease with which he could shift from the critical sharpness of II Corinthians 10–13 to the extravagant warmth of II Corinthians 1–9, which followed hard upon it.

Finally, the idea in Ephesians that the unity of the church is a prerequisite of its being presented to God is a similar explanation, for the benefit of readers who had not heard of it, of a doctrine which was already familiar to the Colossians and to which Paul had alluded in his letter to them: "And you, who were once estranged and hostile in mind, doing evil deeds, he has now reconciled in his body of flesh by his death, in order to present you holy and blameless and irreproachable before him" (Col. 1:21–22). In Ephesians he states the doctrine in full:

> Therefore remember that at one time you Gentiles in the flesh, called the uncircumcision by what is called the circumcision, which is made in the flesh by hands—remember that you were at that time separated from Christ, alienated from the commonwealth of Israel, and strangers to the covenants of promise, having no hope and without God in the world. But now in Christ Jesus you who once were far off have been brought near in the blood of Christ. For he is our peace, who has made us both one, and has broken down the dividing wall of hostility, by abolishing in his flesh the law of commandments and ordinances, that he might create in himself one new man in place of the two, so making peace, and might reconcile us both to God in one body through the cross, thereby bringing the hostility to an end. And he came and preached peace to you who were far off and peace to those who were near; for through him we both have access in one Spirit to the Father. So then you are no longer strangers and sojourners, but you are fellow citizens with the saints and members of the household of God, built upon the foundation of the apostles and prophets, Christ Jesus himself being the chief cornerstone, in whom the whole structure is joined together and grows into a holy temple in the Lord; in whom you also are built into it for a dwelling place of God in the Spirit (Eph. 2:11–22).

This idea is at least as old as Galatians, where Paul had written, "There is neither Jew nor Greek, there is neither slave nor free, there is neither male nor female; for you are all one in Christ Jesus" (Gal. 3:27–28). It is repeated in Romans: "For there is no distinction between Jew and Greek; the same Lord is Lord of all and bestows his riches upon all who call upon him" (Rom. 10:12). And it is expanded in Colossians: "Here there cannot be Greek and Jew, circumcised and uncircumcised, barbarian, Scythian, slave, free man, but Christ is all, and in all" (Col. 3:9–11).

Two final examples of the author's relation to his material deserve mention. The first is to be found in the series of mixed metaphors that occur first in the description of the church as a structure which "is joined together and grows into a holy temple" (Eph. 3:17), and is further developed in the description of the body as it both "grows and is built up in love" (Eph. 4:16). The origin of the mixture is to be found in I Corinthians, where the church is successively a field (I Cor. 3:6–9), a building (I Cor. 3:9–17), and the body of Christ (I Cor. 12:27). In each case the analogy is worked out in a consistent way: the field is planted and watered and yields a crop, the building is set on a foundation and built up, and the body has members which function interdependently. Colossians speaks of Christians as being "rooted" and "built up" in Christ (Col. 2:7), and Ephesians, following Colossians, borrows the building and body analogies and confuses them even further. The building "grows" (Eph. 2:21), the adherents of the church are "rooted" (the plant idea) and "grounded" (the building idea), and the body "is built" (Eph. 3:17; 4:16). The confusion of these ideas is so complete, in fact, as to suggest that it can only have come about as a natural result of Paul's long familiarity with them and his repeated use of them in such close association with each other as to blur the distinction between them.

An even more revealing example of the way in which Paul adapted material from his earlier writing to serve new uses in Ephesians is to be found in the famous passage about the armor of God (Eph. 6:11–17). This figure, borrowed from Isaiah, appears first in Paul's writing in I Thessalonians: "But you are not in darkness, brethren, for that day to surprise you like a thief. For you are all sons of light and sons of the day; we are not of the night or of darkness. So then let us not sleep, as others do, but let us keep awake and be sober. For those who sleep sleep at night, and those who get drunk are drunk at night. But, since we belong to the day, let us be sober, and put on the breastplate of faith and love, and for a helmet the hope of salvation" (I Thess. 5:4–8). It is employed again in Romans: "The night is far gone, the day is at hand. Let us then cast off the works of darkness and put on the armor of light; let us conduct ourselves becomingly as in the day, not in reveling and drunkenness, not in debauchery and licentiousness, not in quarreling and jealousy. But put on the Lord Jesus Christ, and make no provision for the flesh, to gratify its desires" (Rom. 13:12–14).

Parallel to the armor-of-God concept in Paul's writing is a closely related figure, that of putting on the new nature. It appears first in I Corinthians: "For this perishable nature must put on the imperishable, and this mortal nature must put on immortality" (I Cor. 15:53). It is employed more extensively in II Corinthians 1–9: "For we know that if the earthly tent we live in is destroyed, we have a building from God, a house not made with hands, eternal in the heavens. Here indeed we groan, and long to put on our heavenly dwelling, so that by putting it on we may not be found naked. For while we are still in this tent, we sigh with anxiety; not that we would be unclothed, but that we would be further clothed, so that what is mortal may be swallowed up by life" (II Cor. 5:1–4). Galatians identifies the new nature with Christ and relates its putting on to the believer's baptism in the past: "For as many of you as were baptized into Christ have put on Christ" (Gal. 3:27).

Colossians emphasizes that the change from one nature to the other has already occurred: "You have put off the old nature with its practices and have put on the new nature, which is being renewed in knowledge after the image of its creator" (Col. 3:9–10). Colossians also develops the ethical application of the figure: "Put on then, as God's chosen ones, holy and beloved, compassion, kindness, lowliness, meekness, and patience, forbearing one another and, if one has a complaint against another, forgiving each other; as the Lord has forgiven you, so you also must forgive. And above all these put on love, which binds everything together in perfect harmony" (Col. 3:12–14).

Ephesians retains the distinction between the two applications. The ethical it treats at great length and in great detail, beginning with the sentence, "Put off your old nature which belongs to your former manner of life and is corrupt through deceitful lusts, and be renewed in the spirit of your minds, and put on the new nature, created after the likeness of God in true righteousness and holiness" (Eph. 4:22–24). For the doctrinal it reserves the older figure of the armor. But although it still associates the putting on of the armor with the warfare between darkness and day, it omits all mention of reveling, drunkenness, debauchery, licentiousness, quarreling, and jealousy, and gives a wholly theological meaning to the armor itself, which has now become the means whereby the Christian shares in Christ's power. In I Thessalonians only the breastplate and helmet had been named, and these represented the Christian virtues of faith, love, and hope. In Ephesians six articles are enumerated: belt, breastplate, shoes, shield, helmet, and sword; they represent truth, righteousness, the preparation of the gospel of peace, faith, salvation, and the Spirit. The change from the simple list of I Thessalonians is significant. Particularly significant is the substitution of "salvation" for "the hope of salvation." In the earlier letters salvation is spoken of as a process that has begun in the past, continues in the present, and will be completed in the future. In I Thessalonians Paul writes, "For God has not destined us for wrath, but to obtain salvation through our Lord Jesus Christ" (I Thess. 5:9). In I Corinthians Paul speaks of "the gospel . . . by which you are being saved" (I Cor. 15:1–2), and in both I Corinthians and II Corinthians 1–9 he contrasts "those who are being saved" with "those who are perishing" (I Cor. 1:18; II Cor. 2:15). The present aspect of the process is stressed in II Corinthians 1–9: "Behold, now is the acceptable time; behold, now is the day of salvation" (II Cor. 6:2). But the future aspect is still strong in Romans: "Since, therefore, we are now justified by his blood, much more shall we be saved by him from the wrath of God" (Rom. 5:9).

The new eschatology of Colossians, however, according to which the believer has already been raised (Col. 2:12; 3:1) and transferred to the kingdom (Col. 1:13), pictures salvation as already accomplished. The believer looks forward to being presented, "holy and blameless and irreproachable," before God (Col. 1:22). Although Colossians does not mention salvation as such, it implies throughout that salvation, like resurrection, has ceased to be thought of as a future hope and has now become a present state resulting from an act that has already been performed. Ephesians makes this explicit: "But God . . . even when we were dead through our trespasses, made us alive together with Christ (by grace you have been saved), and raised us up with him" (Eph. 2:4–6); and again: "By grace you have been saved through faith" (Eph. 2:8). Therefore it cannot speak of the helmet as representing "the hope of salvation," as in I Thessalonians, but must call it simply "the helmet of salvation." The figure has had to be adapted to bring it into line with Paul's developed theology.

Ephesians, in short, is exactly the sort of letter we should expect Paul to have written at the end of the theological development that the other letters reflect, and it is also exactly the sort of letter we should expect him to have written to serve the special purpose for which it was composed.

Ephesians was clearly written after Colossians, which it constantly expands and completes, but the close resemblances between the two letters suggest that the interval between them may not have been more than a matter of days. Its title, "To the Ephesians," appears to be an editorial guess; it is certainly incorrect. Nor did the words "in Ephesus" appear in the salutation when the letter was first published; they were added in later manuscripts under the influence of the title. Despite the elaborate arguments that have been employed to explain the origin of this textual curiosity, the simplest still seems to be the best. That is, that the original salutation contained the name of the place to which the letter was addressed, but that the text had become corrupted and the name omitted, either deliberately or by accident, in the copy that came into the editor's hands when the letters were collected and published. Marcion identified it as "the letter from Laodicea" (Col. 4:16) and called it "To the Laodiceans" in his edition of Paul. He may well have been right. Paul could easily have written Ephesians (to Laodicea) immediately after Colossians, and then, before the letters were dispatched by the hand of Tychicus, added the final personal greetings to the end of Colossians in which he recommended that the two churches should read both letters.

The chronological list now reads: I Thessalonians, I Corinthians, II Corinthians 10–13, Philippians, II Corinthians 1–9, Galatians, Romans, Colossians, Philemon, Ephesians.

10

II THESSALONIANS

Most critics who accept both of the Thessalonian letters as genuine consider I Thessalonians to be the earlier of the two. This conclusion depends heavily on the evidence of Acts, which tells us that, after his departure from Thessalonica, Paul proceeded to Beroea, where he left Silas and Timothy, while he himself went on to Athens with certain of the Beroean brethren. These brethren returned immediately to Beroea with a command that Silas and Timothy were to come to Paul as soon as possible. After a short stay in Athens, Paul made his way to Corinth, where he was rejoined by Silas and Timothy on their arrival from Macedonia (Acts 17:10–15; 18:1,5).

With this narrative the following series of statements in I Thessalonians is commonly compared: "But since we were bereft of you, brethren, for a short time . . ." (I Thess. 2:17); "Therefore when we could bear it no longer, we were willing to be left behind at Athens alone, and we sent Timothy . . . to establish you in your faith and to exhort you . . ." (I Thess. 3:1–2); "But now that Timothy has come to us from you . . ." (I Thess. 3:6). On the basis of this comparison it is commonly concluded that Paul's instructions to Timothy had not been to come straight from Beroea, as Acts states, but to go back from Beroea to Thessalonica and to proceed south from there. With that relatively minor correction the narrative of Acts is seen to provide a satisfactory occasion for the composition of I Thessalonians.

Once this conclusion has been reached, however, it is very difficult to date II Thessalonians before I Thessalonians. Attempts to do this have invariably been rejected on the grounds that Acts provides no satisfactory occasion for the writing of II Thessalonians between Paul's departure from Thessalonica and his arrival in Corinth, and that the time available is insufficient to allow for the development of the situation with which the letter deals. The inevitable result of this conclusion has been to cast suspicion on the genuineness of II Thessalonians, and it must be admitted that if the letters were actually written in the order usually assigned to them, the acceptance of II Thessalonians as genuine is very difficult indeed.

We have already seen that Acts cannot be used to date the letters in the traditional way, however, and we have also seen that the traditional date of I Thessalonians cannot be correct. It cannot have been written before Paul left Corinth at the end of his first visit. There is thus ample time for II Thessalonians to have been written before it, and we are therefore at liberty to re-examine the evidence that bears on the relative dates of the two letters. This evidence, which began to be amassed by Grotius, and has gradually been added to over the years, has been presented in its fullest and most convincing form by J. C. West,[1] who concludes that II Thessalonians is the earlier of the two letters. If this conclusion is correct it seriously weakens the chief modern arguments against the genuineness of II Thessalonians, which assume that I Thessalonians served as the model for the second letter. (The earlier theory of Baur, that both letters are spurious, has been generally abandoned.)

II Thessalonians is the least edifying of all the letters, but it is the

---

[1] "The Order of 1 and 2 Thessalonians," *Journal of Theological Studies*, XV (1913), 66–74.

easiest of all to interpret in terms of Paul's development. Like I Thessalonians it has no legal theory at all; it was written before the question of law and grace had become a problem in the church. Strictly speaking, it has no Christology either, since its interest is in the work of Christ as distinguished from the person of Christ, and Christ's sole function in the theology of the letter is eschatological. But the very absence of a legal theory and of a doctrine of the person of Christ, combined with the very crude doctrine of the work of Christ and the very primitive eschatology which the letter reflects, suggests very strongly that it was written before the letters in which the developed forms of these doctrines appear.

As we have seen, the development of Paul's eschatology can be traced through a series of successive modifications. In I Thessalonians the modification consists of the introduction of the doctrine of a special resurrection of Christians at the parousia (I Thess. 4:13–18). In I Corinthians it is the introduction of the idea that the resurrection body will be made of spirit, and that the bodies of the living will be changed from flesh to spirit at the parousia (I Cor. 15:44,51). In Philippians it is the idea that the believer's resurrection follows immediately after death (Phil. 1:23). In II Corinthians 1–9 it is that the believer has already received at least a down payment of the body of spirit before death (II Cor. 5:1–5). In Galatians and Romans, developing an idea already suggested in II Corinthians 1–9, it is that the believer has already died (Gal. 2:19–20; Rom. 6:3–11). And in Colossians it is that the believer has not only already died but has also already been raised with Christ (Col. 3:1). In each case the new element is a modification or expansion of the eschatological system just preceding it. Thus, to limit ourselves to the earlier letters, the system of Philippians, for example, presupposes that of I Corinthians, and that of I Corinthians presupposes that of I Thessalonians.

Similarly, the system of I Thessalonians presupposes an earlier system, which it modifies, and since the modification which it introduces has to do with the special resurrection of Christians who have died before the parousia, the earlier system must have been one in which such deaths before the parousia were not contemplated at all. It is precisely this system which we find in II Thessalonians. Indeed,

II Thessalonians itself introduces a modification of a still earlier system, for the letter was written to explain why the parousia had not taken place as soon as Paul had led the Thessalonians to believe it would. It thus tells us of two earlier stages in Paul's eschatology than we have known about hitherto. The first of these is the system which Paul had held on the occasion of his first visit to Thessalonica. It taught that the events leading up to the end had already begun. The rebellion was at hand, and the man of lawlessness was about to be revealed; when he had taken his seat in the temple and proclaimed himself to be God, the Lord Jesus would come and slay him with the breath of his mouth (II Thess. 2:3–8). It was a crudely simple apocalyptic message, but Paul says in so many words that it was what he had told the Thessalonians when he was still with them (II Thess. 2:5).

In II Thessalonians, Paul modifies this system by introducing the idea of the restrainer, who is temporarily preventing the last events from being completed, and thus causing a delay in the parousia (II Thess. 2:6–7). The restrainer had not figured in the original system; he was someone who had made his appearance since that system had been devised. The modification he necessitated was slight, however. The restrainer would only stand in the way temporarily; as soon as he was out of the way the predicted events would resume their course and hasten to their conclusion.

The Christology of the letter is just as primitive as its eschatology. A brief outline of the later modification in Paul's Christology shows once again that II Thessalonians represents the earliest stage of Paul's thinking on this subject. I Thessalonians first mentions the death and resurrection of Christ, because the new eschatology demands this (I Thess. 1:10; 5:10). I Corinthians introduces the idea of Christ as the second Adam, again in an eschatological setting (I Cor. 15:21, 45–49). Philippians develops this idea, seeing significance for the first time in Christ's voluntary resignation of the form of God and in his humiliation and obedience to death (Phil. 2:5–8). It is not necessary to trace the development further; the subsequent steps are familiar, and the over-all direction of the development is clear. Paul's Christological emphasis is constantly shifting toward the past. II Thessalonians stands at the beginning of the series. Its interest is completely futuristic, so much so that it does not refer even to Christ's death and resurrection. In it Christ is viewed as a heavenly being whose function it will be to come at the last day in flaming fire and inflict "vengeance on those who do not know God and who do not obey the gospel of our Lord Jesus" (II Thess. 1:8). Like the eschatology, this Christology is unworthy of the mature Paul, and he was to move steadily away from it as he grew older and his thinking deepened. Its presence in II Thessalonians is evidence of the very early date of the letter.

II Thessalonians has no legal theory as such. Like its companion writing, it dates from the period before the controversy with the Judaizers arose. There was thus no problem in Paul's mind of the relation of law to grace. The Thessalonian Christians, being Gentiles, were not required by Paul to undertake the keeping of the law, and no conservative Jewish Christian had as yet appeared who suggested that they should. The ethical system of the letter, if indeed it can be called a system, is simplicity itself. The Thessalonians have been chosen to be saved "through sanctification by the Spirit and belief in the truth" (II Thess. 2:13). They have only to "stand firm" (II Thess. 2:15). Paul's prayer for them is that the Lord Jesus Christ and God the Father will comfort their hearts "and establish them in every good work and word" (II Thess. 2:17). The one ethical problem with which the letter deals is that of idleness, and Paul reminds his readers that he had laid down a principle for dealing with this problem when he was with them: "If any one will not work, let him not eat" (II Thess. 3:10). Otherwise the assumption of the letter is that the Spirit will guide the believer to behave as becomes a saint. This, of course, is far simpler and more primitive than the ethical outlook even of I Thessalonians, which is forced to deal with such problems as marriage (I Thess. 4:1-8), the impression the Christian community makes on outsiders (I Thess. 4:10-12), and respect for authority in the church (I Thess. 5:12-13).

All three lines of evidence, therefore, point to the same conclusion, that II Thessalonians was written before I Thessalonians and that it is the earliest writing that we possess from Paul's pen. (II Thessalonians 2:15 implies that an earlier letter has been lost.) As we shall see in the following chapter, which deals with the absolute dates of the

Thessalonian letters, this order is borne out by the references to contemporary events which these two letters contain.

With the dating of II Thessalonians the list of the letters in the order of their composition is complete. It reads: II Thessalonians, I Thessalonians, I Corinthians, II Corinthians 10–13, Philippians, II Corinthians 1–9, Galatians, Romans, Colossians, Philemon, Ephesians.

11

ABSOLUTE DATES

So far we have limited ourselves to establishing the order in which the letters were written. The resultant relative chronology is as follows:

II Thessalonians
I Thessalonians
I Corinthians
II Corinthians 10–13
Philippians
II Corinthians 1–9
Galatians
Romans
Colossians, Philemon, Ephesians

We now turn to the question of absolute dates, which hinges on the interpretation of the chronological references in the Thessalonian letters.

I Thessalonians contains a clear reference to a major disaster which had befallen the Jews shortly before the letter was written:

> For you, brethren, became imitators of the churches of God in Christ Jesus which are in Judea; for you suffered the same things from your own countrymen as they did from the Jews, who killed both the Lord Jesus and the prophets, and drove us out and displease God and oppose all men by hindering us from speaking to the Gentiles that they may be saved—so as always to fill up the measure of their sins. But the wrath for the end has come upon them ahead of time! (I Thess. 2:14–16).

The meaning of the last sentence in this paragraph has been the subject of much debate, and a variety of renderings will be found in the standard translations. The usual "has come upon them" is almost certainly wrong; φθάνω was losing its anticipatory meaning by the end of the first century, but it had not done so when I Thessalonians was written. It clearly retains this meaning in the line, "We who are alive, who are left until the coming of the Lord, *shall not precede* those who have fallen asleep" (I Thess. 4:15), and it almost certainly has it as well in the Gospel saying, "If I with the spirit [finger] of God cast out demons, then the kingdom of God has come upon you ahead of time" (Matt. 12:28; Luke 11:20). Jerome plainly understood it in this way in Luke, where he translated *praevenit* (Luke 11:20), and he may also have translated it thus in Matthew, where *pervenit,* the reading of the manuscripts, looks suspiciously like a scribal error (Matt. 12:28). There is no question of Jerome's rendering of the verb in either of its two occurrences in I Thessalonians. In the familiar passage about the resurrection he writes: "nos . . . non praeveniemus eos qui dormierunt" (I Thess. 4:15), and the best manuscripts of the passage under discussion read, "praevenit enim ira Dei super illos" (I Thess. 2:16). There is thus no justification for translating otherwise than as "the wrath . . . has come upon them ahead of time." The meaning of εἰς τέλος is another matter. Jerome translated it "usque in finem" and later translators have variously rendered it "at last," "completely," "for ever," or "unto the uttermost." The phrase would seem to depend, however, on the noun "wrath," and the literal rendering of the three words together would be "wrath for the end." This rendering offers no difficulty. What Paul is saying is that the "wrath for the end," which he also calls the "wrath to come" (I Thess. 1:10), has begun to be visited upon the Jews of Judea "ahead of time."

That the line must refer to some disaster that had recently befallen the Judean Jews has long been understood. Moffatt[1] cites a long list of authorities who take it as a reference to the destruction of Jerusalem in A.D. 70, and who conclude from this either that the whole letter is a forgery or that the line in question (which echoes *Test. Levi* vi. 11) is a later interpolation. But the manuscript tradition contains no evidence that the text of the letter ever existed without the line, and the sole reason for suspecting its originality is the conjectural supposition that it refers to an event that occurred after the end of Paul's life. The alternative supposition—and this is borne out by the textual tradition—is that the line is original. It must therefore refer to a disaster which befell the Jews of Judea between the late 30's and the early 50's of the first century—the outside limits of the period in which I Thessalonians must have been written.

There is really only one event in this period that completely satisfies the requirements of the case. That is the famine that occurred in Judea in the year 46.[2] Josephus speaks of it as an event that could still be remembered a half-century later (*Ant.* iii.15.3). For him it is "the great famine" (*Ant.* xx.5.2), and he recalls it not only because of the magnitude of the disaster that it brought but also because of the magnificent generosity of Queen Helena of Adiabene, who used her personal fortune to purchase shiploads of grain from Egypt and figs from Cyprus in order to save the population of Jerusalem from starvation. Needless to say, a disaster of such proportions must have been a matter of immediate general knowledge outside of Judea, especially among those who had close ties of kinship and religion with the sufferers.

What Paul says about the event makes this identification even more probable. Famine was one of the traditional "woes of the end"

[1] *Introduction to the Literature of the New Testament* (3rd ed.; Edinburgh, 1918), p. 73.
[2] For the date of the famine see K. S. Gapp, "The Universal Famine under Claudius," *Harvard Theological Review*, XXVII (1935), 258–265.

in Jewish apocalyptic, and it figures prominently in early Christian eschatology. It is prophesied explicitly in the Gospel of Mark: "There will be famines: this is but the beginning of the sufferings" (Mark 13:8). Paul himself includes it in his list of the final woes: "Who shall separate us from the love of Christ? Shall tribulation, or distress, or persecution, or famine, or nakedness, or peril, or sword?" (Rom. 8:35). It is, in other words, one of the readily identifiable signs of the approaching end. It is precisely as such that Paul refers to the disaster in I Thessalonians.

The close relationship between I Thessalonians and the Previous Letter to Corinth further bears out this conclusion. I Thessalonians was written at about the same time as the Previous Letter, and the Previous Letter contained the first mention of the collection for the saints, Paul's great campaign to raise funds among the Gentile churches for the Christians of Jerusalem. The letters contain many references to the collection. They state that its purpose was to provide relief for the poor among the saints of Jerusalem, and they ask the members of the Gentile churches to contribute generously and cheerfully. They even explain that the collection was undertaken at the request of James and Cephas and John, who urged "that we should remember the poor" (Gal. 2:10). But they never explain why the need for such a collection had arisen in the first place. This omission has led to several conjectures, none of which are entirely satisfactory. One, that the Jerusalem church was impoverished because it had experimented unsuccessfully with communism, is based on a wholly unwarranted inference from Acts. Another, that Paul hoped to ingratiate himself with the Jerusalem church by means of a "peace-offering" of money, is based on his prayer that his "service for Jerusalem may be acceptable to the saints" (Rom. 15:31); but this is surely to read into the prayer more than Paul intended. As the collection drew to a close, he may have had reason to wonder whether his offering would be welcomed by the Jerusalem church, but he certainly did not undertake the collection in the first place with the intention of placating the enmity of his opponents or of commending himself, or his gospel, to the Jewish Christian church as such. The purpose of the collection from the beginning had been to provide relief for those in want. On that point the letters are clear.

What the letters do not tell us in so many words is why the Jerusalem church should have been in such desperate straits as to require a highly organized large-scale campaign to raise relief funds in the Gentile world, and it is this question which we must answer if we are to understand what really lay behind Paul's decision to undertake the collection. By far the most satisfactory answer is that it was the famine of 46 that brought upon the Jerusalem church the suffering that the collection was undertaken to relieve. All the available evidence points to this conclusion: the recognition that I Thessalonians was written at the close of Paul's first trip to Europe, its reference to a Judean disaster that could be taken as a sign of the "wrath for the end," and its nearness in time to the Previous Letter to Corinth, which announced that the collection was about to begin. If this conclusion is correct, I Thessalonians must have been written while the famine was in progress. It would thus fall in the year 46.

The date of the beginning of Paul's first trip to Europe, as Grotius discovered long ago, can be fixed from II Thessalonians. The writing of II Thessalonians was occasioned by a problem. The members of the church in Thessalonica, or some of them at least, had convinced themselves that the day of the Lord had already come (II Thess. 2:2). How they had come to hold this idea we shall see presently. At the moment we need only establish that they believed it to be true. Paul writes, "Now concerning the coming of our Lord Jesus Christ and our assembling to meet him, we beg you, brethren, not to be quickly shaken in mind or excited, either by spirit or by word, or by letter purporting to be from us, to the effect that the day of the Lord has come" (II Thess. 2:1–2).

Paul's way of meeting this problem is to prove to the Thessalonians that their conclusion is false by demonstrating that it is inconsistent with prophecy. "Let no one deceive you in any way," he writes, "for that day will not come, unless the rebellion comes first, and the man of lawlessness is revealed, the son of perdition, who opposes and exhalts himself against every so-called god or object of worship, so that he takes his seat in the temple of God, proclaiming himself to be God. Do you not remember that when I was still with you I told you this?" (II Thess. 2:3–5).

The ground of this argument is that the day of the Lord could only come after certain preliminary events had taken place. These events, about which Paul had instructed the Thessalonians when he was with them, were first, the rebellion, second, the revealing of the man of lawlessness, and third, the self-exaltation of the man of lawlessness, culminating in his taking his seat in the temple and declaring himself to be God. The point of the argument is that since all of these prophesied preliminaries had not yet taken place, the day of the Lord could not have come.

But had none of them taken place? Close examination of what follows would seem to indicate that one of them, namely, the rebellion, had. Paul does not say this in so many words, but his failure to deny it cannot be without· significance, for the force of his argument depends on his ability to show that the prophecies of these events are still unfulfilled, and he does not attempt to show this in the case of the rebellion. Instead, he begins his demonstration with the second of the predicted events, the revelation of the man of lawlessness. "And you know," he writes, "what is restraining him now so that he may be revealed in his time. For lawlessness is already at work in secret; only it must work in secret until he who now restrains is out of the way" (II Thess. 2:6–7).[3]

In spite of the difficulty of the language in this passage, the progress of the argument can be followed easily enough. The "man of lawlessness" has not yet been "revealed." He is in the offing, no doubt, for lawlessness is already at work under cover. Indeed, he would have put in an appearance before now except for one thing: he is being prevented from doing so. The Thessalonians, moreover, know how to identify "what is restraining him now." And they must realize that the revelation of the man of lawlessness will continue to be deferred until "he who now restrains" is out of the way. This kind of cryptic language has an obvious purpose. It was intended to be meaningless to the uninitiated reader in case the letter fell into the wrong hands. The Thessalonians, however, were expected to be able to understand it without difficulty. All they had to do was to supply the name of "the

[3] For a discussion of the problem of translation see J. B. Lightfoot, *Notes on Epistles of St. Paul* (London, 1895), p. 114.

present restrainer," which Paul says they already knew, and all would be clear.

But who was the present restrainer? Commentators, both ancient and modern, all but universally interpret Paul's words about the restraining power as a reference to the Roman Empire. The Fathers, from Tertullian on, quote the passage to prove that Christianity is not hostile to the state but looks to it as a bulwark against the unchecked activity of lawlessness. All concede that the second expression, "he who restrains," is a personification of the first, "that which restrains," and take it as meaning the emperor, since he was the person in whom the imperial power resided. According to this view Paul meant that the man of lawlessness would be revealed when there was no more emperor, that is, when the empire had fallen. But this view, although its appeal to the Fathers is obvious, cannot be correct. Paul simply did not expect the return of the Lord to be delayed until the end of a succession of imperial reigns. II Thessalonians itself clearly holds out the hope to its readers that when the parousia comes it will burst without warning upon the very persons who are even now persecuting them. The restraining power, therefore, cannot have been the Roman Empire viewed as a continuing political institution, and it cannot have been a long succession of emperors in whom the imperial power resided. It can only have been the particular emperor who sat on the throne at the time. That is to say, the person who appears in II Thessalonians as "he who now restrains" must have been Claudius. What Paul was saying, and what the Thessalonians were expected to understand, was that the restraining power of Claudius had prevented the man of lawlessness from being revealed as soon as they had expected him. And this state of affairs would continue until Claudius was out of the way. What follows in the passage bears this out, for it enables us to identify the man of lawlessness himself and to show how Claudius could be conceived of as restraining his activities.

When the lawless one is revealed, Paul goes on, "the Lord Jesus will slay him with the breath of his mouth and destroy him by his appearing and his coming. The coming of the lawless one by the activity of Satan will be with all power and with pretended signs and wonders" (II Thess. 2:8–9). The passage refers to two "comings," that of the man of lawlessness and that of Jesus, and it uses the same word, parousia, in each case. The sequence is made clear by the context. First there will be the parousia of the man of lawlessness, who will engage in the activities already described and finally declare himself to be God, and then there will be the parousia of Christ, who will slay the man of lawlessness with the breath of his mouth.

What, now, is implied by the term "parousia" in these sentences? In the case of Jesus the answer is well known. He who had once lived on earth was now in heaven, from whence he would shortly appear again. His parousia would thus be a reappearance, or a return. When used in connection with Jesus the term always has this meaning. Is it possible that it also has this meaning in connection with the man of lawlessness? The fact that the parousia of Jesus and the parousia of the man of lawlessness are mentioned in successive clauses in the same sentence would seem to indicate that the term has the same meaning in both. We may reasonably infer, therefore, that when Paul spoke of the parousia of the man of lawlessness he may well have meant not the first appearance of this figure but his reappearance.

The parallelism between what Paul says of Christ and what he says of the man of lawlessness would seem to go even further. When the man of lawlessness appears, it will be as the agent of Satan. When Christ appears, as Paul's readers know, it will be as the agent of God (II Thess. 1:5-8). Again, lawlessness is already at work in the world even before the appearance of the man of lawlessness, just as sanctification by the Spirit (II Thess. 2:13) is at work even before the appearance of Christ. What Paul seems to imply, in other words, is that the career of the man of lawlessness is an exact parallel of the career of Christ.

But what he does not tell us is how far back the parallelism of the two careers extends. Did the man of lawlessness, like Jesus, begin his career with an earthly life? And did his death mark the beginning of the next phase, the secret working of lawlessness? Since we have no positive evidence on which to base an answer to these questions, we must approach them by way of hypothesis. On the one hand, there is the possibility that the man of lawlessness never had a prior earthly existence. In that case we cannot identify him. On the other hand, however, there is the possibility that he not only lived an earthly life but that the Thessalonians knew precisely who he was when he was alive. In that case we should be able to identify him ourselves. If we can do this convincingly, that fact itself must be taken as evidence that Paul may have expected his readers to be able to do the same thing.

As it turns out, the identification of the man of lawlessness is not difficult. We have already established that the present restrainer can only have been Claudius. We have also seen the point at which Claudius' restraint had interrupted the march of those apocalyptic events which would lead to the end, with the result that the man of lawlessness was prevented from finishing the work which was his. The first of the prophesied events, the rebellion, had presumably taken place, or at least had begun. But the second, the self-exaltation of the man of lawlessness, culminating in his taking his seat in the temple and proclaiming himself to be God, had been forestalled. And it would be prevented from being completed until Claudius was out of the way.

This sequence of events is precisely what occurred when Claudius succeeded Caligula in January of the year 41.[4] In the last few months of his reign, Caligula, who had begun to think of himself as divine, conceived the design of erecting a statue of himself in the temple in Jerusalem. The execution of this plan was at first prevented by the deliberate delay of P. Petronius, the governor of Syria, in carrying out the emperor's orders. The inhabitants of Judea, when the affair became public knowledge, had announced to Petronius their firm resolve to die before they would see the statue erected. To back up their threat they proceeded to allow the fields to lie fallow, refusing to sow the season's crop. News of Caligula's intention soon spread over the whole Jewish world. In Alexandria the Jewish community, which had recently suffered a brutal pogrom as a result of its refusal to set up the emperor's image in the synagogues, began to arm itself. When news of these developments reached Agrippa, who happened to be staying in Rome at the time, he became convinced that the erection of the statue could only result in a Jewish war. He therefore courageously intervened

[4] The identification of Paul's "man of lawlessness" with Caligula was originally made by Hugo Grotius. In recent writing it has largely been ignored. But see M. H. Shepherd, "A Venture in the Source Criticism of Acts," *Munera Studiosa*, ed. by Shepherd and Johnson (Cambridge, 1946), p. 96n.

with Caligula and in consequence of the personal friendship that existed between the two men succeeded in dissuading him from pressing the issue. Caligula's murder shortly after this, in January of 41, put an effective stop to the whole design. For a time, however, it had seemed inevitable to the whole Jewish and Christian world that the prophecy of Daniel concerning the desecration of the temple by a king who exalted himself against God was about to be fulfilled. To the Christians especially, already expecting the end of the age and searching the Old Testament for prophecies of its coming, the statue of Caligula seemed the "abomination of desolation" (Mark 13:14) and Caligula himself the apocalyptic figure whose self-glorification heralded the end of the age.

To the identification of Paul's man of lawlessness with Caligula two objections are ordinarily raised. The first is that, to early Christian writers in general, with the exception of the author of the Johannine Apocalypse, and to Paul in particular, the Roman Empire was not a power hostile to Christianity. Therefore, it is argued, Paul could hardly have spoken of the emperor as an Antichrist. This is the argument of Bousset,[5] who believes that the passage in question can have had no specific political application. But while it is perfectly true that early Christian writers urged their readers to respect the authority of government, it is equally clear that for obvious religious reasons all Christians resisted the cult of the deified emperor. Their support of the government was limited to its civil authority; in matters of religion they allowed none of its claims. Bousset's investigation of the long history of the Antichrist legend led him to ask whether the force of the myth depended on the ability of its users to identify the figure of the Antichrist with a known political figure. This question he answered in the negative. But the question which concerns us is not the one which Bousset put but, rather, whether the doings of Caligula had religious significance to the Jews and Christians who observed them. And this question cannot possibly be answered in the negative. It is a documented fact that the Jews placed an immediate and unequivocal

---

[5] *The Antichrist Legend* (Eng. trans., London, 1896), pp. 22, 128. Bousset does admit, however (p. 192), that Paul means the empire when he speaks of the restraining power.

religious interpretation on Caligula's designs with regard to the statue.[6] This being the case, we may safely conclude that the Christians must have done the same thing. The argument that Christians were too loyal to Rome to be able to recognize Caligula as the Antichrist simply does not hold.

The second objection to the identification of Paul's man of lawlessness with Caligula is that Caligula did not actually fulfill the apocalyptic predictions. The statue was shipped to Palestine but it was never actually erected, and of course Caligula did not take his seat in the temple. But this is precisely the point which Paul himself made. His purpose in making it, however, was not to prove that the Thessalonians' identification of the man of lawlessness was mistaken; it was to explain why the man of lawlessness had not returned to complete his work. It was because he was being restrained.

The usual objections to the identification of Paul's man of lawlessness as Caligula, then, must be dismissed. Indeed, it is difficult to see how the Christians, awaiting the advent of this apocalyptic figure, could have failed to recognize Caligula's doings as a fulfillment of the prophecies about the one who would exalt himself against every so-called god or object of worship, so that he takes his seat in the temple of God, proclaiming himself to be God.

The identification of the rebellion is no less easy. Caligula's announced intention of setting up his statue in the temple, it will be recalled, had caused the Jewish leaders in Palestine to threaten a large-scale program of passive resistance. When the Gentiles in Alexandria attempted to force the Jews to place the emperor's image in the synagogues, the Jewish community openly defied the order, and bloody fighting ensued between the two groups. Finally, the news of Caligula's murder was the signal for an open Jewish revolt, not only in Alexandria but also, it seems, in Antioch as well. It would be strange if these events in Palestine, Egypt, and Syria had not seemed to the Christians to be a fulfillment of the prophecies about the rebellion that would mark the beginning of the last days.

---

[6] "The Jews looked on Gaius as a second Antiochus Epiphanes, bent on destroying their race and religion" (M. P. Charlesworth, in *Cambridge Ancient History*, X, 666; see also the references to Jewish sources given there).

156

It was in the midst of these events that Claudius came to the throne. He was not slow to deal with the problems which he had inherited. Immediately on his accession he turned his attention to the task of suppressing the Jewish disturbances and establishing an orderly policy of dealing with this troublesome minority. To the Alexandrians he addressed a letter confirming the former privileges of the Jews, though cautioning them against attempting to extend these privileges. The letter concluded with a sharp warning to both Jews and Gentiles to keep the peace. According to Josephus, Claudius applied the same policy to the Jews everywhere in the empire. Josephus may be suspected of having exaggerated Claudius' favor toward the Jews, but there seems to be no reason for doubting that his general approach to the Jewish problem followed the lines laid down in Alexandria. Suetonius, who may be suspected of having exaggerated Claudius' severity, records that he expelled the Jews from Rome; it seems doubtful that more than a few were actually deported, however, and we may perhaps conclude that here as elsewhere he took repressive measures against them only insofar as these seemed necessary to prevent disorder. In the matter of emperor-worship, Claudius made his position clear at once by refusing to accept divine honors. He publicly referred to Caligula's demands for such honors as the actions of a madman. In short, in matters that affected the Jews, Claudius appeared as the man who had checked the tide of rebellion and halted the course of events which Caligula had set in motion.

Paul's characterization of Claudius, therefore, as the restrainer who had interrupted the course of apocalyptic events and forestalled the activities of the man of lawlessness fits the situation perfectly. As long as the restraining hand of Claudius was in control, he could argue, lawlessness would have to work in secret. Not until Claudius was out of the way would the man of lawlessness reappear. On Claudius' death, however, Paul expected Caligula, having been revived by the power of Satan, to return and finish his work.[7] This, of course, would be the signal for the parousia of Christ.

With this background of events in mind we can now proceed to

[7] The idea of the return of Caligula faded with the passing years only to re-emerge several decades later in the expectation of the return of Nero.

the question of dates. There are two to be considered: the date of Paul's first visit to Thessalonica and the date of the writing of II Thessalonians.

The date of Paul's first visit to Thessalonica can be fixed between rather narow limits. It must have coincided, in part at least, with the last months of Caligula's reign, for Paul says, with reference to the rebellion and the appearance of the man of lawlessness as necessary preliminaries to the parousia of Christ, "Do you not remember that when I was still with you I told you this?" (II Thess. 2:5). These words would seem to indicate that in his preaching to the Thessalonians Paul had interpreted the Jewish uprisings and Caligula's threat to put his statue in the temple as signs that the parousia of Christ was imminent. On the other hand, the visit must have ended before Caligula's death, or at least before Claudius had restored order, for Paul's original preaching had said nothing about the delay which the restraining influence of Claudius would effect in the apocalyptic program. Paul had left the Thessalonians under the impression that they had seen the beginning of the march of events that would swiftly lead to the end of the age. Not until II Thessalonians was written did he explain to them that an unforeseen circumstance had arisen, namely, the restraining activity of Claudius, that was preventing these events from progressing to their conclusion. We shall probably not be far wrong, then, in dating Paul's departure from Thessalonica not later than January of the year 41.

The date of the composition of II Thessalonians can be fixed with similar precision. It will be remembered that the occasion for the letter was the emergence among the Thessalonians of a belief that the day of the Lord had already come. Paul writes, "Now concerning the coming of our Lord Jesus Christ and our assembling to meet him, we beg you, brethren, not to be quickly shaken in mind or excited, either by spirit or by word, or by letter purporting to be from us, to the effect that the day of the Lord has come" (II Thess. 2:1-2). These words would seem to suggest that although Paul was not quite certain how the Thessalonians had been persuaded to accept this belief, whether by a supposed revelation or even by a false report of the event itself, he feared that they might have received a letter, either deliberately forged in his name or purporting to have been sent with his approval, saying that he himself was now teaching that the day of the Lord had come. This interpretation is borne out by the closing sentences of II Thessalonians, which caution Paul's readers against accepting any letter as coming from him unless its closing greetings are in his own handwriting: "I, Paul, write this greeting with my own hand. This is the mark in every letter of mine; it is the way I write" (II Thess. 3:17).

But although Paul seems not to have been sure how the Thessalonians had been finally convinced of the truth of the strange conclusion to which they had come, he plainly knew that they had reached it by calculating the time of the end of the present age. What is more, the method of calculating which they had used was one to which, they had reason to believe on the basis of his original preaching to them, he also subscribed. It is significant that in II Thessalonians he neither denies the validity of this method nor disclaims it as his own, but only argues that the Thessalonians have applied it incorrectly and therefore have come to a false conclusion.

What Paul had told the Thessalonians originally, as we have already seen, was that the march of events leading up to the end of the present age had already begun. He had also identified Caligula as the prophesied king who would "exalt himself and magnify himself above every god" (Dan. 11:36; II Thess. 2:4). There is no evidence that he had gone so far as to name an actual date for the approaching end, and it seems unlikely that he would have been willing to commit himself definitely on this question, the answer to which was traditionally regarded as being known only to God. But the Thessalonians seem to have been less cautious. And as it happens, the means whereby they could at least attempt to calculate the date of the end were available to them in the very prophecies in the book of Daniel to which Paul had directed their attention. For example, the first of the prophecies about the king who would exalt himself reads:

> He shall speak words against the Most High,
>   and shall wear out the saints of the Most High,
>   and shall think to change the times and the law;
> and they shall be given into his hand
>   for a time, two times, and half a time (Dan. 7:25).

Even more explicit is the following:

> And from the time that the continued burnt offering is taken away, and the abomination that makes desolate is set up, there shall be a thousand two hundred and ninety days. Blessed is he who waits and comes to the thousand three hundred and thirty-five days. But go your way till the end; and you shall rest, and shall stand in your allotted place at the end of the days (Dan. 12:11–13).

That it was such passages as these to which the Thessalonians had turned in order to calculate the time of the end is clear from II Thessalonians, the second chapter of which makes constant reference to the sections of Daniel in which they occur. Indeed, once the Thessalonians had identified Caligula as the prophesied king, it is inconceivable that they should have failed to notice that the prophecies about him in two places (Dan. 7:25; 12:7) gave the length of time that would elapse between the culmination of his activities and the end of the age as, in round numbers, "a time, two times, and half a time," that is, three and a half years, and elsewhere (Dan. 12:11–12) stipulated that the last stage of the apocalyptic fulfillment would begin in 1,290 days and be completed in 1,335 days.

The problem in all this was to know when to begin counting. The statue of Caligula was never actually set up in the temple, and as far as we know there was no interruption of the burnt offering (though the threat of this was implicit in the refusal to sow the crops in the fall of the year 40). Another event, however, could serve as a starting point for the necessary calculation. This was Caligula's murder in January of the year 41. The pertinent passage in Daniel reads as follows:

> Yet shall he come to his end, with none to help him. At that time shall arise Michael, the great prince who has charge of your people. And there shall be a time of trouble, such as never has been since there was a nation till that time; but at that time your people shall be delivered, every one whose name shall be found written in the book. And many of those who sleep in the dust of the earth shall awake, some to everlasting life, and some to shame and everlasting contempt. And those who are wise shall shine like the brightness of the firmament; and those who turn many to righteousness, like the stars for ever and ever. But you, Daniel, shut up the words, and seal the book, until the time of the end. Many shall run to and fro, and knowledge shall increase (Dan. 11:45; 12:1–4).

It is obvious from this that Caligula's death could easily serve as the starting point from which to calculate the time of the end. But this is precisely the point at which Paul attacks the reasoning of the Thessalonians. Caligula, he says, has not come to his end; he will have another period of activity on earth: "The parousia of the lawless one by the activity of Satan will be with all power and with pretended signs and wonders, and with all wicked deception for those who are to perish, because they refused to love the truth and so be saved" (II Thess. 2:9–10). This is a reference to such prophecies as, "By his cunning he shall make deceit prosper under his hand," and, "He shall seduce with flattery those who violate the covenant" (Dan. 8:25; 11:32). Paul also makes the point that the final death of the lawless one, the one that really counts apocalyptically, will be brought about by the Lord Jesus, who "will slay him with the breath of his mouth and destroy him by his appearing and his coming" (II Thess. 2:8). This is surely a reference to the prophecy, "He shall even rise up against the Prince of princes; but, by no human hand, he shall be broken" (Dan. 8:25). The point of these references is that the prophesied end of the activity of the lawless one had not come with the murder of Caligula (by a human hand), as the Thessalonians had supposed, but would only come with his second, and final, death, which was still in the future.

What the Thessalonians had done, in brief, was to begin to count the days after the death of Caligula in January of 41. When the final day came, in the summer of 44, and no signs of the parousia of Christ were visible to them, they had concluded that this event must have taken place elsewhere. When Paul heard what had happened, he wrote to assure them that their calculations had been incorrect. The prophecy of the death of the man of lawlessness, which they had taken to be fulfilled in the murder of Caligula, was still unfulfilled—not because Caligula was not the man of lawlessness, but because the death to which the prophecies referred was a future death which the man of lawlessness would suffer after his return to earth.

The date of II Thessalonians, therefore, can be fixed. It cannot have been written before early September of the year 44, for the 1,335 days were not up until then. It can hardly have been written very long after that time either, for it deals with matters that were still a subject of urgent debate. It may safely be placed, therefore, in the fall of the year 44.

We have thus established three absolute dates on the basis of the evidence of the letters: A.D. 41 for the end of Paul's first visit to Thessalonica, 44 for the composition of II Thessalonians, and 46 for the composition of I Thessalonians. Since I Thessalonians is contemporaneous with the Previous Letter to Corinth, which announced Paul's intention of gathering a collection for the relief of the poor Christians in Judea, and since the letters of the collection period were written within the ensuing year (II Cor. 9:2), they may safely be placed in the year 47; I Corinthians in the spring, at Passover; II Corinthians 10–13 and Philippians during the next seven weeks; II Corinthians 1–9 at Pentecost; and Galatians and Romans in the summer and fall. The three remaining letters, Colossians, Philemon, and Ephesians, were written after Romans. There is no way of telling, on the basis of the evidence of these letters, how long after Romans they were written. The marked changes in style and doctrine which they exhibit over the collection letters, however, suggest that they may have been separated from Romans by a considerable interval.

12

SUMMARY:
THE ORDER OF EVENTS IN
THE LETTERS

Historians have for so long assumed that only Acts could supply the narrative outline of Paul's life that it comes as something of a surprise to discover that the letters contain ample evidence on which to base a fairly detailed account of his activities over a considerable part of his missionary career. The most extended autobiographical passage in the letters is found in Galatians, and since it is fundamental to any reconstruction of Paul's life, it may be quoted in full:

> You have heard of my former life in Judaism, how I persecuted the church of God violently and tried to destroy it; and I advanced in Judaism beyond many of my own age among my people, so extremely zealous was I for the traditions of my fathers. But when he who had set me apart before I was born, and had called me through his grace, was pleased to reveal his Son in me, in order that I might preach him among the Gentiles, I did not confer with flesh and blood, nor did I go up to Jeru-

salem to those who were apostles before me, but I went away
into Arabia; and again I returned to Damascus.

Then after three years I went up to Jerusalem to visit Cephas,
and remained with him fifteen days. But I saw none of the other
apostles except James the Lord's brother. (In what I am writing
you, before God, I do not lie!) Then I went into the regions of
Syria and Cilicia. And I was still not known by sight to the
churches of Christ in Judea; they only heard it said, "He who
once persecuted us is now preaching the faith he once tried to
destroy." And they glorified God because of me.

Then after fourteen years I went up again to Jerusalem with
Barnabas, taking Titus along with me. I went up by revelation;
and I laid before them (but privately before those who were of
repute) the gospel which I preach among the Gentiles, lest somehow I should be running or had run in vain. But even Titus,
who was with me, was not compelled to be circumcised, though
he was a Greek. But because of false brethren secretly brought
in, who slipped in to spy out our freedom which we have in
Christ Jesus, that they might bring us into bondage—to them we
did not yield submission even for a moment, that the truth of
the gospel might be preserved for you. And from those who were
reputed to be something (what they were makes no difference to
me; God shows no partiality)—those, I say, who were of repute
added nothing to me; but on the contrary, when they saw that
I had been entrusted with the gospel to the uncircumcised, just
as Peter had been entrusted with the gospel to the circumcised
(for he who worked through Peter for the mission to the circumcised worked through me also for the Gentiles), and when they
perceived the grace that was given to me, James and Cephas and
John, who were reputed to be pillars, gave to me and Barnabas
the right hand of fellowship, that we should go to the Gentiles
and they to the circumcised; only they would have us remember
the poor, which very thing I was eager to do.

But when Cephas came to Antioch I opposed him to his
face, because he stood condemned. For before certain men came
from James, he ate with the Gentiles; but when they came he
drew back and separated himself, fearing the circumcision party.
And with him the rest of the Jews acted insincerely, so that even
Barnabas was carried away by their insincerity. But when I saw
that they were not straightforward about the truth of the gospel,
I said to Cephas before them all, "If you, though a Jew, live like
a Gentile and not like a Jew, how can you compel the Gentiles
to live like Jews?" (Gal. 1:13–2:14).

Volumes have been written on this passage, but its outline is clear at a glance. It tells us that Paul, after his conversion, went first to Arabia, then returned to Damascus, and then after three years went up to Jerusalem. This was his first visit to Jerusalem as a Christian. His second visit took place "after fourteen years." It was apparently not long after the second visit that the break occurred with the Judaizers in Antioch. Galatians was written before the issues which had caused the break had been settled.

But Galatians, as we have already seen, was written during the collection. And the collection, needless to say, was undertaken in churches which Paul had founded before the beginning of the collection trip. The founding of these churches—in Macedonia and Achaia, as well as in Galatia—must therefore have taken place between Paul's first and second visits to Jerusalem.

That Galatians does not say this in so many words need not astonish us. Galatians is not a history book; it is a letter, and letters do not ordinarily tell their recipients what the recipients already know. Paul did not have to tell the Galatians that he had already visited them and converted them. They already knew that. Nor did he have to tell them that after leaving Galatia he had gone to Greece. They already knew that too. What he feared they might not know was where he had been before he appeared in Syria and Cilicia, and what his relations with the Jerusalem church had been during that early period; and he suspected that they had been deliberately misinformed about what had happened during his most recent visit to Jerusalem, after his return from Greece. It is these facts which the letter supplies. Knox seems to be the only critic who has seen this completely clearly. By the time of the second Jerusalem visit, he writes, "Paul had reached Macedonia, Greece and Asia,"[1] and it may be added, he had very probably been to Illyricum as well (Rom. 15:19).

That Paul had been to Europe before the second visit to Jerusalem is now perfectly clear. Equally clear is the correctness of those translations of Galatians 2:10 in which the force of the Greek tenses is respected, with results more or less as follows: "Only they requested that we should continue to remember the poor, which very thing I made haste to do." These words, as Knox has pointed out, can only refer to

[1] *Chapters in a Life of Paul* (Nashville, 1950), p. 59.

the collection mentioned in the Corinthian letters and Romans, and they establish that the collection began immediately after the second visit to Jerusalem. That the collection trip ended with a third visit to Jerusalem is also clear from Romans, in which Paul writes, "At present, however, I am going to Jerusalem with aid for the saints" (Rom 15:25).

The letters thus tell us of three visits. Knox has called the first "Acquaintance," the second "Conference," and the third "Offering," and these names have now become standard. "Acquaintance," of course, is the first visit to Jerusalem, three years after the conversion; "Conference" the second, "after fourteen years"; and "Offering" the third, at the close of the collection trip. We have also heard of two trips. The first, which took place between the first two Jerusalem visits, we may call "Foundation," since it was the occasion for the founding of churches in Galatia, Macedonia, and Achaia. The second, which took place between the second and third Jerusalem visits, we may call "Collection," since its chief purpose was to collect money for the relief of the Christians in Judea. This sequence of events may be outlined as follows:

1. Conversion
2. Acquaintance visit to Jerusalem, "after three years"
3. Foundation trip to Syria, Cilicia, Galatia, Macedonia, and Achaia
4. Conference visit to Jerusalem, "after fourteen years"
5. Collection trip to Syria, Galatia, Asia, Macedonia, and Achaia
6. Offering visit to Jerusalem

That the trips and the visits were related to each other in this way is beyond question. Moreover, we are now in a position to describe the trips in considerable detail. After his first visit to Jerusalem, Paul traveled first to Syria, where his work undoubtedly centered in Antioch. From there he extended the field of his operations to Cilicia. Galatians tells us this in so many words, and it also tells us by implication that from Cilicia Paul went to Galatia.

We find him next in Macedonia, where he first visited Philippi and then Thessalonica. He writes, "You Philippians yourselves know that in the beginning of the gospel, when I left Macedonia, no church entered into partnership with me in giving and receiving help except you only; for even in Thessalonica you sent me help once and again" (Phil. 4:15–16). This first visit to Thessalonica, as we have seen, ended not much later than January of the year 41.

From Macedonia, Paul proceeded to Achaia. To the Corinthians he writes, "We were the first to come all the way to you with the gospel of Christ. . . . And when I was with you and was in want, I did not burden any one, for my needs were supplied by the brethren who came from Macedonia" (II Cor. 10:14; 11:9). How long he stayed in Achaia we do not know, but he very possibly went from there to Illyricum, for he was later to write in Romans, "From Jerusalem as far round as Illyricum I have fully preached the gospel of Christ" (Rom. 15:19). We do know that in the fall of the year 44, three and a half years after his departure from Thessalonica, he heard that the Thessalonians had persuaded themselves that the parousia had already taken place, although they had not seen any of the outward signs that would accompany this event. He therefore wrote to the Thessalonians to assure them that they were mistaken and to explain why the parousia was being delayed. This letter, which we know as II Thessalonians, is the earliest writing from Paul's pen that we possess.

From this point on the story of Paul's activity begins to emerge in a clearer light. Before leaving Europe at the close of the Foundation trip he paid a second visit to Corinth, the "painful visit" (II Cor. 2:1; 13:2). His intention at that time was to pay a second visit to Thessalonica as well, but this proved impossible. He therefore remained behind in Athens while Timothy proceeded to Macedonia. When Timothy rejoined him, bringing a report of conditions in Thessalonica, he wrote I Thessalonians. The year was now 46.

In the same year, after his return from Europe, Paul paid his second visit to Jerusalem. The account of this visit in Galatians has been discussed at great length by commentators, who have tended to see in it greater difficulties than it really contains. The principal points it makes are: (1) that Paul went to Jerusalem "by revelation," that is, that he felt divinely inspired to go and was not summoned by the Jerusalem church; (2) that he laid before the leaders of the church the gospel he had been preaching among the Gentiles; (3) that the leaders did not require Titus to be circumcised, though he was a Greek; (4) that they "added nothing" to what Paul had been preaching; (5) that James, Cephas, and John agreed that Paul and Barnabas should go to the Gentiles and they to be circumcised; and (6) that they should remember the poor, presumably of the Jerusalem church.[2]

The nature of the agreement between the Jewish and Gentile missions is clear: having been separate and distinct until this time, they were to continue so. Paul and Barnabas were not to be required to accommodate their gospel to the prejudices of the extreme conservatives among the Jewish Christians, but were to accept Gentile converts on the same terms as before, that is, without requiring that they be circumcised and without requiring that they observe the traditional Jewish dietary regulations. These terms are not spelled out in the account of Paul's meeting with James and Cephas and John, but subsequent events prove that they had been agreed upon.

Shortly after Paul returned to Antioch from Jerusalem, Cephas also came to Antioch. At first he followed the custom of the Antioch church and ate with the Gentiles. But when "certain men came from James" he separated himself, since he feared "those of the circumcision." This shows plainly that Paul's agreement with the Jerusalem church recognized the right of Gentile converts to remain uncircumcised and to ignore the dietary regulations, but the agreement had not taken into account the possibility that Jewish Christians might also ignore the dietary regulations when they were with Gentiles. Peter's visit to Antioch, in short, exposed the weakness of the assumption that the two missions could simply be treated as separate and distinct enterprises, and it may well be that the "false brethren secretly brought in" and the "certain men" who "came from James," far from being the trouble-making busybodies whom they are depicted as having been, were in fact the only persons who realized from the beginning that the easy agreement arrived at in Jerusalem was bound to give rise to discord.

[2] The supposed difficulties in this passage are two in number. Some scholars have suggested that the line, "even Titus . . . was not compelled to be circumcised," may mean that he submitted to circumcision voluntarily rather than under compulsion, but this is surely looking for problems where none exist. The following clauses are admittedly an incomplete sentence, but their meaning again is clear. Certain "false brethren" did attempt to influence the Jerusalem leaders against Paul, but their efforts were unsuccessful.

in any case, discord ensued. Paul accused Cephas and Barnabes, who had also separated himself from the Gentiles, of insincerity. He went further than that. He proceeded to maintain that the law was no more binding on Jewish Christians than on Gentiles. From that moment the Judaizers could not fail to recognize Paul as their chief enemy.

The final stipulation of Paul's agreement with the leaders of the Jerusalem church had been that he and Barnabas should "remember the poor, which very thing," he adds, "I made haste to do." He was referring, of course, to the great effort to raise money among the Gentile churches which took him on the Collection trip. The trip began from Antioch shortly after the conflict with the Judaizers, and he probably went first to Galatia. So much is implied in his later instructions to the Corinthians: "Now concerning the collection for the saints, as I directed the churches of Galatia, so you also are to do" (I Cor. 16:1). Either from Antioch, before setting out, or from Galatia he also penned the Previous Letter to Corinth, in which he told the Corinthians of the forthcoming collection and asked them to contribute. At this time his plan seems to have been to travel to Ephesus and take ship from there to Corinth. From Corinth he would go briefly to Macedonia and return to Corinth for the close of the collection. By the time he arrived in Ephesus, however, he had altered this plan. Instead of going to Corinth first he would go to Macedonia and proceed from there to Corinth. In I Corinthians, written from Ephesus in the spring of 47, he explains his change of plan to the Corinthians: "For I do not want to see you now just in passing; I hope to spend some time with you, if the Lord permits" (I Cor. 16:7).

The Corinthians were not pleased by what Paul had written in I Corinthians, and Paul soon learned that at least one faction among them was in open rebellion against his authority. Accordingly, he wrote them a second letter from Ephesus, sharper in tone than I Corinthians. This letter, which we know as II Corinthians 10–13, he dispatched by the hand of Titus. When Titus had delivered the letter and observed its effect, he was to travel to Macedonia, where Paul expected to be by the time of his arrival.

Before his departure from Ephesus, however, Paul found himself the victim of a persecution of great severity. He was arrested and imprisoned, and for a time he even believed that he had been sentenced to death. During this imprisonment he also received news of the further activities of the Judaizers, who were now, it would seem, telling Paul's Gentile converts, probably in Galatia, that the law was binding on all Christians, Jews and Gentiles alike. This was no more than the reverse of what Paul had said in Antioch, that the law was not binding on either Jews or Gentiles, but Paul took it otherwise. "Some," he wrote to the Philippians at this time, "preach Christ from envy and rivalry . . . out of partisanship, not sincerely but thinking to afflict me in my imprisonment" (Phil. 1:15,17). Later in the same letter he warned his readers: "Look out for the dogs, look out for the evil-workers, look out for those who mutilate the flesh. For we are the true circumcision, who worship God in spirit, and glory in Christ Jesus, and put no confidence in the flesh" (Phil. 3:2–3). There was now open warfare between the Judaizers and Paul.

How Paul secured his release from prison in Ephesus and escaped the death which he believed to be imminent we do not know. We only know that he succeeded in leaving Ephesus and journeyed to Troas and from there to Macedonia. There he met Titus, whom he had sent to Corinth as his emissary. Since Titus had made a promising beginning of the collection in Corinth, and since the Macedonians wished to contribute also, Paul decided to remain in Macedonia and to send Titus back to Corinth. Titus took with him II Corinthians 1–9, in which Paul further developed his antilegal position, apparently with the thought that the Corinthians should be forearmed against a possible incursion of Judaizers in their midst.

Shortly after the writing of II Corinthians 1–9 Paul appears to have heard that the Judaizers had not only followed him to Galatia but had achieved some success in persuading his Galatian converts that they should be circumcised and should undertake the keeping of the whole law. In an effort to counteract this influence he wrote Galatians, in which he took the strongest antilegal position to be found in all of his writing, arguing that the law had not been given by God at all, but was the instrument of lesser beings, having been imposed by angels.

It was a brilliant argument, but it could not be maintained. Not only did it deny the immediacy of God's absolute sovereignty, itself a serious heresy, but it also brought into question the direct inspiration of a large part of the Old Testament, a fundamental assumption of Christian as well as Jewish thought. Paul therefore realized that the position he had taken in Galatians had to be modified, and after he had moved on to Corinth, but before he had set out for Jerusalem to deliver the collection, he wrote Romans, in which he revised his whole antilegal position by combining the principal arguments of II Corinthians 1-9 with those of Galatians. In the process he omitted the extreme statements of both letters, or altered them in such a way as to remove their offensive implications.

By this time, however, Paul had concluded that he no longer had "any room for work in these regions" (Rom. 15:23) and resolved to transfer his activity to Spain. After delivering the collection to Jerusalem he would first visit Rome, and then proceed from there to the west. He closed his letter to the Romans with an appeal for their prayers on his behalf, that he might be delivered from the unbelievers in Judea and that his offering to the Jerusalem church might be acceptable to the saints, so that he might make his way to Rome with joy.

It is usual to assume that immediately after the writing of Romans, Paul proceeded to Jerusalem, delivered the collection to the church, and was arrested and imprisoned. That, at any rate, seems to have been the understanding of the author of Acts, and it has all but invariably been followed by later students of Paul's life. The letters, however, give no indication that Paul was arrested in Jerusalem at the close of the collection. On the contrary, they seem to indicate that he left Jerusalem and went, not to Rome and then to Spain, but back to Asia. These indications are to be found in Colossians, Philemon, and Ephesians, all of which were clearly written after Romans, and all of which have an Asian background. It is only as a result of preconceptions wholly derived from Acts that the composition of these letters is placed in Caesarea or Rome instead of in Asia. If it were not for Acts they would naturally be placed in the neighborhood of Colossae, Laodicea, and Hierapolis, places which they imply are within a short distance of the location of the prison from which they were written.

The three letters in question reflect the background of a fairly extensive Asian ministry, with Paul at its head. Paul's fellow workers and associates in this ministry are Timothy (Philem. 1:1), Epaphras (Col. 1:17; Philem. 23), Tychicus (Col. 4:7; Eph. 6:21), Aristarchus (Col. 4:10; Philem. 24), Mark (Col. 4:10; Philem. 24), Jesus Justus (Col. 4:11), Luke (Col. 4:14; Philem. 24), and Demas (Col. 4:14; Philem. 24); we also hear of Philemon (Philem. 1), Apphia (Philem. 2), Archippus (Col. 4:17; Philem. 2), Onesimus (Col. 4:9; Philem. 10), and Nympha (Col. 4:15). Except for Timothy, these are all persons whom the letters have never named before. They do not figure in Paul's references to the founding of the Gentile churches, and their names do not appear in connection with the collection. They seem to be a group of missionary assistants and leading converts who did not begin to be associated with Paul until after the collection was over. Moreover, the sphere of their activity is clearly Asia, a locality in which Paul's previous work had apparently been limited to a brief beginning in Ephesus while the collection was in progress (I Cor. 16:8).

Equally telling is the very strong impression one gains from these letters that the churches to which they are addressed had never been immediately involved in the conflict with the Judaizers. When Paul writes to the Colossians about "questions of food and drink, or with regard to a festival or a new moon or a sabbath" (Col. 2:16), he undoubtedly recalls the older issue of the keeping of the Jewish law by Gentile Christians, but he does not argue this current question by referring to it. Apparently it had never been an issue with the Colossians. He can even mention "the elemental spirits of the universe" (Col. 2:20) without implying a connection with the older argument of Galatians in which these beings had been identified with the angels who imposed the law. Apparently the Colossians had never been familiar with that argument.

The evidence of Ephesians is even more telling in this regard. That letter's over-all theme is unity. "For he has made known to us in all wisdom and insight the mystery of his will, according to his purpose which he set forth in Christ as a plan for the fulness of time, to unite all things in him, things in heaven and things on earth" (Eph. 1:9–10). The Gentiles, who were once "separated from Christ, alienated from the commonwealth of Israel, and strangers to the covenants of promise," have been "brought near in the blood of Christ . . . who has made us both one, and has broken down the dividing wall of hostility . . . that he might create in himself one new man in place of the two . . . and might reconcile us both to God in one body through the cross, thereby bringing the hostility to an end" (Eph. 2:12–16). The Gentiles are therefore "fellow citizens with the saints and members of the household of God" (Eph. 2:19). This household, moreover, is "built upon the foundation of the apostles and prophets" (Eph. 2:20), to whom the Spirit has now revealed what was not previously known, namely, "how the Gentiles are fellow heirs, members of the same body, and partakers of the promise in Christ Jesus through the gospel" (Eph. 3:4–6). These passages echo the leading arguments which Paul had developed in Galatians and Romans in opposition to the Judaizers, and Paul must have remembered the circumstances in which they had arisen. But now they appear, not as arguments but as statements, with no reference to the former conflict out of which they had come. Once again, it would seem, the recipients of the letter could be assumed never to have been directly touched by the great issue of the earlier period of Paul's ministry.

What this seems to mean is that before the founding of the churches to which Colossians, Philemon, and Ephesians were addressed, Paul's differences with the Judaizing element in the Jerusalem church had been settled, once and for all, and in Paul's favor. This settlement did not rest on the basis of the earlier agreement according to which the Jewish and Gentile missions were to remain separate, but on the basis of a new agreement according to which Paul's theory of the inheritance, as finally developed in Romans, had been recognized as the revealed gospel for the Gentile world. Once that agreement had been reached, the Judaizing movement among Paul's churches was bound to collapse, and in fact we never hear of it again. With its collapse, moreover, Paul's reason for thinking that he should transfer his activity to Spain, since he no longer had room for work in the east, ceased to have force. The plan to leave the east is first mentioned in Romans. Only a few months previously, Paul had written to the Corinthians that he hoped to spend the following winter with them and be sped on his way by them, wherever he should go (I Cor. 16:6), and shortly thereafter he had written to the Philippians, "To remain in the flesh is more necessary on your account. Convinced of this, I know that I shall remain and continue with you all, for your progress and joy in the faith" (Phil. 1:24–25). The plan of Romans, to travel to Spain, therefore, was hastily arrived at. Once Paul's differences with the Jerusalem church had been settled, it would seem to have been just as quickly given up. All the evidence of the letters indicates that after leaving Jerusalem following the delivery of the collection, he went to Asia.

With Colossians, Philemon, and Ephesians the story of the letters ceases. Briefly it tells us that between his first and second visits to Jerusalem, Paul traveled to Syria, Cilicia, Galatia, Macedonia, Achaia, and probably Illyricum. Immediately after the second visit to Jerusalem he engaged in the collection for the saints, during the course of which the controversy with the Judaizers arose. At the close of the collection he visited Jerusalem for the third time, and on this occasion the controversy was settled in Paul's favor. After this he returned to Asia Minor, where he engaged in further missionary work, very probably in Ephesus.

The chronology of most of these events is not difficult to ascertain. We have seen that Paul must have paid his first visit to Thessalonica not later than January of the year 41, and that II Thessalonians was written three and one-half years afterward, in the fall of 44. I Thessalonians was written in 46, the year of the famine, shortly before the beginning of the collection. It can hardly come before the fall of 46, by which time the severity of the famine would have been generally known. The second visit to Jerusalem would thus fall toward the end of the year, and the composition of the Previous Letter to Corinth shortly thereafter. By the following spring at Passover, Paul was in Ephesus. At Pentecost he was in Macedonia. And by fall he was back in Jerusalem. The collection thus was completed before the end of 47. How long after this third visit to Jerusalem he wrote Colossians, Philemon, and Ephesians, the letters do not tell us.

The early chronology of Paul's life, however, can be reconstructed on the basis of what we have discovered so far. If the second visit to

Jerusalem took place in 46, the first visit must have taken place in 35, and the conversion in 32.[3] The results may be summarized in outline form as follows:

- **32** Conversion
  Arabia and Damascus

- **35** First visit to Jerusalem (Acquaintance)
  Syria (Antioch), Cilicia

- **40/41** Galatia, Macedonia (Philippi, Thessalonica)
  Achaia (Corinth), Illyricum

- **44** Composition of II Thessalonians

- **46** Achaia (Corinth, Athens)
  Composition of I Thessalonians
  Second visit to Jerusalem (Conference)
  Antioch: Conflict with the Judaizers
  Composition of Previous Letter to Corinth

  } Foundation trip

- **47** Galatia
  Ephesus: Composition of I Corinthians,
  II Corinthians 10–13, Philippians
  Macedonia: Composition of II Corinthians 1–9,
  Galatians
  Achaia: Composition of Romans

  } Collection trip

  Third visit to Jerusalem (Offering):
  Settlement of controversy with Judaizers

- **48–?** Asia: Composition of Colossians, Philemon, Ephesians

[3] This takes the "fourteen years" of Gal. 2:1 as an inclusive figure, which it must be, since we now know the second visit to Jerusalem to have taken place in 46, the year of the famine; an interval of seventeen years would require that the conversion be dated in 29, a conclusion that seems highly unlikely.

PART **II**:

  THE EVIDENCE OF
ACTS

13

THE ACTS OF THE APOSTLES

So far, we have attempted to arrive at a Pauline chronology without making use of Acts. The theoretical justification for this approach to the problem is that the letters, being a primary source, must take precedence over Acts, which is only a secondary source, however good. The practical justification is that every attempt to solve the problem of the Pauline chronology by fitting the letters into the framework of Acts invariably ends in failure. The letters simply will not fit.

Acts, however, cannot be left out of account. Although not contemporaneous with the letters, it obviously rests to a considerable extent on sources of information which were compiled, if not during Paul's lifetime, at least not long after his death. It may very well contain eyewitness accounts of some of the events in his ministry. It certainly agrees with the letters more often than it disagrees with them. In short, it appears to know what it is talking about.

The main problem of Acts is not that it is ignorant of the facts which we learn from the letters or that it habitually distorts them, but that it relates them in the wrong order. For example, we know from the letters that between Paul's first and second Jerusalem visits he journeyed through Macedonia and Achaia. Acts also knows of the Missionary Journeys that took Paul to these places, but it does not begin to tell of them until after it has given an account of the second Jerusalem visit. Again, we know from the letters that Paul's great conflict with the Judaizers arose after his second Jerusalem visit, reached its peak during the Collection trip, on which he briefly revisited the churches of Macedonia and Achaia, and was still unresolved as he turned his steps toward Jerusalem for the third time. Acts also knows of this conflict with the Judaizers—it even says that it was settled by a Council, which is more than we can discover from the letters—but it places the conflict and the Council before the founding of the very churches in Macedonia and Achaia which contributed to the collection.

Examples of this kind could be multiplied almost indefinitely. They all, however, point to the same general conclusion which has been reached by practically every investigator of the problem—that Acts has failed to coordinate the Jerusalem visits with the rest of Paul's career. The precise nature of the displacement and its extent can best be shown by means of a comparison of the chronology of the letters with that of Acts.

LETTERS	ACTS
CONVERSION	CONVERSION
Arabia	
Damascus	Damascus
JERUSALEM *A* (Acquaintance)	JERUSALEM *a* (Acquaintance)
Galatians 1:18–20	Acts 9:26–30
Syria	Cilicia
Cilicia	Syria
Galatia ⎫	
Macedonia ⎬ Foundation Trip	
Achaia ⎭	

LETTERS	ACTS
JERUSALEM *B* (Conference)	**JERUSALEM *b* (Famine) 11:27–30**
Galatians 2:1–10	
Syria Galatia Asia Macedonia Achaia } Collection Trip	
JERUSALEM *C* (Offering)	**JERUSALEM *c* (Completion)**
Romans 15:25–32	Acts 12:25
	Syria
	Cyprus Southern Asia Minor } First Missionary Journey
	Syria
	JERUSALEM *d* (Council)
	Acts 15:1–33
	Syria
	Southern Asia Minor Macedonia Achaia Asia } Second Missionary Journey
	Syria
· · · · Asia · · · · · · · · } Farewell Trip	Asia Macedonia Achaia Macedonia } Third Missionary Journey
	JERUSALEM *e* (Arrest)
	Acts 21:15ff.

Jerusalem Visits and Missionary Journeys

Two major disagreements are at once apparent between these chronologies. The first has to do with the number of Jerusalem visits which each contains. The letters tell us of only three, Acquaintance, Conference, and Offering. Acts, on the other hand, tells us of five, Acquaintance, Famine, Completion, Council, and Arrest.

The first and second of the Acts visits, Acquaintance and Famine, can easily be equated with Acquaintance and Conference of the letters. True, the Acts account of the Famine visit does not describe a conference as such, but like Galatians it represents the visit as Paul's first formal contact with the Jerusalem apostles since the beginning of his work in Antioch; and although the Galatians account of this visit does not mention the famine, we now know that Galatians was written during the collection for the saints, which followed this visit and was occasioned by the famine. The next visits, however, are a puzzle, for Acts seems to have too many. Ancient editors were aware of this difficulty, and as early as the fourth century more than one of them had attempted to deal with it by reducing the number of the Acts visits. This they accomplished by the simple, though drastic, expedient of altering Acts 12:25 in such a way as to make the third visit (Completion) disappear. The original had read: "And Barnabas and Saul returned to (ϵἰς) Jerusalem when they had completed the mission . . . ." In addition to this reading the manuscripts offer us three others, each of them the contribution of some ancient editor who sought to improve matters by tampering with the text. One made the line read "returned *from* Jerusalem" by changing ϵἰς to ἀπό. Another got the same result by changing ϵἰς to ἐξ. A third boldly wrote "returned to Antioch." But attractive as these conjectures may have seemed to their originators, they cannot be taken seriously now. This visit is not to be done away with merely by pretending that Acts does not record it.

Modern investigators have tended to settle on another solution, that of taking Famine and Council as a doublet. The attractiveness of this suggestion cannot be denied. Not only does it eliminate a troublesome extra visit, but it also seems to bring Acts into line with the letters by moving Council up from fourth place (Jerusalem *d* of Acts) to second place (Jerusalem *b* of Acts), where it can be equated with Conference (Jerusalem *B* of Galatians). This solution, however, though it attacks the problem at the right point, does not really bring the Jerusalem visits into line with the letters after all, for it leaves us with three visits, Acquaintance, Famine-Council, and Completion, before the start of the First Missionary Journey, and this cannot be. Galatians insists that between Conversion and the writing of the letter, Paul had made only two visits to Jerusalem, and Galatians is not datable before the start of the First Missionary Journey.

This difficulty, which arises not from the total number of the visits but from their distribution within the framework of the Missionary Journeys, should not blind us to the fact that the elimination of the extra visit by taking it as a doublet of one of the others is doubtless the first step toward the correct solution of the problem. The question is, which two of the three middle visits in question, Famine, Completion, and Council, are to be identified as doubleted accounts of a single event?

This question is not as difficult to answer as it may seem. The original text of Acts 12:25 reads as follows: "And Barnabas and Saul returned to Jerusalem when they had completed the mission (διακονίαν), bringing with them John who was also called Mark." Where we are to place this visit depends, of course, to a large extent on what we make of the phrase, "when they had completed the mission." What "mission" is meant? If we had nothing but the record of Acts to go on, we should probably decide that the mission must have been the ministry of Barnabas in Antioch, in which he was assisted by Paul (Acts 11:22ff.). Barnabas had been sent to Antioch by the Jerusalem church. Presumably he might have returned to Jerusalem when his mission was completed, bringing Paul and Mark with him. On the basis of this interpretation we should have no choice but to place Completion after Acquaintance and identify it with Jerusalem *B* of Galatians.

The letters, however, tell us of another "mission" that ended with a return to Jerusalem. This was the collection for the saints. What is more, the letters use the noun διακονία, or its verb, to describe this mission. For example, in Romans, Paul writes, "Just now I am making my way to Jerusalem with aid (διακονῶν) for the saints" (Rom. 15:25). A little later he asks the Romans to pray that "my service (διακονία) for Jerusalem may be acceptable to the saints" (Rom. 15:31). The same use of διακονία to denote the collection may be found in I Corinthians

16:15 and in II Corinthians 8:4. In view of these facts it seems probable that Acts 12:25 means nothing more nor less than that Barnabas and Paul returned to Jerusalem when they had completed the collection.

But if Completion comes at the end of the collection, it cannot, either as a separate visit or as one member of a doublet, be identified with Jerusalem *B* of Galatians (Conference), which we now know took place immediately before the collection. It can only be identified with Jerusalem *C* of the letters (Offering), when the collection was finished. By the same token, Council cannot be identified with Jerusalem *B* of Galatians (Conference) either, for the Council settled the controversy with the Judaizers, and this controversy did not arise until the collection was in progress and was not settled until the collection was over. Council, therefore, has an equal claim to be identified with Jerusalem *C* of the letters (Offering). These two visits, therefore, would seem to be the doublet we are seeking.

This solution is borne out by the fact that the letters strongly suggest that the great famine was already in progress when I Thessalonians was written. At that time Paul had completed the Foundation trip and was either on the point of returning to Antioch or had actually arrived there. Immediately thereafter he paid his second visit to Jerusalem and then set out on the Collection trip. This second visit would thus be the same as the Famine visit of Acts.

The correspondences between Acts and the letters at these points confirm the correctness of this analysis. Acts tells us that Paul and Barnabas went to Jerusalem at the time of the famine because a prophet named Agabus had "foretold by the Spirit" that the famine was coming (Acts 11:28); Paul says he went "by revelation" (Gal. 2:2). Acts says that Paul and Barnabas brought relief to the brethren in Judea (Acts 11:29–30); Paul says that James, Cephas, and John, the chief apostles in Jerusalem, asked him and Barnabas, as they were leaving, to "remember the poor," and he adds, "which very thing I made haste to do" (Gal. 2:10). The "very thing" to which Galatians refers was the collection for the saints in Jerusalem. It is referred to again, and in detail, in I and II Corinthians and Romans, where it is called a "contribution for the poor" (Rom. 15:26), and its conclusion, as we have seen, is recorded in Acts: "And Barnabas and Saul returned to Jerusalem when they had completed the mission" (Acts 12:25). Nor do the correspondences end here. Acts tells us that Council settled a conflict that had arisen in Antioch when "some men came down from Judea and were teaching the brethren, 'Unless you are circumcised according to the custom of Moses, you cannot be saved'" (Acts 15:1); Paul tells us that his own conflict with the Judaizers, which took place during the collection, had arisen in Antioch when "certain men came from James." The presence of these visitors had been enough to cause Cephas and Barnabas and the other Jews to decline to continue to eat with the Gentiles. In Paul's own words, they "acted insincerely," and they did so, he explains, following the example of Cephas, who feared "those of the circumcision" (Gal. 2:11–13). That this conflict had to wait for settlement until the end of the Collection trip is clear from all the letters that were written while it was in progress. Acts tells us that it was settled in Paul's favor at the Council, over the objections of "some believers" who felt that Gentile Christians should be circumcised and should be required to keep the law of Moses (Acts 15:4–33). These strict Jewish Christians, incidentally, were Pharisees (Acts 15:5), a circumstance which would seem to be not unrelated to Paul's repeated insistence on his own Jewish birth and upbringing in the letters of this period and more especially to his specific mention in one place of the fact that he was himself a Pharisee (Phil. 3:5). And finally, both Colossians and Ephesians, which were written after the collection was finished, look back on the controversy not only as being over and done with but also as having been settled in Paul's favor.

The initial problem of the visits, therefore, appears to find its best solution in the recognition of Completion and Council as a doublet. This allows the first three visits of Acts to be identified with the first three visits of the letters in a straightforward manner as follows:

LETTERS	ACTS
Acquaintance	Acquaintance
Conference	Famine
Offering	Completion-Council

We may now turn to the second major disagreement between the letters and Acts, that concerning the Missionary Journeys.

Comparison of the chronology of Acts with that of the letters not only reveals that the number of Jerusalem visits in Acts is greater than it should be. It also reveals that Acts has put the Missionary Journeys later in Paul's career than they belong. For example, Acts does not begin the First Missionary Journey until after the third Jerusalem visit (Acts 12:25). The letters, on the other hand, tell us plainly that even before the second Jerusalem visit Paul had traveled as far as Macedonia and Achaia, places that do not make their initial appearance in Acts until the Second Missionary Journey. Again, Acts has plainly confused the Collection trip, which ended with the third Jerusalem visit, with a later Missionary Journey, over much the same ground, which ended with Paul's fourth and final visit to Jerusalem. The letters, on the other hand, suggest that the Collection trip did not end with Paul's arrest, for the "Asian ministry," which produced Colossians, Philemon, and Ephesians, cannot possibly be dated either before or during the collection period and must therefore be placed after it.

These examples are enough to indicate the nature of the problem. As we have seen in connection with the visits, it is largely a question of the order of events, complicated by an additional question as to the precise number of events with which we have to deal. But whereas in the case of the visits we had one event too many, in the case of the Journeys we have one too few. At first glance this may not seem as obvious as the fact of the extra visit. But it is not difficult to demonstrate.

We may begin with a universally recognized correspondence between the letters and Acts. The letters reveal that at one stage in Paul's career he set out from Syria and Cilicia, the scene of his first missionary labors, and embarked on a trip that took him first to Galatia (the exact location of the area to which Paul applies this term is not important here), then to Macedonia and Achaia. In these last two provinces he founded churches in Philippi, Thessalonica, and Corinth, in that order. This invasion of Europe, to which we may give the name "Foundation trip," appears in Acts as the Second Missionary Journey (Acts 15:36–18:22). The identification of Foundation trip with Second Missionary Journey is both logically necessary (since first trip to Europe in the letters can only equal first trip to Europe in Acts) and consistent with the evidence (since Acts bears out precisely what the letters tell us actually occurred). We may therefore use it as a safe starting point.

The letters now tell us that after the Foundation trip Paul revisited the churches which he had founded, his purpose being to collect relief for the poor in the Jerusalem church. This return to the churches of Galatia, Macedonia, and Achaia, to which we have given the name "Collection trip," followed the same general route which Paul had taken on the Foundation trip, with the exception that this time he went from Galatia to Macedonia by way of Ephesus, where certain friends of his from Corinth were now living. He did not stay long in Ephesus, probably not more than two or three months at most, but proceeded from there to Macedonia, then to Achaia, then (presumably by ship) to Jerusalem, to deliver the money he had collected. Paul was not arrested and sent to Rome on this occasion. Of this we can be reasonably certain, since we have three letters—Colossions, Philemon, and Ephesians—which date after the letters of the Collection period. These letters reflect the background of an "Asian ministry," which took place after the collection. In other words, the letters lead us to believe that Paul went back to Ephesus after the collection was completed, and since this return was apparently a part of the last trip which he made before his arrest, we may call it the "Farewell trip."

We are now in a position to state the problem of the Journeys in simple terms, using as a starting point the first trip to Europe. (What happened before this does not concern us at the moment.) The letters tell us that Paul made three missionary trips in the period in question —Foundation, Collection, and Farewell. Acts tells us that he made only two—Second Missionary Journey and Third Missionary Journey. The conclusion is inescapable that Acts has one Journey too few.

As we have said, this fact is not commonly recognized. Therefore the problem of the missing Journey has no such long history of solutions as has the problem of the extra visit. The reason for this neglect is not hard to find. Until the problem of the visits is correctly solved, the problem of the Journeys does not appear in its true colors. One of the classic starting points for the study of the Pauline chronology has been the identification of the last Jerusalem visit in Acts (Arrest) with the third visit of the letters (Offering). The attractiveness of this identification is understandable, since Paul is made to say in Acts that he had come to Jerusalem on his last visit (Arrest) "to bring to my nation alms and offerings" (Acts 24:17). Its immediate effect, however, is to reduce the number of the Jerusalem visits to three instead of the four which are demanded if the arrest did not occur at the close of the Collection trip. This error, which is widely held, is chiefly responsible for obscuring the fact that Acts really has one Journey less than the letters.

To speak of the deficit in Acts as a "missing Journey" is perhaps somewhat misleading. It is true that Acts does have only one Journey, the Third Missionary Journey, where the letters require two, Collection and Farewell. But it is obviously not true that Acts has entirely omitted either Collection or Farewell. Instead it has combined the two. It has done this by omitting the end of Collection and the beginning of Farewell. In other words, the first part of the Third Missionary Journey is really the first part of the Collection trip and the second part of the Third Missionary Journey is the end of Farewell.

Apparently the mistaken combination of parts of Collection and Farewell had already been made in one of Luke's sources. That source, the so-called Journey source, seems to have followed the curious method wherever possible of telling all of the incidents connected with a particular place as though they had occurred on a single visit to that place.[1] Other visits to the same place it usually dismissed with a summary. Ordinarily this method yielded relatively harmless anachronisms, for it does not greatly matter if Paul, for example, displeased "the devout women of high standing" on his first visit to Pisidian Antioch, where the source places this incident (Acts 13:50), or on a subsequent visit.

But the application of this method to the incidents connected with Ephesus had serious consequences. The letters lead us to believe that Paul visited Ephesus at least twice. The first of these visits took place during the Collection trip. On this occasion he stayed not longer than two or three months. The second visit took place during the Farewell trip, and this time Paul seems to have stayed for a considerably longer period. The letters do not tell us how long it was, but they make clear

[1] We are indebted for this suggestion to H. J. Cadbury.

that it was long enough to allow not only for Paul's missionary activity in Ephesus itself but also, at least on the part of his assistants, in Colossae and Laodicea as well. If these two visits to Ephesus are combined into one, as they seem to have been in the Journey source, the result can only be the confusion of the Collection trip with the Farewell trip. This confusion is precisely what we find in Acts.

The marks of the conflation of the two Ephesian visits in the nineteenth chapter of Acts are not difficult to discern. The introduction of Apollos (Acts 18:24–19:7; cf. I Cor. 16:12) clearly belongs to Collection, as does Paul's first attempt to present Christianity to the Ephesian synagogue "for three months" (Acts 19:8; cf. I Cor. 16:8). Conversely, the daily argument in the hall of Tyrannus "for two years" (Acts 19:9f.) just as clearly belongs to Farewell. But Luke apparently had no way of knowing that his source at this point was playing him false. He took over the conflated Ephesian section from the Journey source and, this done, embarked immediately on the account of Paul's last trip to Jerusalem, which really followed the second, and longer, of the two visits to Ephesus.

The Journey source almost certainly followed the account of the Ephesian residence by giving its customary summary of the itinerary which took Paul to his next important stopping place, in this instance from Ephesus to Jerusalem by way of Macedonia, Greece, and Macedonia again. But Luke possessed a far more detailed source of information about Paul's last trip from Ephesus to Jerusalem. This was the diary of one of Paul's companions. Since it seems to have concerned itself chiefly with the sea voyage, it is perhaps better called a Log. The Log apparently took up the story of the last voyage in detail at the point where Paul and his companions left Macedonia, after the last visit to Greece, and began moving toward Jerusalem. At this point, therefore, Luke interrupted the Journey source, turned to the Log, and irrevocably committed himself to the false combination of the Collection trip and the Farewell trip into a single Third Missionary Journey.

The recognition that the Third Missionary Journey is a conflation of the two last trips of the letters—Collection and Farewell—enables us for the first time to relate the events of Acts to those of the letters at a great number of points, as follows:

LETTERS	ACTS
CONVERSION	CONVERSION
Arabia, Damascus	Damascus
JERUSALEM *A* (Acquaintance)	JERUSALEM *a* (Acquaintance)
Syria, Cilicia	Tarsus, Antioch
(. . . .)	First Missionary Journey
Galatia, Macedonia, Achaia (Foundation)	Second Missionary Journey
JERUSALEM *B* (Conference)	JERUSALEM *b* (Famine)
Galatia, Ephesus, Macedonia, Achaia (Collection)	Third Missionary Journey (1st part)
JERUSALEM *C* (Offering)	JERUSALEM *c-d* (Completion-Council)
Asia (Farewell)	Third Missionary Journey (2nd part)
	JERUSALEM *e* (Arrest)

The extent to which this is possible suggests that the ultimate solution to the chronological problem of Acts lies in a comparatively simple revision of the order in which two of its sources have been employed.

The Sources of Acts

Critics have long recognized the existence of sources underlying Acts.[2] But although there is general agreement on the proposition that the sources exist, there is less willingness to employ source analysis as one of the major tools for the historical criticism which Acts requires. The reasons for this are not difficult to see. In the first place, Luke has all but completely obliterated any distinguishing marks of language and

[2] The best treatment of the sources in Acts will be found in J. Dupont, *The Sources of Acts* (Eng. trans., London, 1964).

style which the sources may have shown originally. In the second place, the letters were for so long misdated, on the supposed evidence of Acts, that they were of no use as a means of testing the accuracy of Luke's chronology.

The stylistic obstacle will always remain. But the misdating of the letters can be altered. When this is done we discover, as has already been shown, that very large sections of Acts agree with the order of events which the letters reflect. And by placing the events of the letters side by side with the events of the sections of Acts that correspond with them, we can perform an operation that resembles the placing of Mark side by side with one of the other Synoptic Gospels.

We have already seen that one starting point for this kind of comparison is the identification of the Foundation trip of the letters with the Second Missionary Journey of Acts. The account of this Journey begins at Acts 15:36 and ends at Acts 18:22. The source on which it depends is usually called the Journey source, as we noted earlier. Two other sections of Acts are commonly recognized as having depended primarily on this source. They are the account of the First Missionary Journey (Acts 13:1–14:28) and part of the account of the Third Missionary Journey (Acts 18:23–20:3). It is comparatively easy to see that the source begins at Acts 13:1. It is not so easy to tell just where it leaves off.

The Journey source employs a characteristic formula. Paul and Barnabas, or Paul and Silas, as the case may be, journey to a town where the Christian gospel is unknown. On the Sabbath they enter the synagogue and proclaim that Jesus is the Messiah. The majority of the Jews reject the message. Paul and his companions, therefore, "turn to the Gentiles," who hear it gladly and are converted. This angers the unbelieving Jews, who drive the missionaries from the town. Occasionally they go so far as to stir up the whole district against them. But wherever Paul and his companions go they leave behind a group of converts who are mostly Gentiles.

Another feature of the Journey source is its interest in the legal status of the Christian mission in the Roman world. On the island of Cyprus a Jewish magician seeks to influence the proconsul against

Paul and Barnabas. But the magician is shown to be a mountebank and the proconsul is converted (Acts 13:6–12). In Philippi the owners of a fortune-telling slave girl, angered because Paul has driven out the "spirit of divination" that had possessed her, falsely accuse Paul and Silas of advocating customs which are unlawful for Romans. For this supposed crime the magistrates have them beaten and thrown into prison. But after an earthquake has given the jailer an opportunity to see what good men these are, and the authorities have learned that they are Roman citizens, they are released and even receive an apology from the magistrates (Acts 16:16–40). In Thessalonica the unbelieving Jews, jealous of Paul's success, stir up a riot against the Christians and drag one of them, a certain Jason, before the city authorities, to whom they accuse the missionaries of having "turned the world upside down" and of acting against the decrees of the emperor by saying "that there is another king, Jesus." The authorities take security from Jason and the rest and let them go (Acts 17:5–9).

In Corinth the unbelieving Jews accuse Paul before the proconsul of persuading people to worship God contrary to the law; but the proconsul, realizing that the disagreement involves no wrongdoing or vicious crime but is merely a matter of "words and names and your own law," orders the accusers to leave the court (Acts 18:12–17). In Ephesus the silversmiths, afraid that Christianity will hurt their trade in religious souvenirs of the temple of Artemis, start a riot against the Christians. The Asiarchs, who are Paul's friends, beg him not to show himself to the angry mob which has gathered in the theater, and the town clerk finally disperses the crowd by insisting that the silversmiths, if they have any real charges to bring, should bring them before the regular courts (Acts 19:23–41).

A third feature of the Journey source, to which we have already referred, is its practice wherever possible of recounting all the incidents connected with a particular place as though they had occurred during a single visit to that place, usually the first. This habit of the source is so little remarked by investigators, and it is of such great importance, that we may profitably examine the evidence in some detail. Following is a list of the places visited more than once, with the length of the account of each visit indicated; those that occur in a summary (*s*) are so identified.

	1st visit	2nd visit	3rd visit
Pisidian Antioch	13:14–51	14:21 (*s*)	
Iconium	14:1–6	14:21 (*s*)	
Lystra	14:8–20	14:21 (*s*)	16:1–3
Derbe	14:20–21 (*s*)	16:1 (*s*)	
Philippi	16:12–40	20:2 (*s*)	20:3–6
Thessalonica	17:1–10	20:2 (*s*)	
Corinth	18:1–18	20:2–3	
Ephesus	18:19–21	19:1–20:1	

It will readily be seen from the above list that in most cases the account of the first visit to any of these places is a good deal longer than the account of any subsequent visit. Exceptions are Derbe, where each of the two visits is dismissed in a summary, and Ephesus, where the second visit is substantially longer than the first. It will also be seen that wherever the account of a visit subsequent to the first contains any incident at all instead of being a bare summary, the incident itself is of such a nature as to forbid its having been included in the account of an earlier visit. Thus the circumcision of Timothy and his enlistment as a companion of Paul and Silas (Acts 16:1–3) is placed on the third visit to Lystra; it could not have been placed on the first or second visit because the rest of the record showed that Timothy did not enter the picture until the Second Missionary Journey. Again the plot of the Jews which forced Paul to return from Greece by way of Macedonia instead of by sailing to Syria (Acts 20:2–3) could not have been placed in the account of the first visit to Corinth, since the record showed that on the former occasion he actually had sailed to Syria from Cenchreae. Finally, the account of the first visit to Ephesus reads as follows: "And they came to Ephesus, and he left them there; but he himself went into the synagogue and argued with the Jews. When they asked him to stay for a longer period, he declined; but on taking leave of them he said, 'I will return to you if God wills,' and he set sail from Ephesus" (Acts 18:19–21). This in itself demands that any incidents connected with an Ephesian stay of any length should be deferred until a later visit.

The bearing of these facts on the chronological trustworthiness of the Journey source is at once apparent. The letters lead us to believe that the source is probably accurate as regards the itinerary of the various Missionary Journeys. But the source itself reveals that it cannot be relied on with respect to the placement of specific incidents. This means that we must abandon such inferences as the dating of Paul's first visit to Corinth during the proconsulship of Gallio, for although the trial before Gallio is included in the account of the first visit, this by no means proves that it occurred then. Indeed, the chronology of the letters tells us that it cannot have occurred until long after the first visit.

The Journey source, then, is the document that can be identified without too much difficulty as underlying Acts 13:1–14:28 and 15:36–20:3. (It almost certainly continues beyond this point, having been conflated with the Log, and it very probably contains an insertion from the Log in Acts 16:10–16.) As its name implies, it tells the story of the Missionary Journeys. Its hero is Paul, who, together with Barnabas, Silas, and Timothy, takes the gospel from Antioch to Cyprus, Southern Asia Minor, Macedonia, Achaia, and Asia—in other words, into the Roman world. Its villains are (1) a Jewish mountebank on Cyprus, who tries unsuccessfully to influence the proconsul against the missionaries; (2) the Jews of the dispersion in various places in Southern Asia Minor, who reject the gospel and drive the missionaries out of their towns; (3) two Roman entrepreneurs in Philippi, who have lived on the earnings of a fortune-teller, a female slave of theirs, and who take revenge on Paul for ridding her of her "spirit of divination" by falsely accusing him before the magistrate of teaching customs that are unlawful for Romans; (4) the unbelieving Jews of Thessalonica, who, jealous of Paul's success in making converts, accuse the Christians before the city authorities of treason against the emperor, on the ground that they have said that there is another king, Jesus; (5) the unbelieving Jews of Corinth, who bring Paul before the proconsul and accuse him of persuading people to worship God contrary to the law; and (6) the silversmiths of Ephesus, who try unsuccessfully to turn the city against the Christians because they pose a threat to the trade in religious souvenirs.

The geographical anchor of the Journey source is Antioch, where the Journeys begin and end. It makes no reference to Christian missionaries from Jerusalem, and it omits all mention of Paul's earlier Jerusalem visits. The end of the Journey source has been conflated with the Log, as we have seen, so it is difficult to tell just how much material it may have contributed to the final chapters of Acts. The Arrest almost certainly comes from it, at least in part, for the connection between the "Jews from Asia" who cause Paul's arrest in Jerusalem and the unbelieving Jews of the dispersion who are among the principal villains of the earlier Journeys is very plain to see. We shall have more to say about the composition of the last chapters of Acts further on. At present we are chiefly concerned with the identification of the Journey Source in the earlier portions, where it appears without conflation.

It has already been remarked that with the aid of the chronology of the letters we can perform a critical operation on Acts which resembles the removal of the Marcan material from the other Synoptic Gospels. We are now in a position to do this. If we remove the earlier identifiable blocks of the Journey source (Acts 13:1–14:28; 15:36–20:3) which agree with the order of events in the letters, from their surroundings, we are left with the account of the Council (Acts 15:1–33) preceded immediately by the summary of the Completion visit (Acts 12:25). This in turn is preceded by the story of Herod's persecution of the church, which ended in his death (Acts 12:1–23). And this is preceded by a long block of material which is usually identified as coming from a document called the Hellenist source (Acts 6:1–11:30). Since the account of Herod's persecution (Acts 12:1–23) is commonly recognized as an insertion, we may leave it to one side. What we have left, then, is composed of the following: Acts 6:1–11:30; 12:25; 15:1–33.

This document, which may very well appear substantially entire in these sections, is a work of a very different kind from the Journey source. The Journey source is principally interested in the relationship between the Christian mission and the non-Christian world, whether this world be made up of Jews or pagans. The Hellenist source, on the other hand, is interested solely in the relationship between Jewish Christians and Gentile Christians and between the leading churches of each group, Jerusalem and Antioch. Both works are apologetic in purpose. But whereas the Journey source presents the general Christian defense against the charge that the church was an illegal or subversive movement in the empire, the Hellenist source presents the specific defense of the church in Antioch against the charge that it was not a legitimate branch of the true church, since it was neither apostolic in foundation nor orthodox in teaching and practice. We know, of course, who the people were who made this charge about the church in Antioch. They were a group of conservative Jewish Christians, members of the church in Jerusalem and of the mission churches which had sprung from it, who took it upon themselves at one point to Judaize the church in Antioch and its Gentile missions. Their position was that Gentiles who became Christians must be circumcised and must keep the Jewish law, and they made a concerted effort to impose this view upon the Gentile Christian churches during the period of the collection. Paul's response to their activities is familiar from the letters of the collection period, which were written during the height of the controversy. The reply of the church in Antioch, written later, took the form of a pamphlet. The Hellenist source is that pamphlet.

It answers the charges by making four points: (1) The church in Antioch did not represent an independent, nonapostolic foundation, since it had been formed by members of the Jerusalem church who had left Jerusalem and settled in Antioch after the persecution in which Stephen was martyred. Furthermore the early days of its growth had been watched over by Barnabas, whom the church in Jerusalem had sent to Antioch for this very purpose. (2) Paul (the source calls him Saul), whom Barnabas had brought to Antioch from Tarsus, had been converted by nothing less than a vision of the risen Lord and had been accepted by the apostles in Jerusalem upon his return there. (3) The practice of the church in Antioch to which the Judaizers objected—reception of Gentile converts without requiring that they accept circumcision or undertake to keep the Jewish law—was once the practice of the Jerusalem church and had been approved by the apostles in the early days. (4) This approval had been reaffirmed for the church in Antioch and its missions by the Council of Jerusalem. Thus, without saying so in so many words, the pamphlet actually accuses the Jewish

Christian church of having abandoned the position of its own founders. The church in Antioch, on the other hand, it represents as having preserved the doctrine and practice of the original apostles.

The pamphlet makes these points by means of a historical narrative. It begins with the appointment of the seven and proceeds at once to the persecution that began with the death of Stephen and resulted in the scattering of the church. It then presents a series of incidents involving the remaining apostles, in which the mission of the Jerusalem church is extended, step by step, until it includes Gentiles. First Philip, one of the seven, converts "multitudes" of Samaritans (half-breed Israelites, so to speak). The apostles, when they hear of this, journey to Samaria and lay their hands on the baptized converts, who receive the Holy Spirit (Acts 8:4–25). Then Philip converts an Ethiopian eunuch (no Israelite he) who is only a Jew by adoption (Acts 8:26–40). Here the series is interrupted while the pamphlet tells of the conversion of Paul on the road to Damascus and of his return to Jerusalem, where Barnabas introduces him to the apostles, who not only receive him but make possible his escape to Tarsus when the Hellenists seek to kill him (Acts 9:1–30). This done, it returns to the series about the Jerusalem apostles with three stories about Peter. At Lydda he heals a man who has been bedridden for eight years. And "all the residents of Lydda and Sharon" are converted (Acts 9:32–35). At Joppa he raises Dorcas from the dead. And "many" are converted (Acts 9:36–43). Still at Joppa he has a dream in which the voice of God tells him that he need not observe the Jewish laws of clean and unclean meats. Meanwhile a Roman centurion, Cornelius, stationed at Caesarea, is instructed by an angel to send to Joppa for Peter. Peter goes, enters the house of the Gentile soldier, and proclaims the gospel. The Holy Spirit falls on all the Gentiles present, so Peter baptizes them and remains as a guest in the house for several days (Acts 10:1–48). On his return to Jerusalem he is called to account before the church by "those of the circumcision" for having gone to uncircumcised men and eaten with them. But when they have heard Peter's story, all are convinced that "to the Gentiles also God has granted repentance unto life" (Acts 11:1–18).

The pamphlet now turns its attention to Antioch. It does this by going back to the persecution that followed Stephen's death. Some of the members of the Jerusalem church, it explains, who had been forced to flee at that time, had settled in Antioch, where they began to preach to Greeks as well as Jews. When the Jerusalem church heard of this, they sent Barnabas to Antioch. Barnabas was pleased with what he saw. Needing help in the growing church, he went to Tarsus, found Paul, and brought him to Antioch, where the two men labored together for a year.

Up to now relations between the two churches had been unmarred by controversy. Antioch, under the leadership of Barnabas and Paul, had been accepting Gentile converts, but this was only what Jerusalem had also done. The continuing friendship between the two churches is illustrated by the generous action of Antioch in sending relief to Jerusalem at the time of the famine (Acts 11:27–30) and by the "mission" of Barnabas and Paul which ended in their return to Jerusalem (Acts 12:25).

But, we now learn, in spite of the practice of the Jerusalem apostles of accepting Gentile converts without requiring that they be circumcised and become subject to the Jewish law, and in spite of the Jerusalem church's having approved of this policy when the question arose over Peter's baptism of Cornelius, a conservative minority persisted in holding to a more narrow view. Certain members of this group even went so far as to try to persuade the church in Antioch that the conservative position was the only orthodox Christian position, and the confusion that resulted from their interference in the affairs of the Antioch church made necessary a formal appeal to Jerusalem. When the apostles and elders heard what had happened, they repudiated the actions of these men, referring to them as "some persons from us . . . although we gave them no instructions," and reaffirmed the apostolic policy of accepting Gentile converts without requiring that they become Jews. With this formal decree the pamphlet, or at least the narrative portion of it that served as the Hellenist source, ends.

The skill and artistry with which the pamphlet was composed are considerable. Obviously it was written after the Council, perhaps some time later. Just as obviously it would not have been written at all unless the Gentile church were still under attack from Jewish

Christians. But the author has successfully avoided identifying the persons against whom the pamphlet is aimed. Instead, his villains are a shadowy group out of the past, who at one time had resisted the apostles when the latter decided to accept Gentiles as members of the church. These men appear only three times in the story: first, at the very end of the series of incidents involving the Jerusalem apostles, where they are called "those of the circumcision" (Acts 11:2); second, in the introduction to the account of the Council, where they are called "some men . . . from Judea" who tried to teach the Christians of Antioch that circumcision was necessary for salvation (Acts 12:1); and third, in the account of the Council itself, where they are called "some believers who belonged to the party of the Pharisees"; here they say of Gentile Christians that "it is necessary to circumcise them, and to charge them to keep the law of Moses" (Acts 15:5). In the first and last of these places they are introduced so casually that the incautious reader might suppose them to be quite incidental to the story. And wherever they are introduced they appear as nothing more sinister or dangerous than a group of conservative Christians of whom the worst that might be said is that they honestly disagreed with the more liberal opinions of the apostles.

The reader's difficulty in identifying these men as the real villains of the pamphlet results not only from the lateness of their introduction and the casualness of their treatment, however. It is prepared beforehand. In the early part of the pamphlet, the author introduces a group of wicked and violent men, who bring about the death of Stephen and set in motion a severe persecution of the church. They are Jews, members of four Jerusalem synagogues—the Synagogue of the Freedmen, that of the Cyrenians, that of the Alexandrians, and that of those from Cilicia and Asia—and they cause Stephen's death by falsely accusing him of having spoken "blasphemous words against Moses and God" and of having said that Jesus would destroy the temple and change the customs of the Mosaic law. In other words, they are villains of a familiar and easily identifiable type, Jews who reject the gospel themselves and are willing to go to any lengths to prevent its proclamation to others. The reader of the pamphlet could be expected to recognize them immediately. Once having done so, he would be slow to suspect that the real villains of the piece were another group of men entirely, and members of the Christian church at that.

But the earlier set of villains bears a subtle relationship to the later. In order to understand this relationship we must first identify the hero of the pamphlet. Unlike the Journey source, in which the hero is Paul, the pamphlet has no human hero. Its protagonist is the Holy Spirit. The various human characters in the story are divided into two groups— those who are illumined and guided by the Spirit and those who resist its promptings. Stephen, we are told, is "full of the Spirit and of wisdom" (Acts 6:3). The Jews who try to overcome him in argument cannot stand up against "the wisdom and the Spirit" with which he speaks (Acts 6:10). Stephen, "full of the Holy Spirit," looks into heaven and sees the glory of God, and Jesus standing at God's right hand (Acts 7:55). The Jewish villains, in other words, are guilty of resisting the Holy Spirit.

This is precisely what "those of the circumcision" do, of course, although the author never says so in so many words. It is the Spirit which puts the seal of approval on Philip's baptism of the Samaritans (Acts 8:17); it is the Spirit which prompts Philip to approach the Ethiopian eunuch (Acts 8:29); it is the Spirit, falling on the household of Cornelius, which convinces Peter that these Gentiles are to be baptized (Acts 10:44–48). Yet "those of the circumcision" criticize what has been done (Acts 11:2). Similarly, in connection with the church in Antioch we are told that Barnabas, who guided the infant church, was "full of the Holy Spirit" (Acts 11:24). Peter testifies at the Council that God has borne witness to the Gentiles by "giving them the Holy Spirit" (Acts 15:8). And the decree of the Council requires of Gentiles only what "has seemed good to the Holy Spirit" and to the apostles and elders in Jerusalem (Acts 15:28). Yet "some believers" have been maintaining all the while that Gentile converts must be circumcised and must keep the law of Moses (Acts 15:5). The inference is plain. These Christians have resisted the Spirit just as Stephen's murderers had done.

It can hardly be doubted that the pamphlet, although produced by the church in Antioch, was intended to be read by Jewish Christians in Judea. For one thing, it scrupulously avoids saying anything uncomplimentary about the rank and file of Jerusalem Jews. Those who falsely accuse Stephen are carefully identified as Jews of the dispersion (Acts 6:9). Those who examine and condemn him are the high priest and the council, the same authorities who had examined and condemned Jesus (Acts 6:12; 7:1). In Damascus it is "the Jews" who seek Paul's life (Acts 9:23), but when he returns to Jerusalem it is "the Hellenists," Jews of the dispersion (Acts 9:29). Those "of the circumcision," we are informed, are members of "the party of the Pharisees" (Acts 15:5). Even Stephen's speech, which would seem to be an integral part of the pamphlet, is not directed against Jews as such, but only against those who have disobeyed God and resisted the Holy Spirit. Although it betrays a familiarity with arguments first worked out in Galatians, it carefully avoids those parts of the arguments that may offend Jewish Christians, and where it accuses "our fathers" of wrongdoing, it is careful to document its accusations with quotations from the Old Testament (Acts 7:2–53). The role of Paul is written with extreme care, undoubtedly to avoid giving offense to Jewish Christians. His conversion is not complete on the road to Damascus. He must have Christian hands laid upon him in order to regain his sight and be filled with the Holy Spirit (Acts 9:17). He is baptized (Acts 9:18). He is accepted by the Jerusalem church as a "disciple" (not an "apostle") only after Barnabas vouches for him (Acts 9:26f.). When his life is in danger, the Jerusalem Christians send him to Tarsus for safety (Acts 9:30), and he comes to Antioch only at the bidding of Barnabas (Acts 11:25f.). In Antioch, he is Barnabas' subordinate (Acts 11:30; 12:25). Probably to emphasize his Jewishness, he is called Saul instead of Paul, although the other sources of Acts as well as the letters lead us to believe that he was not generally known by that name.

This was the document on which Luke had to depend for his information about the founding of the church in Antioch and the beginning of Paul's life as a Christian. Its advantages as a source were obvious. It told a simple, straightforward story and it appeared to stick to the facts. Although it was tendentious in the extreme, its bias was artfully concealed. Most important of all, it proved that Paul, though he may have been hated by unbelieving Jews of the dispersion, had been on good terms with the Jewish Christians of Jerusalem and with the original apostles.

The two disadvantages of the pamphlet as a source were (1) its lack of any exact chronological data, and (2) its lack of interest in the missionary journeyings of Paul and Barnabas beyond Antioch. The lack of chronological data did not matter so long as the pamphlet was talking about events in Judea. Whether the span of time between the death of Stephen, say, and the conversion of Cornelius was thought of as one year or ten could make no possible difference. But chronology did matter in connection with Antioch. The pamphlet suggested that the church in Antioch had been founded shortly after the death of Stephen. It gave no real indication, however, of the span of time between that point and the next event which it described, the Famine visit to Jerusalem. Indeed, it gave the impression, unintentionally no doubt, that the Famine visit came at the end of the "whole year" during which Barnabas and Paul met with the church (Acts 11:26), when in fact it did not come until perhaps eleven years later, in the year 46.

At all events the pamphlet misled Luke at this point. He should, as we know, have placed the account of the First and Second Missionary Journeys before the Famine visit, that is, between Acts 11:26 and 11:27. But he did not. He continued to follow the pamphlet through the account of the famine. In all probability he did this because the pamphlet gave every appearance of telling a straightforward and complete story, and it certainly said nothing about any missionary journeying on the part of Barnabas and Paul. But whatever may have led him to follow the pamphlet past the point where he should have broken off, Luke was too good a historian not to see that something was wrong. After all, a famine in the reign of Claudius, who did not come to the throne until 41, could hardly have followed as closely on the death of Stephen as the pamphlet seemed to indicate. But Luke was also too good a historian to play fast and loose with the facts as his sources gave them. He reported what the pamphlet said, doing his best to explain to the reader how the curious sequence of events might have been possible. The famine, he explained, had not occurred as early as this, it had only been prophesied. The narrative style of this explanation is so unlike that of the rest of the pamphlet as to reveal that the source has been entirely recast at this point, undoubtedly to soften the anachronism which it contained. Indeed, the construction of Acts 11:27–30 is such an exact reproduction of that of Luke 2:1–4 as to leave little room for doubt that it is largely Luke's own free composition.

But no amount of explanation would suffice for the next difficulty which the pamphlet presented, for after a passing reference to the "mission" which immediately followed the Famine visit, it proceeded to the Council, which took place on the completion of the "mission." How Luke may have known that the Council could not have taken place before the beginning of the Missionary Journeys we can only guess. It is not impossible that his personal knowledge of Paul's later career was enough to tell him that the Council belonged after the time where the pamphlet seemed to put it. Perhaps common sense told him, as it tells us, that if Barnabas and Paul came to the Council after completing a "mission," some sort of journeying on the part of the two men must have gone on, at least in the interval between the Famine and Council visits. Perhaps the address of the apostolic decree, "to the brethren who are of the Gentiles in Antioch and Syria and Cilicia," was enough to suggest that the account of the Council should be deferred until something had been said about missionary work among Gentiles outside of Antioch. Any one of these reasons would have been sufficient.

The pamphlet, however, had to be respected. Therefore, after pausing to tell of the last days of Herod, Luke dutifully recorded the return to Jerusalem (Acts 12:25) immediately after the Famine visit, where the pamphlet said it belonged. He did this in a summary of one sentence, which cannot possibly be all that the pamphlet told about the visit. (The pamphlet was not interested simply in listing visits; its purpose was to show how friendly they were.) Then he turned to the Journey source, took from it the account of the First Missionary Journey, and only after this was firmly in the record did he return to the pamphlet for the account of the Council.

It was a serious blunder. But it appears to have been an honest one. Some investigators, seeing that the Council is introduced too early in Acts, have suspected the misplacement of being deliberate on Luke's part. His interest, they say, was to show that Paul was reconciled with the Jerusalem church very early in his missionary career, whereas the fact was that the reconciliation only took place on his last Jerusalem visit, if it took place at all. It is only fair to say that this judgment is unavoidable if the traditional dates for the letters are accepted. But, as we have seen, these traditional dates can no longer be upheld. And with the abandonment of the old chronology of the letters must also go the abandonment of the notion that the disorder of Acts was deliberately contrived in order to conceal an unpleasant truth.

Once the blunder was committed, however, there was no way of repairing the damage. The pamphlet apparently ended with the Council, and Luke had no choice but to follow it with the account of the Second Missionary Journey—far too late, alas. This done, he could only continue to follow the Journey source as it proceeded to recount the beginning of the Collection trip. By this means he arrived at the nineteenth chapter of Acts. To his credit it should be pointed out that he did not obliterate the one bit of evidence in his sources that still indicated that something was wrong. The pamphlet had said, at the end of the account of the Council, that Silas, after delivering the decree to Antioch, had returned to Jerusalem (Acts 15:33). The Journey source made it clear that Silas was in Antioch at the beginning of the Second Missionary Journey (15:40). Luke faithfully recorded what both sources said, even though it would have been a simple matter to omit the reference to Silas' return to Jerusalem or to add a sentence to the effect that he stayed in Antioch (the latter was the way in which some early editors attempted to remove the difficulty). Such candor should put us on our guard against the too easy assumption that Luke played fast and loose with the facts as he found them.

To recapitulate, then, Luke had two sources for the early part of Paul's career. One was a pamphlet, the so-called Hellenist source, which purported to give an account of the early relations between the churches of Jerusalem and Antioch. This source told of two visits of Barnabas and Paul to Jerusalem, the Famine and Council visits. It gave no indication of the date of either visit or of the lapse of time between them. Nor did it mention the missionary activity of Barnabas and Paul outside of Antioch, except for a brief reference to the "mission" which the two men completed between the Famine and Council visits. The other source was a narrative of the Missionary Journeys.

Although its incidents were for the most part arranged topographically rather than chronologically, it gave a faithful account of the itinerary of the Journeys. It had no interest, however, in the relations between the churches of Jerusalem and Antioch and it made no reference to Paul's early visits to Jerusalem. (The Famine visit, for example, belongs between Acts 18:22 and 23. It is not there.)

Luke's problem was to weave these two sources together. He should have placed the first two Missionary Journeys (Acts 13:1–14:27; 15:36–18:22) between the founding of the church in Antioch (Acts 11:19–26) and the Famine visit (Acts 11:27–30). He should also have placed the Collection trip (the first part of which is covered in Acts 18:23–19:8) between the Famine visit and the Council (Acts 15:1–33). Unfortunately he did not. He waited too long before beginning the Missionary Journeys. The result of this mistake was to introduce an enormous anachronism into the account of Paul's life.

The Last Chapters

The twentieth chapter marks a break in the book of Acts. It not only marks a break in that it contains a transition from one source to another. More important, it is the occasion for a change in the method of the author. Prior to the twentieth chapter he has depended on easily identifiable sources, and it is comparatively simple to find the points where they are joined together. He has used these sources in large blocks—the Hellenist source in two such blocks, Acts 6:1–11:30 and 15:1–33, with a summary depending on this source in 12:25; and the Journey source in two more, Acts 13:1–14:28 and 15:36–20:3, with an intrusion from the Log in 16:9–15. But in the last chapters of the work this familiar method seems to be abandoned. Instead of great blocks of material taken over directly from the sources, we find what looks more like an original piece of writing, in which the author, although he may make use of sources, is not by any means wholly dependent on them for the shape of the narrative. The early chapters may be compared to old-fashioned milk; the later chapters are "homogenized."

Take, for example, the source which is variously called the "we-sections," the "Diary," and the "Log." This source makes a brief appearance as an intrusion in the Journey source at Acts 16:9–15. In the later chapters it reappears in the following places: Acts 20:4–16; 21:1–17; 27:1–28:16. These passages, if put together, give all the stops on a voyage from Troas to Philippi and return, and from there to Puteoli, by way of Tyre, Caesarea, and Malta, and points between. It can hardly be doubted that this is the account of a single voyage, in spite of the displacement of its first section (Troas to Philippi) in Acts 16:9–15. (The reason for this displacement is easy to see. The Log gave the impression that this was Paul's first trip to Macedonia.) Obviously the Log is not "Luke's diary." If it were he would have known better than to displace its first section.

Luke does not use this source exactly as he used the Hellenist and Journey sources in the earlier chapters. In the three places where it appears in the last nine chapters of the book it contributes only 90 out of the total of 304 verses; and one block, which contains the story of the shipwreck (Acts 27:1–28:16), accounts for 60 of these. In the two earlier blocks (Acts 20:4–16 and 21:1–17) its purpose is simply to move Paul to the next place where an important scene is set. Thus the first of these takes him to Miletus, where he addresses the Ephesian elders, and the second takes him to Jerusalem, where the climax of the book takes place. The third block, notwithstanding the suspense of the shipwreck, is really used to keep the interest going during a necessarily long stretch of falling action. Doubtless Luke was glad to have such a source, but it is in no sense true that he "depended" on it for the important matters with which he dealt in the last nine chapters of Acts.

These important matters are handled in two blocks. The first (Acts 20:17–38) contains Paul's speech to the Ephesian elders, with its setting. This is almost certainly an original composition of Luke. The second (Acts 21:18–26:32) contains everything connected with Paul's arrest, from his arrival in Jerusalem to his departure from Caesarea for Rome. This also appears to be an original composition of Luke. That is not to say that he used no sources. In several places he quite clearly reused material from the Hellenist source, for example. Thus, when Paul comes to Jerusalem (Acts 21:17–25), James and the elders remind him of things which we have already learned (and Luke has already used) from the account of the Council. Again, on two occasions (Acts 22:1–21 and 26:2–23,25–27,29) Paul tells the story of his conversion on the road to Damascus, which Luke has already used in the early part of the book. And before Felix, Paul explains his presence in Jerusalem by saying that he had come "to bring to my nation alms and offerings" (Acts 24:17), a reason which would seem to have been suggested by the earlier reference to the "mission." These examples, it is true, occur in speeches, where the author was allowed a great deal of freedom, but the speeches are an integral part of the story. The first (Acts 21:20–25) actually carries the plot.

Luke also used material from the Journey source, which almost certainly underlies the account of Paul's actual arrest at the gate of the temple and the events that follow it (Acts 21:26ff.). The familiar interests of the Journey source are there in profusion. Jews from Asia raise the outcry against Paul (Acts 21:27; cf. Acts 19:8f.); the tribune is afraid when he learns that Paul is a Roman citizen, for he has bound Paul and ordered him to be scourged (Acts 22:24–29; cf. 16:37–39); Paul is accused of being "a pestilent fellow, an agitator among all the Jews throughout the world" (Acts 24:5; cf. 17:6f.).

But although it is comparatively easy to see the influence of these sources in the section under discussion, it is by no means easy to disentangle them. The conclusion is almost inescapable that this conflation is the work of Luke himself. So it is with the rest of the account of Paul's last visit to Jerusalem, his arrest, and his imprisonment in Caesarea. The themes of the earlier sources are there; sometimes the narrative style is so reminiscent of one or the other that we are almost certain we can identify it, but when we try to find the seams where the sources join we discover that they do not exist. We pass back and forth between straight narrative, dramatic dialogue, and formal speeches, and nowhere is there a sign of a break in the smooth flow of the story. Although Luke used sources for this section, he seems to have completely rewritten them, employing a method which he used nowhere else, either in the Gospel or in the earlier chapters of Acts.

What may have caused this change of method is open to conjecture. It is possible, of course, that as he approached the climax of his work Luke simply lavished more artistry on it than he had felt the earlier sections demanded. But knowing what we do about his respect for recorded facts, we shall have considerable difficulty in making this suggestion seem plausible. Even less probable is the chance that a hitherto undetected and unsuspected source underlies the account of Paul's last days in Jerusalem and Caesarea, as a non-Marcan source, for example, underlies Luke's passion narrative. The problem of the section in question is not that it sounds like a new source; it is precisely that it sounds so much like the familiar ones.

One possibility, however, does seem to be worth serious consideration. That is that Luke felt free to abandon his usual method of handling sources in the story of Paul's last Jerusalem visit because he was himself an eyewitness to much of what had happened then. When he came to write his book he might still have used written sources for this section—a competent historian, even though he may be an eyewitness, does not necessarily feel that he is the only witness who has anything to say—but his use of such sources would of necessity have been very different from his use even of the same sources for events about which he had no independent information. It is such a transition as this, from utter dependence on the written record to a much freer adaptation of whatever in the record seemed useful, that we observe as we move into the last chapters of Acts. The likelihood that Luke may have been his own principal source for a great deal of the material in these chapters, therefore, can never be completely ruled out.[3]

Going on the assumption that Luke was a witness of at least some of the events that took place on Paul's last Jerusalem visit, we may profitably ask where his first-hand acquaintance with Paul began. Obviously it cannot have been as early as the Council. If it had been, he would have been able to put together the Hellenist and Journey sources in the proper order. It cannot have been later than Paul's arrival in Jerusalem on his last visit. This leaves only the period of

[3] See H. J. Cadbury, "The Knowledge Claimed in Luke's Preface," *Expositor*, XXIV (1922), 401–420.

the Asian ministry. It seems reasonable to suppose, therefore, that Luke may have entered the picture during Paul's last residence in Ephesus. He did not accompany Paul on his last visit to Greece, and his summary account of this trip (Acts 20:1–3) reveals his ignorance of the events of that period of three months or more. From that point on, however, he is the master of his material.

This supposition allows us to frame what appears to be a satisfactory hypothesis about the making of the book of Acts. As Luke approached his task, let us say, he possessed a first-hand acquaintance with only the final events in the story which he planned to write. Specifically, he knew that Paul had been active in Ephesus, that after a final series of visits to churches in the Aegean area he had gone to Jerusalem, and that he had been arrested there, imprisoned in Caesarea, and finally sent to Rome. The earlier events in Paul's life were by no means so familiar to him, since he had not been present when any of them took place.

He possessed written sources, however. One of these, the Hellenist source, told of Paul's conversion, his first visit to Jerusalem, his association with Barnabas in Antioch, the Famine visit, the "mission," and the Council. The other, the Journey source, told of the Missionary Journeys: first to Cyprus and southern Asia Minor (Galatia); then to southern Asia Minor, Macedonia, and Achaia; then to southern Asia Minor, Ephesus, Macedonia, Achaia, and back to Jerusalem for the arrest. Each of these sources had a fault. The Hellenist source omitted any reference to the first two Missionary Journeys, which took place before the Famine visit. The Journey source, following its practice of telling everything connected with a particular place as though it had happened on a single visit to that place, conflated the earlier Ephesian residence (Collection) with the later one (Farewell) and thus combined two trips into one Journey.

It was these faults in the sources that betrayed Luke into making his mistakes. The first of these mistakes, as we have seen, was the placing of the first two Missionary Journeys too late in relation to the Famine visit. The second was the omission of the end of the Collection trip and the beginning of the Farewell trip. Probably his own familiarity with the end of the story helped to betray him in the latter instance. If he himself could identify some of the incidents in the Journey source's account of Paul's Ephesian residence as having happened on Paul's last visit there, he might well have been persuaded that the source could be relied on for the proper placement of the others. He can hardly be blamed for not having seen that the end of the Collection trip, the Council visit to Jerusalem, and the beginning of the Farewell trip all belong somewhere between the eighth and tenth verses of the nineteenth chapter. Once these mistakes were made, however, the present shape of Acts was a foregone conclusion.

Was the Luke who is mentioned in the letters as "the beloved physician" (Col. 4:14) and as one of Paul's "fellow workers" (Philem. 24) the author of Acts? There can be no positive proof that he was, since the possibility cannot be ruled out that there may have been two Lukes, one the companion of Paul and the other the author of Acts. On the other hand, the Luke of the letters makes his first appearance in the story of Paul's career during the "Asian ministry," which is reflected in Colossians, Philemon, and Ephesians, the precise point in the story where the author of Acts seems to have ceased to depend entirely on documentary sources and to have begun to write as an eyewitness. This being the case, the supposition that there were two Lukes would seem to require us to assume that they both entered the picture at the same time and place, and in the same relation with Paul, and while it is perhaps conceivable that such a coincidence occurred, there is no particular reason for believing that it did. It is also conceivable, if we are not dealing with two Lukes, that the Luke of the letters may have been the author of the Log, and that the final work, which comprises both the Gospel and Acts, was wrongly attributed to him for that reason, but there is no evidence of any kind that the attribution of the Gospel and Acts is incorrect. When we now see that the Luke of the letters seems to have entered Paul's life at precisely the point where the final author of Acts begins to write as though he had been an eyewitness of the events which he is describing, the probability would seem to be substantially enhanced that they were one and the same man

The Chronological Sequence of the Pauline Sections of Acts

Thanks to Luke's integrity in setting down what his sources recorded, it is only a scissors-and-paste job to rearrange the three sources —Hellenist (H), Journey (J), and Log (L)—in the Pauline sections of Acts in the chronological order of the letters:

1. Conversion, first Jerusalem visit, etc. 6:1–11:26 (H)
2. First Missionary Journey 13:1–14:28 (J)
3. Second Missionary Journey 15:36–18:11,18–22 (J)[4]
4. Famine visit 11:27–30 (H)
5. Collection trip (beginning) 18:23–19:8 (J)
6. Collection trip (end) and Council 12:25; 15:1–33 (H)
7. Ephesian residence 19:9–20:1 (J)
8. Macedonia 20:1(J); cf. 16:11ff. (L)[5]
9. Greece 20:2–3 (J); 18:12–17(J)
10. Macedonia to Rome 20:4–28:31 (Luke, conflating J and L)

The Datable Events

Acts connects four datable events with Paul's life:

1. Claudius' expulsion of the Jews from Rome (18:2)
2. The famine (11:28)
3. The proconsulship of Gallio in Achaia (18:12)
4. The arrival of Festus in Judea (24:27)

[4] Acts 18:12–17 is omitted here since it cannot have taken place so early.
[5] Acts 16:9–15 is an insertion from the Log. It probably replaces a sentence in the Journey source to the effect that Paul and his companions sailed from Troas to Neapolis and made their way from there to Philippi. Its use at this point is probably an honest mistake. On the other hand, Luke's Gospel contains just such a displacement in its use of the rejection at Nazareth (Luke 4:16–30) as an introduction to the account of the Galilean ministry, although Mark had put it after the residence in Capernaum (Mark 6:1–6), and Luke's account still shows that that is where it belongs: "What we have heard you did at Capernaum, do here also in your own country" (Luke 4:23). Apparently Luke did not feel that the order of his sources always had to be preserved.

There is no problem about the last three of these. The famine cannot be dated before 45 or after 47; it very probably occurred in 46;[6] Gallio's proconsulship must have fallen between the summer of 51 and the summer of 53;[7] and the summer of 55 is the most probable date for the arrival of Festus in Judea.[8] The date of Claudius' expulsion of the Jews from Rome, however, requires some discussion.

Suetonius in his life of Claudius (xxv) says that "Claudius expelled the Jews from Rome when they kept on rioting at the instigation of Chrestus," but he does not tell us when. Dio Cassius (lx.6.6) confirms this, adding that the decree was not carried out: "He did not expel the Jews, since they had again grown so numerous that they could hardly have been driven out of the city without disorder on the part of the mob of them, but only forbade them to assemble according to their ancestral custom." Dio includes this among the events of the year 41, and it is in that year that we should expect to find it, for one of the first problems with which Claudius had to deal was the unrest which Caligula's madness had stirred up in the Jewish world. His letter to Alexandria, which dates from this year, states his policy: if the Jewish disorders cease, there will be no further punishment; if they continue, the consequences will be severe. The evidence for the date of Claudius' decree, therefore, would seem to be consistent, and Lake remarks, "If there were no reason to the contrary it would probably be put down to A.D. 41." [9]

The reason to the contrary is that Acts says that when Paul arrived in Corinth he found Aquila and Priscilla, who had recently come from Italy because "Claudius had commanded all the Jews to leave Rome" (Acts 18:2), and 41 has always seemed too early a date for Paul's arrival in Corinth.

Some historians, therefore, have concluded that Dio Cassius must be wrong about the date, and they have cited Orosius, a historian of the fifth century, as their authority for dating Claudius' decree in 49. But Orosius does not date the decree then. What he actually says is:

---

[6] See K. S. Gapp, "The Universal Famine under Claudius," *Harvard Theological Review*, XXVIII (1935), 258–265.
[7] See K. Lake, *Beginnings of Christianity*, V, 460ff.
[8] *Ibid.*, pp. 464ff.
[9] *Ibid.*, p. 459.

"Josephus reports that the Jews were expelled from the city by Claudius in the ninth year of his reign, but I am more moved by Suetonius, who says, 'Claudius expelled the Jews from Rome when they kept on rioting at the instigation of Chrestus'" (viii.6.15). Since no surviving writing of Josephus mentions the expulsion of the Jews, we cannot form an independent judgment of his supposed dating of the event in the ninth year of Claudius, if indeed he did date it then and Orosius is citing him accurately. Orosius himself believed the date to be incorrect, and he apparently understood the statement of Suetonius to be in conflict with it. Unfortunately, he does not tell us whether the date he accepted as correct was earlier or later than the ninth year of Claudius.

The situation may be summed up briefly as follows: Suetonius gives no date for the expulsion; Dio Cassius places it in 41, adding that it was not carried out; and Orosius says that despite Josephus' having placed it in 49 this date was incorrect. The letters bear out the evidence of Dio Cassius, for 41 is precisely the date when they put Paul in Corinth for the first time. Acts, therefore, would seem to be completely accurate in placing Aquila and Priscilla there at the same time.

With these dates, which confirm the evidence of the letters, we can easily reconstruct the remainder of the chronology of Paul's missionary career. At the close of the third visit to Jerusalem (Completion-Council) Paul probably returned to Antioch. From there he went to Ephesus. His stay in Ephesus lasted at least two years, and probably three,[10] and at the end of it he set out on his last journey to Greece, where he stayed three months (Acts 20:3). During this stay he was tried before Gallio in Corinth and dismissed. This can have happened either in the winter of 51/52 or in the winter of 52/53. If it was in the latter, then the remainder of Acts offers no problems. After the

---

[10] Acts 19:10 says that Paul argued in the school of Tyrannus for two years. This did not cover his whole stay in the city, however. Acts 20:31 says the whole stay lasted three years. The former passage comes from the Journey source, the latter from a speech. The curious discrepancy between the two suggests the interesting possibility that although Luke knew the figure in the source to be incorrect, he nevertheless reproduced it in his narrative and only introduced the correct figure in a speech, which the knowledgeable reader would recognize as the author's composition and not something drawn from a written source.

trial Paul left Greece for Macedonia. He set sail from Philippi in the spring, "after the days of Unleavened Bread" (Acts 20:6), with the intention of reaching Jerusalem by Pentecost (Acts 20:16). Shortly after his arrival in Jerusalem he was arrested. Only a few months had elapsed since the trial before Gallio; therefore the time was the late spring of 53. Paul remained a prisoner in Caesarea for two years, until Felix was succeeded by Porcius Festus (Acts 24:27). Festus probably arrived in the summer of 55, and he sent Paul to Rome in the late summer of the same year, too late, as it turned out, for the voyage to be completed before the onset of the winter storms (Acts 27:9-12).

In the present state of our knowledge this is probably as close to an exact chronology as we can hope to come. We cannot be absolutely certain of Gallio's and Festus' dates, and we cannot be sure that Acts gives all the intervals, or even that those it does give are more than approximations in round figures. Assuming the dates and intervals to be substantially correct, however, Paul's long residence in Ephesus, which ended in 52, began in 49, two years after the Council. Since neither Acts nor the letters tell us anything about this interval, we are at a loss to know how it was spent. For the rest of Paul's life, however, we have at least the foundation of a consistent and workable chronology which accords with all the evidence of Acts and the letters. This chronology may be summarized as follows:

32 Conversion
Arabia and Damascus

35 First visit to Jerusalem (Acquaintance)
Syria (Antioch), Cilicia

40/41 Galatia, Macedonia (Philippi, Thessalonica)

41 Achaia (Corinth)

44 Composition of II Thessalonians

46 Achaia (Corinth, Athens)
Composition of I Thessalonians
Second visit to Jerusalem (Conference = Famine)
Antioch: Conflict with the Judaizers
Composition of Previous Letter to Corinth

47 Galatia

Ephesus: Composition of I Corinthians, II Corinthians 10–13, Philippians

Macedonia: Composition of II Corinthians 1–9

Composition of Galatians

Achaia (Corinth): Composition of Romans

Third visit to Jerusalem (Offering = Completion-Council)

49–52 Ephesus: Composition of Colossians, Philemon, Ephesians

52/53 Greece: Trial before Gallio

53 Fourth visit to Jerusalem (Arrest)

55 Arrival of Festus: Paul sent to Rome

PART **III**:

 SYNTHESIS

14

THE MAN WHO HAD SEEN
THE LORD

Paul's gospel, from first to last, was a reflection of his experience of Christ. "Am I not an apostle?" he asks the Corinthians. "Have I not seen Jesus our Lord?" (I Cor. 9:1). Later, reminding them of the fundamentals of "the gospel, which you received, in which you stand, by which you are being saved," he gives a list of the appearances of the risen Christ; he ends, "Last of all, as to one untimely born, he appeared also to me" (I Cor. 15:1–2,8). He expresses the same thought, at greater length and with greater emphasis, in Galatians: "For I would have you know, brethren, that the gospel which was preached by me is not a gospel according to man. For I did not receive it from man, nor was I taught it, but it came through a revelation of Jesus Christ." This occurred "when he who had set me aside before I was born, and had called me through his grace, was pleased to reveal his Son in me, in order that I might preach him among the Gentiles" (Gal. 1:11–12, 15–16). His vision of the risen Christ, in short, had been the decisive event in Paul's life.

The importance of this event for the understanding of Paul's subsequent career was just as clear to the author of Acts as it is to the modern reader of Paul's letters. Acts tells the story of the conversion three times, always in great detail, and always with the purpose not merely of explaining how Paul was changed from an unbelieving Jew into a follower of Christ, but of showing how he was changed from a persecutor of the infant church into an apostle, who "proclaimed Jesus, saying, 'He is the Son of God'" (Acts 9:20). The first of the Acts accounts begins as follows:

> But Saul, still breathing threats and murder against the disciples of the Lord, went to the high priest and asked him for letters to the synagogues at Damascus, so that if he found any belonging to the Way, men or women, he might bring them bound to Jerusalem. Now as he journeyed he approached Damascus, and suddenly a light from heaven flashed about him. And he fell to the ground and heard a voice saying to him, "Saul, Saul, why do you persecute me?" And he said, "Who are you, Lord?" And he said, "I am Jesus, whom you are persecuting; but rise and enter the city, and you will be told what you are to do." The men who were traveling with him stood speechless, hearing the voice but seeing no one. Saul arose from the ground; and when his eyes were opened, he could see nothing; so they led him by the hand and brought him into Damascus. And for three days he was without sight, and neither ate nor drank (Acts 9:1–9).

The two other Acts accounts (Acts 22:4–16; 26:9–18) tell substantially the same story, the former repeating from the subsequent scene in the first account the detail about Ananias' healing of Paul's blindness, the latter, however, omitting mention of the blindness and its cure. The purpose of all three accounts is to explain Paul's career as the consequence of his vision of the risen Christ. In this respect Acts and the letters are in complete agreement.

The longest and most detailed description of a vision of the risen Christ from Paul's own pen is in II Corinthians 10–13:

> I must boast; there is nothing to be gained by it, but I will go on to visions and revelations of the Lord. I know a man in Christ who fourteen years ago was caught up to the third heaven —whether in the body or out of the body I do not know, God

knows. And I know that this man was caught up into Paradise
—whether in the body or out of the body I do not know, God
knows—and he heard things that cannot be told, which man
may not utter. On behalf of this man I will boast, but on my
own behalf I will not boast, except of my weaknesses (II Cor.
12:1–5).

Is this a description of the vision on the Damascus road?

It is not difficult, at first glance, to persuade oneself that it is not.
To begin with, it does not sound like the conversion as that experience
is described in Acts. The setting and the circumstances, both of which
are important in the story of the conversion, are not given; Paul's
companions are not referred to; and the two most significant elements in the story in Acts, the seeing of the light and the hearing of
the words of Jesus, "Saul, Saul, why do you persecute me? . . . I am
Jesus whom you are persecuting," are not mentioned.

Nor does the passage in question claim to be an account of the
conversion. It seems merely to describe one of what may have been a
number of "visions and revelations of the Lord," perhaps of the kind
that is mentioned elsewhere in Acts:

> When I had returned to Jerusalem and was praying in the
> temple, I fell into a trance and saw him saying to me, "Make
> haste and get quickly out of Jerusalem, because they will not
> accept your testimony about me." And I said, "Lord, they them-
> selves know that in every synagogue I imprisoned and beat those
> who believed in thee. And when the blood of Stephen thy witness
> was shed, I also was standing by and approving, and keeping the
> garments of those who killed him." And he said to me, "Depart;
> for I will send you far away to the Gentiles" (Acts 22:17–21).

There is nothing in the passage in II Corinthians 10–13 that suggests
that the vision of which it speaks was other than an experience of
this sort; it certainly is not represented as having changed Paul from
a persecutor into an apostle.

And finally it is explicitly said to have occurred "fourteen years
ago." Earlier students of Paul's life tended to regard this consideration
as decisive, since the traditional date of II Corinthians 10–13 was toward
the end of the Third Missionary Journey, not many months before
Paul's arrest, and it was impossible to date the conversion such a

short time before the arrest, because Galatians testified that at least fourteen years (and possibly seventeen) had intervened between the conversion and the second visit to Jerusalem.

Impressive as these reasons may sound, however, they will not stand up under cross-examination. To begin with the last, it not only depends on the assumption that the letters can be dated by being fitted into the existing chronological framework of Acts, but it also dates the framework itself on the assumption that a specific incident, in this case the trial before Gallio, which Acts puts in the Second Missionary Journey, is properly placed there. Neither of these assumptions can be upheld. We now know that Acts has confused the Collection trip with the Third Missionary Journey, and that the Journey source, which contained the account of the trial, regularly includes all incidents connected with a particular place in its account of Paul's first visit to that place; it only attaches an incident to a subsequent visit when the content forbids its being attached to the first. Consequently there is no real reason for believing that Paul's trial before Gallio occurred on his first visit to Corinth, and thus no reason for dating II Corinthians 10–13 after Gallio's proconsulship. The evidence of the letters, on the other hand, tells us that Paul probably arrived in Corinth as early as 41. II Corinthians 10–13 was written in the spring of 47, during the Collection trip, and Galatians, which gives fourteen years as the smallest possible interval between the conversion and the second Jerusalem visit (which immediately preceded the Collection trip), was written in the summer of the same year. The chronological evidence, therefore, suggests very strongly that the experience which Paul dates fourteen years before the writing of II Corinthians 10–13 was not some postconversion vision of the Lord but the conversion itself.

While the passage does not explicitly claim to be an account of the conversion, the argument that it may describe one of a number of "visions and revelations" on Paul's part likewise depends in large measure on inferences drawn from Acts, which alone speaks of such a postconversion vision of the Lord to Paul (Acts 22:17–21). Elsewhere in the letters when Paul speaks of his having seen the Lord, he always seems to refer to the conversion (I Cor. 9:1; 15:8; Gal.

2:15–16). Even in the passage under discussion the reference to "visions and revelations" is not necessarily a claim that Paul had had more than one such experience himself. It may well have been the "false apostles" against whom Paul was writing who had made such a claim. Indeed, some of the peculiarities of expression in the passage could well be a reflection of the actual language of these opponents of Paul. This is particularly true of such expressions as "caught up to the third heaven" and its apparent equivalent, "caught up into Paradise," as well as the repeated phrase, "whether in the body or out of the body I do not know, God knows," all of which are unparalleled in Paul's other writing and sound rather like echoes of the familiar jargon of the professed ecstatic.

Nor can it be convincingly argued that the later words, "And to keep me from being elated by the abundance of revelations" (II Cor. 12:7), necessarily support the view that Paul had had an abundance of such experiences. The Greek text is corrupt at this point, but even as it stands it can be understood in quite another way: "And as regards the greater abundance [ὑπερβολή usually implies the exceeding of a quantitative or qualitative limit] of the revelations . . . therefore, that I should not exalt myself above measure, there was given to me a thorn in the flesh, a messenger of Satan, to harass me, that I should not exalt myself above measure. Three times I besought the Lord about this, that it should depart from me; and he said to me, 'Sufficient for you is my grace, for power is made perfect in weakness'" (II Cor. 12:7–9). Here again it may be the "greater abundance" of the revelations of Paul's opponents which is meant. What follows would seem to bear this out, for it is a series of implied contrasts between these opponents and Paul. Unlike them, he does not exalt himself above measure; unlike them, he has learned from the Lord to depend wholly on his grace; unlike them, he has also learned from the Lord that power is made perfect in weakness. Is he also implying that, unlike them, he has had no need of an abundance of revelations of which to boast? He concludes, "I will all the more gladly boast of my weaknesses, that the power of Christ may rest upon me" (II Cor. 12:9).

Furthermore, the one experience of his own of which Paul actu-

ally speaks is clearly the one on which he rested his claim to apostleship. In the part of the letter in which it occurs Paul is heaping scorn
on a group of missionaries who had invaded Corinth, claiming an
apostolic authority equal to his own. He writes:

> And what I do I will continue to do, in order to undermine
> the claim of those who would like to claim that in their boasted
> mission they work on the same terms as we do. For such men
> are false apostles, deceitful workmen, disguising themselves as
> apostles of Christ. And no wonder, for even Satan disguises
> himself as an angel of light. So it is not strange if his servants
> also disguise themselves as servants of righteousness. Their end
> will correspond to their deeds (II Cor. 11:12–15).

Paul then undertakes to counter the boasting of these men with a
series of boasts of his own: "Whatever any one dares to boast of—I
am speaking as a fool—I also dare to boast of that" (II Cor. 11:21).
Are they Israelites? So is Paul. Are they servants of Christ? Paul is a
better one; he has suffered far more than they. The argument proceeds
in this vein without a break. Finally it reaches a climax: "I must boast;
there is nothing to be gained by it, but I will go on to visions and
revelations of the Lord" (II Cor. 12:1). But instead of boasting to have
had an equal or a greater number of such visions himself, he counters
by describing a single vision, superior to the "visions and revelations"
of the false apostles. This is not one among many visions; it is the
single all-important vision that had come to Paul "fourteen years ago"
and made him a true apostle.

The experience itself is clearly delineated. Paul was "caught up
to the third heaven, into Paradise, and heard words that cannot be
uttered, which it is not permitted to a man to speak." Nothing is said
about the object of the vision, but "caught up to the third heaven"
implies that what Paul saw was a dazzling glory rather than a clearly
defined figure. This is borne out by his reference in II Corinthians 1–9,
written shortly afterward, to the Israelites, who "could not look at
Moses' face because of its glory" (II Cor. 3:7), followed by the statement: "And we all, with unveiled face, beholding the glory of the
Lord, are being changed into his likeness from one degree of glory
to another" (II Cor. 3:18). The auditory image being described is of

the same order. Paul is certain that he was being spoken to, and he is equally certain of the meaning of what was said, but he cannot quote the actual words. They were not the words of men at all.

This is precisely the kind of experience which is described in Acts. Only there it is put into the third person instead of the first. The visual image is described as "a light from heaven" (Acts 9:3), but the voice speaks actual words, since it is impossible to record "words that cannot be uttered." The recorded words, however, are a translation, so to speak, of what Paul had heard, into the language of men. "Saul, Saul, why do you persecute me? . . . I am Jesus, whom you are persecuting," expresses perfectly Paul's sudden conviction that his persecution of the church was a persecution of one whom he now knew to be the living Lord. And, "Rise and enter the city, and you will be told what you are to do," exactly conveys the mixture of certainty and uncertainty which Paul must have felt at the time—certainty as to his present surrender to Christ and uncertainty as to his future course as a chosen instrument of Christ's purpose. That Luke understood this to be the source's intention is clear from his refusal to commit himself to a further objectification of the phenomena in his later accounts of the event. The source had said that Paul had fallen to the ground, and that those who were traveling with him had heard the voice but had seen no one (Acts 9:4,7). In the second and third of Luke's accounts he alters these details. In the second Paul still falls to the ground, but the men who are with him now see the light but do not hear the voice (Acts 22:7,9); in the third they all fall to the ground (Acts 26:14). These alterations must be recognized as deliberate on Luke's part, and their purpose is plain. The source had made it clear that it was attempting to describe a spiritual experience in the language of objective observation, and Luke was enough of a historian to recognize this, and enough of an artist to know how to avoid the falsification of the record which would have been inevitable if he had reinforced the imagery of the source by repeating it three times literally. He therefore preserved Paul's part unchanged, but he altered the details as they affected the observers who were traveling with Paul. In the first account they remain standing and hear but do not see; in the second they still remain standing, but now they see but do not hear;

and in the third they all fall down. It is an extraordinarily skillful handling of a difficult problem.

Our two sources, then, would seem to be in agreement. Paul's conversion was such an event as is described in the first person in II Corinthians 10–13 and in the third person in Acts, and the former of these is the only eyewitness account of a resurrection appearance of Christ that we possess. It is not necessary to decide whether the resurrection appearances to the original apostles were exactly the same as the one which Paul experienced. The Gospels have certainly emphasized their physical nature at the expense of their spiritual aspect, but it is entirely possible that the original apostles, having known Jesus in the flesh, saw him as a recognizable figure in the appearances to them. Paul, however, did not. His chief impression of the risen Christ was one of dazzling glory, and this feature left its mark on all his subsequent thought.

Its initial effect, as was only natural, was on his Christology and eschatology. Paul had doubtless heard the story of the earthly Jesus; as a persecutor of the church he must inevitably have known something of Jesus' life and ministry as well as of the circumstances of his death. He must also have known that his followers believed that he had risen from the dead. But the character of Jesus' life had clearly not persuaded Paul that Jesus had been the Messiah, and he certainly had not believed the reports of his resurrection. To Paul, the Jesus of whom he had heard must have been at least a heretic, as well as the leader of a subversive movement, who had been put to death as a criminal. Paul was not converted to Christianity, at least consciously, by being drawn to this Jesus; on the contrary, he was repelled by him. He was converted by a vision of the exalted and glorified Christ, and it was inevitable that it should have been this Christ of whom he spoke when he began "preaching the faith he once tried to destroy."

It was also inevitable, initially at least, that he should have looked on the significant work of Christ as lying in the future rather than in the past. Whatever Christ may have accomplished in the past, it had not contributed to Paul's salvation, at least as far as Paul could see. He had not been made a new man by hearing Jesus teach, or by witnessing his power to heal, or by experiencing his forgiveness. His vision of the exalted and glorified Christ, therefore, had not been to him the authentication of a past experience at all. Instead it had been the proof of the Christian belief that Christ was even then preparing to return to earth, and a preview of his promised parousia. Indeed, if one were seeking a single word to describe the dominant note in Paul's apprehension of Christ at this stage in his career, it might well be "nearness." Christ was near enough, in terms of space, to have made himself visible to Paul on the Damascus road (the "third heaven" being less than halfway to the seventh, topmost heaven), and by inference, near enough, in terms of time, to return at any moment.

This idea of Christ and his work found its natural background in the setting of Jewish apocalyptic thought. The apocalyptic movement, which flourished from the publication of the book of Daniel in 165 B.C. to the virtual extinction of the Jewish national hope in the erection of the Gentile city of Aelia Capitolina on the former site of Jerusalem in A.D. 131, was not a single organic system but an attempted synthesis of two quite separate and distinct (and in some important respects, incompatible) philosophies of history. One of these was the outgrowth of the Hebrew prophetic movement; the other was imported from Persia, where it had originated in the religion of Zoroaster. Reduced to their essentials, the two can be readily distinguished. The Hebrew hope was for the restoration of Israel, either as an ideal religious commonwealth with God as its king, or as a monarchy ruled by an anointed king of the house of David. The Persian hope was for a supernatural savior who would appear from heaven, bring the present age to an end with a general resurrection and a final judgment, and inaugurate a new age of eternal blessedness. No two versions of the synthesis between these quite disparate philosophies are exactly the same, but they all follow similar lines. From the Hebrew tradition comes the idea of a period of suffering followed by a happy and peaceful Messianic reign, usually some centuries in length. To this conception is tacked on, as a sequel, the Persian idea of the coming of the heavenly savior, the general resurrection and last judgment, the end of the present age, and the establishment of the age to come. Not all apocalyptic writers give the system in full, and not all use the same names for its several parts. But the same general outline can be discerned behind all the various forms of the synthesis.

It can also be discerned behind the Christology and the eschatology of Paul's earliest letters. Only there the ruler of the Messianic kingdom and the heavenly savior are the same person, and the judgment of the living takes place at the beginning of the Messianic age rather than after the general resurrection at the end (II Thess. 1:6–10; cf. I Cor. 3:12–15). A single modification, the special resurrection of Christians at the parousia, is introduced into this system in I Thessalonians (4:3–17), and the modified system is defended in detail in I Corinthians. The resurrection of Christ, Paul explains, had begun the apocalyptic fulfillment. Then at his parousia those who belonged to Christ would be raised. After this Christ would reign until he had put all enemies under his feet. The last enemy to be destroyed would be death (thus bringing about the general resurrection for the last judgment). Only then would Christ deliver the kingdom to God the Father, and the Son himself would also be subjected to the Father, that God might be all things to every one (I Cor. 15:23–28).

The Christology of the early letters has the same starting point. In II Thessalonians it is heavily futuristic. There Christ is the super-natural savior who comforts and establishes the believers (II Thess. 2:16,17), but because the letter was addressed to a community that was undergoing persecution, its chief emphasis is on Christ's role as the agent of "vengeance upon those who do not know God and upon those who do not obey the gospel of our Lord Jesus" (II Thess. 1:8). His function is thus viewed as mainly destructive, but that is probably a one-sided statement of the case to be attributed to the special circumstances which brought the letter forth.

I Thessalonians strikes a new Christological note. Instead of betraying an almost exclusively futuristic interest in the work of Christ, it speaks of him as having "died for us so that whether we wake or sleep we might live with him" (I Thess. 5:10). This is the first mention in the letters of the work of Christ in the past. It is important to note, however, that it was dictated by an eschatological interest. Some of the Thessalonian Christians had died, and Paul is here citing the death and resurrection of Jesus as proof that Christians who have died will be raised from the dead before the general resurrection at the end of the Messianic reign.

The developed Christology of I Corinthians is a further enlargement of this idea. There Christ is treated as the second Adam, who by dying in the flesh and rising in the spirit becomes the prototype of a new humanity, which having borne the image of the man of dust, will also bear the image of the man of heaven. Again the interest is primarily eschatological.

But the language of this expanded Christology is not all eschatological. The significant words which it employs are "flesh" and "spirit," which make their first appearance as a Pauline antithesis in I Corinthians. This antithesis is not introduced in connection with the resurrection, but as a part of the argument of the first four chapters of the letter, which deal primarily with epistemology. Reduced to its bare essentials the argument is as follows: Paul's gospel of Christ crucified was a gospel of "weakness" and "foolishness" to those in the flesh; to those in the spirit, however, it signified the power of God and the wisdom of God. The Corinthian factions, in distinguishing between this gospel and that of Apollos or Cephas, showed that they were judging by fleshly rather than spiritual standards. Therefore, "if any one thinks that he is wise in this age, let him become a fool that he may become wise" (I Cor. 3:18), for "we have received not the spirit of the world, but the Spirit which is from God, that we might understand the gifts bestowed on us by God. And we impart this in words not taught by human wisdom but taught by the Spirit, interpreting spiritual truths to those who possess the Spirit" (I Cor. 2:12–13). Here, the function of the spirit is to enable its possessor to understand the "secret and hidden wisdom of God" (I Cor. 2:7), which "no eye has seen, nor ear heard, nor the heart of man conceived" (I Cor. 2:9).

This function of the spirit had been part of Paul's thought from the beginning. He writes in II Thessalonians, "But we are bound to give thanks to God always for you, brethren beloved by the Lord, because God chose you from the beginning to be saved, through sanctification by the Spirit [or 'sanctification of spirit'] and belief in the truth" (II Thess. 2:13). In I Thessalonians he expands this idea:

"For we know, brethren beloved by God, that he has chosen you; for our gospel came to you not only in word, but also in power and in the Holy Spirit and with full conviction" (I Thess. 1:4–5). The contrast between the perception of those who have received the spirit and the lack of perception of those who have not received the spirit is doubtless implicit in these passages, but the explicit identification of the uncomprehending as men of flesh (σαρκικοί) and the comprehending as men of spirit (πνευματικοί) does not appear before I Corinthians: "But I, brethren, could not address you as men of spirit, but as men of flesh . . . for you were not ready for it; and even yet you are not ready, for you are still of the flesh. For while there is jealousy and strife among you, are you not of the flesh, and behaving like ordinary men? For when one says, 'I belong to Paul,' and another, 'I belong to Apollos,' are you not merely men?" (I Cor. 3:1–4). It is as an extension of this line of thought that Paul treats the resurrection in terms of flesh and spirit in I Corinthians 15. Once again, however, it is his apprehension of Christ that makes the new application possible. The Christ who had died had been a being of flesh; the Christ who had appeared to Paul had been a being of spirit. The resurrection had marked the change from the one nature to the other. Therefore, if men were to live with him they would have to undergo a similar change, either by actually dying and rising or by being transformed.

Thus the characteristic Christology and eschatology of the three earliest letters are a reflection of the experience of Christ that came to Paul at his conversion. The doctrine of these letters must not be read as a series of partial statements of Paul's developed thought, but as the working out of the implications of his earliest apprehension of Christ as the exalted and glorified Lord who had appeared to him on the Damascus road. Particularly is this true with regard to the references to Christ's death, which are set in an eschatological background and are only beginning to be treated in connection with the atonement in I Corinthians 15. II Corinthians 10–13 goes theologically with I Corinthians, being an intensification of the first four chapters of that letter. It adds nothing new to the teaching of the earlier letter, and it is significant that its most explicit Christological passage is still a description of the appearance of Christ to Paul at his conversion.

This early group of four letters—II Thessalonians, I Thessalonians, I Corinthians, and II Corinthians 10–13—was succeeded by four others —Philippians, II Corinthians 1–9, Galatians, and Romans—which differ from them very markedly. Not only are their eschatology and Christology easily distinguishable from Paul's earlier teaching on these subjects, but they also introduce a new theme, the relation of law to grace, which they develop so extensively that succeeding generations have come to look upon it as the most distinctive feature of Paul's thought.

The change from the thought of the first four letters to that of the succeeding four was not a gradual process. It was brought about by an experience of Paul's which was to contribute fully as much to his understanding of the meaning of Christ as had the conversion itself. The early doctrine, shaped by the experience of the conversion, is almost exclusively concerned with the risen Christ. It bases nothing on his pre-existence or his coming into the world, it betrays little interest in his life and ministry, and when it mentions his death at all, it is either to admit that it is inexplicable (a stumbling block to Jews and foolishness to Gentiles) or to point out that it was the necessary prelude to his resurrection (what you sow does not come to life unless it dies). The later doctrine, on the contrary, is chiefly interested not in what the resurrected Christ was about to accomplish at his parousia, but in what Jesus had already accomplished in his life and death on earth. And it was in the working out of the relationship between this Jesus of history and the cosmic Christ that Paul made his most original and most lasting contribution to Christian thought.

A single event in Paul's life seems to have awakened in him the realization that the full meaning of Christ could not be found in the apprehension of him solely as the exalted and glorified Lord who would soon descend from heaven and accomplish the work of salvation, but must be found in the understanding, and sharing, of his earthly life of sacrifice. This was Paul's arrest during the persecution in Asia and his belief for a time that he was under sentence of death and was about to be executed (II Cor. 1:8–9). Acts knows nothing of this experience, since it omits the end of the Collection trip, when it took place, but the letters contain a good deal of information about it. This is to be found in Philippians, written while Paul was still in prison, and II Corinthians 1–9, written shortly after his release The occasion for the imprisonment was a persecution, but how this arose we are not told. The imprisonment itself must have lasted for several weeks, long enough for an exchange of letters with Philippi, and Philippians seems to have been written shortly before its end. By that time Paul was beginning to believe that the death sentence would not be carried out after all (Phil. 1:19,25). But he had earlier thought otherwise, and he had come to look on his suffering and his threatened death as having a positive meaning and as actually serving to advance the gospel. He had found this positive meaning in his own suffering by reflecting on its similarity to the suffering and death of Jesus, and in the light of that reflection he had suddenly found himself with a new hope, quite unlike the earlier hope that he would live until the parousia, or if he had died, that he would be raised on that day. His new hope, he writes, is "that I may know him and the power of his resurrection, and may share his suffering, becoming like him in his death, that if possible I may attain the resurrection from the dead" (Phil. 3:10–11).

This was a new apprehension of Christ. It was completely different from the vision on the Damascus road. To begin with, it was unlike the earlier experience in form. That had been the sort of apprehension that could only be described in terms of seeing and hearing, one that had suddenly impinged on the outward senses. This was the kind of awareness that came in a quieter and more inward way, and it is significant that in Philippians Paul does not speak of "seeing" Christ but of "knowing" him. It was also unlike the earlier experience in content. That had disclosed the exalted and glorified Christ, victorious over death, and about to triumph over his enemies. This recalled Jesus of Nazareth, despised and rejected by men, and put to death on a cross. But if it was not a vision of Christ in the literal sense of the word, it was one figuratively, for Paul now saw Jesus in a new light, and, viewed in that light, his earthly life had taken on new meaning. The change is clearly visible in the letters. Just as the Christology of II Thessalonians, I Thessalonians, I Corinthians, and II Corinthians 10–13 had been a reflection of the vision of Christ that had come to Paul in his conversion on the Damascus road, so the Christology of Philippians, II Corinthians 1–9, Galatians, and Romans is a reflection of the new awareness of Christ that had taken shape in his mind as he lay in prison in Ephesus during the persecution in Asia.

The change begins to appear in Philippians, where the recipients of the letter are counseled to model themselves on Christ, who resigned the form of God and came into the world in the form of a slave and died on the cross. Paul himself, he tells them, had already begun to do this in giving up his own claim to worldly respectability as a well-born Hebrew, a practicing Pharisee, a zealous persecutor of the church, and a blameless example of the righteousness in the law. He was now continuing the process by sharing Christ's sufferings, and he was ready to complete it by becoming like him in his death, that if possible he might attain the resurrection from the dead. The phrase, "if possible," comes as something of a surprise, until we realize that Paul has now ceased to think of resurrection as automatic and inevitable, the natural consequence of being a member of the new humanity of which Christ was the prototype. Paul is now attempting to think with the mind of the earthly Jesus, and it has occurred to him that Jesus, having resigned the prerogatives of a being "in the form of God," had gone to his death without any guarantee that he would be restored to life before the general resurrection. The "faith of Christ" to which Paul refers here is the faith on the part of Jesus that God would look on his life of perfect obedience as worthy of full acceptance now, without the necessity of undergoing judgment at the last day, and would therefore raise him from the dead immediately. This faith, of course, had been justified in the case of Jesus. Paul's hope, in Philippians, was that a like faith on his part might be justified in the same way. His desire, he writes, is "to depart and be with Christ," not as one of many who would be raised up at the parousia, but immediately after his death.

It is his own resurrection which Paul has had in mind at first, but he also hopes that the faith to which he has attained may become the faith of his followers. He realizes, however, that this new idea of an immediate resurrection will be strange to his readers, since it has only just been revealed to him, and this is the first time he has communicated it to them. Therefore he writes, "Let those of us who are mature think thus; and if you think differently in any way, God will reveal this also to you" (Phil. 3:15). For those who live until the parousia, however, the older system of I Corinthians still applies: "But our commonwealth is in heaven, and from it we await a Savior, the Lord Jesus Christ, who will change our lowly body to be like his glorious body, by the power which enables him even to subject all things to himself" (Phil. 3:20–21). Philippians is thus a transitional letter in the sense that it introduces the new eschatology and Christology alongside of the old. II Corinthians 1–9, Galatians, and Romans, not only develop this new eschatology and Christology, but also bring the two together into a single system.

The process begins in II Corinthians 1–9, with the statement that "God was in Christ." That is to say, the human Jesus had not "emptied himself," as Philippians had maintained. During his earthly life he had possessed a divine nature and a human nature simultaneously. The human Jesus whom Paul had come to know in the prison in Ephesus had not been merely human after all. He had already possessed the divine nature of the exalted Christ who was to appear to Paul on the Damascus road. And since Christians were called to a life like his, they must also possess, at least in some measure, the divine nature which would be fully theirs when they had put aside the body of flesh. This measure of the divine nature they had received in the down payment of the spirit.

But the most striking feature of the new Christology of these four letters is not simply that it reflects a new apprehension of the meaning of the earthly life of Jesus, but that this meaning is stated in legal terms rather than in eschatological terms. That this should have been so was not solely due to the character of the new apprehension itself. Its immediate cause is to be found in the fact that during the period when these letters were written Paul was engaged in the controversy with the Judaizers over the relation of law to grace.

The controversy had arisen shortly after Paul's second visit to Jerusalem, when a group of conservative Jewish Christians from Jerusalem had begun to maintain that the Gentile members of the Antioch church and its missions should be required to be circumcised and to undertake the keeping of the Jewish law. These men had made their presence felt in Antioch shortly before the beginning of the Collection trip; by the time it was over they had penetrated Paul's Galatian churches, where they had apparently persuaded at least some of Paul's converts of the rightness of their views. The effect of their activities on Paul's thinking begins to be evident as early as I Corinthians, where we find Paul maintaining the principle on which he had always acted, and which he thought had been ratified and approved at his conference with James and Cephas and John in Jerusalem only a few months previously. With Jews he had acted "as one under the law," but to "those outside the law" he had become "as one outside the law," so that he might "by all means save some" (I Cor. 9:19–23). Later in the same letter he makes a stronger statement: "The sting of death is sin and the power of sin is the law" (I Cor. 15:56). This remark is thrown in as an aside, and the interpreter must beware of reading more into it than is there. But it would seem to be the starting point from which Paul developed his full-blown theory of sin and death as sovereigns hostile to the sovereignty of God, and of the law as the instrument of sin (cf. Rom. 7:7–11). Regardless of how it is expanded in detail, however, the intent is clear. It is a vigorous and angry denial of the claim that the law brings salvation, and an assertion that on the contrary it brings death.

Philippians gives fuller expression to this idea. In that letter there can be no question but that Paul has the Judaizers in mind. He writes, "Look out for the dogs, look out for the evil-workers, look out for those who mutilate the flesh. For we are the true circumcision, who worship God in spirit, and glory in Christ Jesus, and put no confidence in the flesh" (Phil. 3:2–3). And he contrasts the righteousness which is "based on law" with the righteousness "which is through the faith of Christ, the righteousness from God that depends on faith" (Phil. 3:9). Here the new apprehension of Christ as the one who went to his death in the faith that God would accept him as righteous and raise him from the dead is brought into direct connection with the contention of the Judaizers that true righteousness is a matter of keeping the law. From this point, the two ideas were never to be separated in Paul's mind. He would maintain to the end that righteousness could only come from God, as a gift of grace to those who had been united with Christ.

The point at issue, of course, was circumcision: Paul did not require his Gentile converts to be circumcised; the Judaizers maintained that they must submit to the rite. Before the Judaizers made this assertion Paul had been quite indifferent to the matter, and the Mosaic law as such had presented him with no problem. II Thessalonians does not mention either circumcision or the law, but this silence is not surprising, since the problem with which the letter deals did not involve the question of the law one way or another. The silence of I Thessalonians, on the other hand, is more significant. That letter contains one of Paul's most bitter attacks on the Jews, "who killed both the Lord Jesus and the prophets, and drove us out, and displease God and oppose all men by hindering us from speaking to the Gentiles that they may be saved —so as always to fill up the measure of their sins" (I Thess. 2:15–16), but there is no mention here of the law or of circumcision. The issue apparently had not yet arisen. I Corinthians, as we have had occasion to notice, deals with the law in general; it also deals specifically with circumcision. The uncircumcised Christian is advised not to be circumcised (and the circumcised not to attempt to conceal the marks of his circumcision), since the time is too short to make such changes worthwhile. But there is certainly no suggestion in any of this that the Christian who has undergone the rite has forfeited the benefits of his Christianity. Even II Corinthians 10–13 maintains this attitude of indifference. Paul's antagonists in this letter are a group of missionaries who have invaded the church of Corinth boasting of apostolic qualifications at least equal to his own. While not Judaizers, they are clearly Jewish Christians, and Paul counters their claim by boasting that his own credentials as a Jew are fully equal to theirs (II Cor. 11:22). He does not rest his claim to apostolic authority on this kind of prestige, of course, but neither does he deny that it is genuine prestige as far as it goes. And he certainly does not suggest that, because it involves a respectability that is inextricably bound up with the keeping of the law, it is incompatible with Christian faith. Galatians even contains a suggestion—though it is hardly more than that—that at one time in his early career Paul may actually have condoned the circumcision of some Gentile converts. He writes, "But if I, brethren, still preach circumcision, why am I still persecuted?" (Gal. 5:11). This would seem to imply that the Judaizers had told the Galatians that Paul had once preached circumcision, in some situations at least, and in fact still preached it in other places. Paul denies only the second of these charges, and in doing so he leaves room for the question whether the first may not have been true. The author of the Journey source in Acts clearly believed that it was, at least in the special case of Timothy, the son of a Greek father and a Jewish mother, and he tells us that Paul "took him and circumcised him because of the Jews that were in those places, for they all knew that his father was a Greek" (Acts 16:3). It is hard to see why a biographer of Paul should have invented this incident if it had not actually occurred. It must therefore be ranged on the side of the evidence that Paul's indifference to circumcision had once been so great that he not only permitted it, but on the principle that "to those under the law" he should become "as one under the law," even encouraged it as a matter of cultural conformity in places where its omission might prove a stumbling block to the effectiveness of his preaching of the gospel.

It seems fairly clear in any case that if circumcision raised any questions for Paul in his early ministry, they were not theological questions. Circumcision only became a theological issue for him when it was preached as a theological necessity, and that happened for the first time when the Judaizers began to invade the predominantly Gentile centers of Christianity in the Antioch church and its missions.

By the time Philippians and II Corinthians 1–9 were written, the lines of the controversy were clearly drawn, and in these letters Paul has already taken the position that Christianity involves the rejection not only of circumcision but of the law in general. Philippians, as we have seen, is primarily a Christological document, and the attack on the law which it contains is introduced into it in a distinctly abrupt way (so abruptly, indeed, as to have suggested to some critics who were unaware of its underlying unity of thought that the letter mght be a conflation of two separate writings). But the legal theory of the letter is an exact reflection of the Christology, being based on a comparison of Paul's career with Christ's. Christ had voluntarily surrendered the status of one who was in the form of God, when he came into the world in the form of a slave. Paul had made a similar surrender in terms of his own life. He had begun as a Jew, and a Jew especially aristocratic in descent, zealous for his religion, and blameless in his observance of the law. By surrendering this status Paul had taken the first step on the course of salvation laid out by Christ, and he counts the advantages he had thus given up as nothing in comparison with the prospect of gaining Christ and sharing in his resurrection. What he seeks is not a righteousness of his own, based on the law, but one that comes from God and is based on trust (Phil. 3:4–11). Thus the legal theory of Philippians—Paul's first attempt to deal with the issue of the Mosaic law as such—is really a restatement of the Christology of the letter.

But Philippians makes a significant contribution to the later legal theory in the contrast which it draws between the righteousness that comes from the law and the righteousness that comes from God through Christ's trust. In Philippians the word "trust" refers to Christ's confidence that God would vindicate him and raise him from the dead, as well as to a similar confidence on Paul's part, based on what God had done for Christ. In Galatians and Romans, "trust" acquires a more complex meaning, but the setting in which it is used in these letters is still that of the contrast between the two kinds of righteousness which first appears in Philippians.

The legal theory of II Corinthians 1–9 is considerably more involved with extraneous theological concerns than that of Philippians—ironically, in view of the fact that this letter's doctrine of the sufficiency of Christ's work of salvation was to form the substantive basis of Paul's final legal theory. As we have seen, II Corinthians 1–9 carries over from I Corinthians the idea that man needs a change in his nature if he is to be fitted for eternal life. The major innovation that it introduces is the teaching that, as a result of the death of Christ, the Christian is already dead and has already gained possession of a down payment of the spiritual nature necessary for eternal life, which he enjoys simultaneously with his original nature of flesh and blood, which is now wasting away. This teaching marks a significant change in emphasis in Paul's theology as over against the thinking of I Corinthians. In the earlier letter Christ had "died for our sins in accordance with the scriptures" (I Cor. 15:3). Here Paul's reference is apparently to the general Old Testament theory of the atoning sacrifice, and he very probably also has in mind the earlier application of this theory to the death of the servant in Isaiah 53. But in this system the death of Christ only begins his work of salvation as it affects the believer. The really significant change in the believer's nature will not take place until the parousia, when he will be raised with a new body of spirit if he has died, or be transformed from flesh to spirit if he is still alive. The three events in which Christ's work is accomplished are still death, resurrection, and parousia, of which parousia is still the climax. This system is at least partially preserved in Philippians, where the significant change in the living still does not take place until the parousia: "But our commonwealth is in heaven, and from it we await a Savior, the Lord Jesus Christ, who will change our lowly body to be like his glorious body, by the power which enables him even to subject all things to himself" (Phil. 3:20–21). But with II Corinthians 1–9 the parousia ceases to be the event which effectuates the all-important change in the believer's nature. Christ's death and resurrection, which have already taken place, are all that are required to bring it about; it now begins when a man "turns to the Lord" (II Cor. 3:16) and is completed when he dies and takes up his residence "with the Lord" (II Cor. 5:8).

It is this aspect of the teaching of II Corinthians 1–9 that is really relevant to the issue of the law, for the law represented a system of salvation to be earned, whereas the doctrine of II Corinthians 1–9 represents a system of salvation already effectuated as a gift. But the legal theory of II Corinthians 1–9 is still framed in terms of the natural concepts held over from Paul's resurrection teaching in I Corinthians rather than in terms of the legal sufficiency of Christ's work, with which the idea of an earned salvation is incompatible. The new covenant of the Christian (prefigured by Jeremiah) is a ministry of the Spirit, and gives life; the old covenant is a ministry of the letter, and kills; the new covenant is recorded in an epistle of Christ, written on men's hearts, not in ink but with the Spirit of the living God, while the old is engraved on stones; the new is of a permanent and greater glory; the old is of a lesser glory already fading when Moses delivered it to the Israelites, and destined from the beginning to be done away with completely at Christ's coming (II Cor. 3:2–11). This conception of the Mosaic law is obviously parallel to the conception of the Christian's possession of two natures simultaneously, but with the movement running in the opposite direction. The Christian has at once a body of flesh and one of spirit, of which the former will eventually disappear to be entirely replaced by the latter. The law had, until Christ's death and resurrection, a similarly double constitution, consisting of the tables of stone on which it was recorded and its own kind of glory; but in its case it was the glory that was destined to pass away, leaving nothing but its material nature, now dead.

This argument depends on an extraordinary exegesis of Exodus; but quite aside from that, it is based not on the juridical issues of the law's validity or of the way in which it functions as law, but on its nature—upon what it was made of—a line of argument which Paul was soon to abandon. What Paul omits from the legal argument of this letter is quite as significant as what he includes. If our salvation has been fully worked by Christ's death, without any act of our own whatever, then the law, which is a means of achieving righteousness, can have no part in the saving process. But, perhaps because the truth of Christ's saving work was so newly discovered by Paul, he failed to state this conclusion in II Corinthians 1-9. He would soon fully develop it in Galatians, however, in which he was to deal for the first time with the issue of circumcision in a letter addressed to a congregation which had been persuaded of its legal necessity.

Galatians presents Paul with an immediate and well-defined problem, and he limits his argument to this precise problem and bases it on the specifically juristic concepts that are intrinsic to it rather than, as in II Corinthians 1-9, on concepts that were originally eschatological and therefore not very closely related to the legal issue to begin with.

If we are to understand the legal argument of Galatians we must keep in mind two aspects of its teaching: it deals specifically with circumcision, and it treats circumcision as a legal requirement. The fact that this teaching is concerned with an initiatory rite fixes the scope of Paul's argument; its juridical nature fixes the juridical framework in which that argument is couched.

The Judaizers' argument must have been comparatively simple: a man must be righteous to be saved; righteousness consists in obeying

God's law; and God's law requires circumcision. Paul had no wish to deny the necessity of righteousness, but he could not accept his adversaries' simple view of its nature. Therefore, he set out to show that its source is not in obedience to law, but in the free gift of God, a gift that takes effect through Christ's death. His demonstration is couched in terms just as juristic as his adversaries'—if considerably more complicated.

All people, Galatians tells us, receive righteousness on exactly the same terms, through trust. Abraham trusted God, and his trust was accounted to him for righteousness; moreover, as a guarantee that all men, Jews and Gentiles alike, should receive righteousness through trust, Abraham was promised that in him all nations should be blessed (Gal. 3:6-9). This promise to Abraham was in the form of a testamentary trust, and it was addressed directly to two persons only, Abraham and a single descendant of his, Jesus Christ. But they received the promise in trust for all nations, who were by its original terms to be made beneficiaries by adoption through Christ as sons of God and descendants of Abraham. Christ had accepted this trust and by his death had satisfied all the accumulated obligations of the intended beneficiaries. Thus he had freed them for adoption. The adoption of each individual Christian is completed in his baptism, which makes him an heir of the promise on exactly the same terms as all other Christians. In the process he has shed his old juridical personality and acquired an entirely new and different one.

In reading Galatians one cannot but be struck with Paul's skill in preserving the substantial theological concerns of II Corinthians 1-9, while recasting them in legal language and indeed in a whole new legal framework. Christ's death is still, as in the earlier letter, the sole cause of our salvation, but it is now death thought of in exclusively legal terms. It is always referred to as crucifixion, a legal execution, and not simply as the dissolution of a natural body of flesh and blood. Its effect is juridical; it satisfies obligations which if unsatisfied would have kept the adoption and heirship from taking effect. In Galatians, as in II Corinthians 1-9, man's personality still stands in need of a radical change, but this change is completely juridically conceived; instead of needing to put off a naturally corruptible body in favor of one that is naturally incorruptible, he now needs to put off a juridical personality that is subject to the law and forfeit to its penalties in favor of one that is entirely new and free.

But if the argument of Galatians is precise and appropriate because the issue is clearly defined, its scope is limited by this very fact. The claim that circumcision is a legal precondition to salvation forces Paul to show how the Christian life is initiated, because circumcision is a rite of initiation. It does not force him to deal theologically with the way in which that life is lived after its initiation. Instead, it inspires in him a thoroughgoing aversion (however temporary) to the word "law," which in Galatians is always used in a pejorative sense. Galatians is, of course, concerned with ethical questions. But it does not deal with these questions in juridical terms, nor does it coordinate its treatment of them with its treatment of circumcision and the law. Instead, it still deals with them in the naturalistic terms of II Corinthians 1–9: vices are simply the works of the flesh, and virtues the fruits of the Spirit (Gal. 5:19–23). In this respect it differs from Romans, where legal theory and ethics are finally brought together in a single system.

All the earlier epistles had been written to congregations founded by Paul himself; Romans was written to a congregation that he had not even visited. He was, however, planning to come to them, stopping in Rome on his way to a missionary expedition in Spain, and he hoped that the Romans would contribute to the expenses of that trip. Although Paul did not know the congregation personally (and indeed did not seem to know the proportions of Jews and Gentiles that composed it) he apparently believed that reports of his teaching, particularly with respect to the law, had already reached them. Romans is Paul's introduction of himself and of his gospel.

In writing Romans, Paul had to deal with a number of problems. Some were implicit in his immediate position in relation to the congregation; some arose out of dangerous theological positions already taken in earlier letters (and particularly in Galatians); and some were necessarily involved in the process of synthesizing in a single coherent presentation the various doctrines which he had developed in response to several, and very different, kinds of challenges.

Implicit in his immediate relations with the Romans was the need to demonstrate that all men, without exception, stood in need of Paul's gospel, and conversely that that gospel fully satisfied their need. This meant that the scope of Romans must be much broader than that of Galatians. In the earlier epistles he had only to prove to a particular group who had been persuaded of the necessity of circumcision that they need not and indeed must not accept it. In Romans, in order to persuade the congregation to accept him and to share in the support of his wider missionary work, he must prove that all men, whether they were conscious of the need or not, must hear his gospel in order to be saved. And the more universal teaching of Romans must carry its own conviction, because the Roman congregation had been founded by another apostle, and Paul could not, as he could in Galatians, rely on his personal authority to carry his point.

This last consideration made it particularly important for Paul to develop a more complete and self-contained legal theory to present to the Romans. The legal theory of II Corinthians 1–9 had been based on concepts only distantly related to the immediate issue; that of Galatians had seemed by implication to leave in doubt the immediate sovereignty of God and the inspiration of Scripture as a whole; moreover, Galatians had failed to demonstrate the way in which God's sovereignty regulates the Christian life; it had failed to develop a doctrine of Christian law. These defects in the earlier legal theory had to be repaired in Paul's introduction of his teachings to the Romans.

But it was a summation of all his teachings, and not just his legal theory, that Paul must introduce. His theology had been, up to now, much more a series of answers to particular concrete questions than a systematic exposition of the relationship between God and man; the several aspects of this theology had therefore been couched in various different concepts, each appropriate to the question in response to which he had used it, and not related in any explicit, or even obvious, way to the others. Thus, Paul had dealt with the problem of death and resurrection in terms of corruptible and incorruptible bodies; he had dealt with the problem of the law in legal terms. In presenting his whole theology to the Romans, Paul must develop a single coordinate system in which these diverse concepts were interrelated.

The basic concepts of Romans, as of Galatians, are juristic; but Paul introduces juristic concepts not used in the earlier letter in the process of making his argument more universal in its application and of coordinating his ethic with his doctrine of salvation. God is now a sovereign and a judge rather than just a testator; man is now a guilty defendant rather than simply an incompetent devisee waiting for his inheritance. These new concepts raise new problems, notably the problem of theodicy and the problem of how the same rule of law can work evil in an evil legal system and good in a good one.

Universal need for salvation, put in juridical terms, is universal guilt. The Gentiles are guilty because they have wantonly refused to recognize that it is God's glory that shines in the created universe, and have worshiped what was created rather than the creator; this freely chosen confusion of the natural order has resulted in the abominable confusion of their own lives. The Jews are guilty because God has explicitly revealed his will to them and they have refused to do it. Thus, no one standing as defendant before God as judge can deserve acquittal on the basis of his own innocence. But acquittal is just what the Christian receives through Christ.

This raises a problem: if God is a just judge, how can he acquit the guilty? The answer is that he does so not by violating the law, but by satisfying its demands. The law imposes alternative penalties, either the death of the transgressor or the prescribed act of atonement, and God has provided Christ to be the atoning sacrifice. Thus, justice having received what it requires, the law has no further demand to make; it has been vindicated, not violated (Rom. 3:21–31).

Salvation, in Romans as in Galatians, comes as a gift transmitted through trust; it has been promised to Abraham and effectuated by Christ's death. The promise was trusted by Abraham, whose trust was accounted to him for righteousness; it was for the benefit not of Abraham's natural descendants but of all who share in his trust; and it results in adoption and heirship as well as in the declaration of the Christian's righteousness. But in Romans the testamentary trust is fitted into a scheme which is at once broader than that of Galatians in that it incorporates the Mosaic law rather than flatly denying its validity, while at the same time demonstrating that this law has no further claim to make upon the Christian. God is still the giver; it is he who has set forth Christ to be the atonement through his blood; and precisely because this is his gift, its function is not only to bring righteousness to the Christian, but at the same time to vindicate God's righteousness as judge. But this system of trust which satisfies the law nevertheless does so without the works of the law; and it is still, as in Galatians, wholly incompatible with any system of earning salvation by works of any kind.

The same situation that forces Paul to assert universal guilt makes it impossible for him to treat sin as nothing more than the individual's wrongdoing. Paul is perfectly conscious of the fact that every human act is powerfully influenced—often decisively influenced—by the social context in which the actor finds himself. No one acts in isolation from other people. And his very doctrine of a salvation worked vicariously by Christ forbids him to think of the sin from which Christ saves us as a purely individual matter, for if sin is nothing more than the individual's decision to do the wrong thing, there is nothing, in theory at least, to prevent the individual's changing his mind and consistently doing the right thing, quite independently of Christ. If Paul is to prove the absolute necessity of salvation through Christ for every man, he must show that sin is imposed on every man in such a way that he cannot escape it—that he is enslaved to it—whatever his personal decision may be. Paul therefore extends his concept of the relationship between man and God. Man is not simply an individual transgressor standing before God's tribunal; he is in his natural state an enemy of God, since he inhabits a world which has become subject to the sovereignty of sin and death. Sin is personified as a conquering sovereign. He has been admitted to this world by Adam; once admitted he brings death (also personified) in with him, and together they rule over everyone in this world, and not just those who have connived at their entrance—just as Hitler ruled over everyone in occupied Norway, and not just over the quislings who had betrayed their country to him. And, since sin can be imputed to the individual only if there is a law that he has broken, the law has been introduced into the kingdom of sin and death, to the end that each of their human subjects may participate in the process of his own condemnation (Rom. 5:12–14,20).

The concept of the law as the instrument of the sovereignty of sin is alluded to briefly in I Corinthians: "The sting of death is sin, and the power of sin is the law" (I Cor. 15:56). It is extended, in a direction which Paul was quickly to abandon, in Galatians: the law "was ordained by angels," while "the scripture consigned all things to sin" (Gal. 3:19,22). It is only fully developed in Romans.

In Romans, Paul conceives of the sovereign jurisdiction of sin and death, and therefore of the law which they enforce, as limited; their jurisdiction is limited to this world, over which they reign as a result of Adam's action. By dying to sin Christ has passed out of this jurisdiction; he is subject neither to sin nor to its law. By identification with Christ in his death—by baptism—the Christian has also passed out of their jurisdiction; he is free both of sin and of the law (Rom. 6:1–2,4). But if he subjects himself to either, whether by sinning with his members or by accepting the jurisdiction of the law (by being circumcised, for example), he again enslaves himself; he is back where he started (Rom. 6:15ff.).

The Christian has not only been removed from one jurisdiction; he has also been brought into another, that of God's immediate sovereignty. And this sovereignty, too, has its law, the law of trust, the law of the Spirit (Rom. 3:27;8:2). Thus the scheme of Romans incorporates two entirely separate systems of law, one the instrument of the sovereignty of sin, the other the instrument of the sovereignty of God. The latter governs the life of the Christian after baptism. In Romans the concept of righteousness plays an important part in the transition from salvation to continuing Christian life. The righteousness of Galatians is primarily a formal quantity, the thing that the law falsely claims to provide, the thing that is in fact transmitted through trust; the righteousness of Romans has a separate significance of its own—has, indeed, a double significance. It is both the declaration by God of the Christian's status as a righteous man—his acquittal, accomplished through Christ's trust—and his transformation into a man who acts righteously. Righteousness in short is Romans' juridical expression for both the event of the Christian's salvation and the quality of his life thereafter; it is the concept by which salvation and ethic are coordinated.

It is in terms of the conception of two systems of law, functioning as the instruments of two antithetical sovereignties, that Paul answers the obvious question which is implicit in his rejection of the Mosaic law, but which he has not faced in Galatians: How does one deal with the fact that some of the law's commands are obviously good? Paul's answer is based on the distinction between law in the sense of a whole legal system and law in the sense of a particular rule of law. The goodness or badness of a rule of law depends not simply on what it commands or forbids, but on the way in which it actually operates in the legal system of which it forms a part—and within the sovereignty of which it is the instrument. This means that a rule which would operate for good in a good legal system under a good sovereign operates for evil in an evil legal system under an evil sovereign. This is a proposition with which everyone living in an age of political unrest is sure to be confronted. For example, when Hitler occupied France he promulgated a great many rules regulating individual conduct—prohibiting personal violence, providing for the distribution of available foods, etc.—which were practically identical with the rules promulgated by the Third Republic for the regulation of the same areas of conduct. But these rules in the context of the occupation could work nothing but evil. If the individual violated them he would be punished by the Germans; if he obeyed them he would contribute to the strength of the German regime and would besides make himself liable to the charge of collaboration when the legitimate French regime was restored. He was enslaved to a situation in which any decision he made could lead only to death. In Romans, Paul sees the Jews in a similar situation.

But Paul is not content with a purely formal juristic answer to the question; he is also a subtle psychologist. He knows that in the context of evil the best rule can constitute an incitement to its own violation. It is only the inexperienced mother who does not know that "Don't touch the fresh cookies on the second shelf in the pantry," when spoken to a child, constitutes a temptation to do the very thing it forbids. Thus it is not the commandment in itself, but the context in which it is given and in which it is to be acted upon, that determines its effect.

Although the over-all argument of Romans is fitted into a juristic framework—a framework of sovereignty and jurisdiction—the naturalistic concepts held over from the Corinthian letters play at least as significant a part in the argument of Romans as they do in that of Galatians. In Galatians, Christ's death is always treated juridically, as crucifixion, legal execution. In Romans it is referred to simply as death; but this death has a juristic as well as a natural significance. It is the passage from this natural world, but this passage has a juridical consequence in removing Christ, together with those identified with him in baptism, from the sovereignty of sin into the sovereignty of God. And death has become a relative quantity; one is not simply dead in the naturalistic sense, one is either dead to sin and alive to God, or vice versa. Life and death are now not simply a characteristic of the individual himself, but his relationship with another being. This conception of death enables Paul to incorporate into the argument of Romans the positive value attributed to natural death in Philippians —though death is not of course a way to earn salvation, as in the earlier letter, but is the way in which the Christian is removed from the sovereignty of sin to that of God. Romans also relies heavily on the flesh-spirit dichotomy inherited from the Corinthian letters, but this dichotomy is now wholly moralized. Flesh is the seat of man's evil impulses, and spirit the source of the Christian's ability to obey God's law (Rom. 8:1ff.). Thus, the very language originally adopted by Paul to deal with the naturalistic problem of the substance of earthly and resurrection bodies is incorporated in the synthesis of Romans into a scheme of sin and atonement that is basically normative.

The conception of sovereignty, on which so much of the argument of Romans is based, carries with it a converse diminution of the natural autonomy of the individual man. Because he lives in this world he cannot escape the sovereignty of sin and death, which have entered it as sovereigns through Adam's betrayal. His sin is not simply his own act, it is also an inevitable slavery consequent upon the situation of the world in which he finds himself. And there is nothing whatever that he can do for himself to deliver himself from that slavery. Nor can anything in the natural state of any man equip him for salvation. Neither by inheritance nor by any action of his own can man deserve the salvation that comes as a gift through trust. The beneficiaries are chosen by God at his absolute good pleasure, as God chose Jacob over Esau while they were both yet unborn. God's sovereign will must prevail whether man obeys or disobeys him. His glory is shown in the pride and tyranny of Pharaoh, because God can by destroying Pharaoh show himself even mightier. The Jews, with their special position in the divine scheme, have refused the real righteousness that comes through trust, trying instead to earn their own righteousness by works, but this does not frustrate God's purpose. On the contrary, Paul believes that the Jews, seeing the inheritance go to the Gentiles, will finally change their minds and be willing to accept it themselves on God's terms. Paul does not go quite as far as Augustine in denying all freedom of choice to man, but he makes it abundantly clear that whatever man's choice may be, God's purpose will be realized through that choice.

With Romans, Paul's doctrine of law and grace reached its final form. But his over-all thought was to undergo one further significant development. And as on the two former occasions when a decisive experience had so filled his mind with a particular apprehension of Christ that all of his thinking became a reflection of that apprehension, so this final phase of his theological development was brought about by a similarly decisive experience. This was Paul's reconciliation with James and the leaders of the Jerusalem church at the time of the settlement of the controversy with the Judaizers.

Students of Paul's life have usually assumed that the controversy with the Judaizers lasted for a considerable length of time. Those critics who have imagined Galatians to be the earliest of the letters have even thought that it lasted for the whole of his missionary career. In point of fact, however, it was confined to a single year, the year of the Collection trip, and it had a definite beginning and a definite end. It began shortly after Paul's second visit to Jerusalem, when the Judaizers appeared in Antioch, and it ended when Paul returned to Jerusalem to deliver the collection. The settlement of the controversy is not described in the letters, but it is fully dealt with in Acts 15:1–33. This account, which comes from the Hellenist source, is undoubtedly a piece of history with a purpose, the purpose being to prove that the conservative tendencies of the later Jewish Christian church did not represent the principles of the original apostles. But there is no reason to doubt the substantial accuracy of the facts it relates. These are that both Peter and James declared themselves to be in agreement with Paul's position that Gentiles were not required to undertake the keeping of the whole law. James then suggested that "we should not trouble those of the Gentiles who turn to God, but should write to them to abstain from the pollutions of idols and from unchastity and from what is strangled and from blood." This suggestion met with the approval of "the apostles and elders, with the whole church," and James's suggestion was embodied in a letter "to the brethren who are of the Gentiles in Antioch and Syria and Cilicia." The letter began: "Since we have heard that some persons from us have troubled you with words, unsettling your minds, although we gave them no instructions, it has seemed good to us in assembly to choose men and send them to you with our beloved Barnabas and Paul, men who have risked their lives for the sake of our Lord Jesus Christ." The men chosen were Judas and Silas, and they delivered the letter in Antioch in person.

Before discussing the event itself, it may be well to speak briefly of two points that are commonly raised in connection with this account of it. The first of these is that the language of Peter's speech sounds too Pauline to be taken as an accurate representation of what he actually said. To this it may be answered that although the speech is not a verbatim report of Peter's remarks, there is no real reason for doubting that it represents Peter's position. Peter always takes the liberal position in the Hellenist source, and nowhere in the New Testament does he appear as the leader of a Jewish Christian faction antagonistic to Paul. The second point that is commonly raised about the Acts account of the Council is that the apostles' letter containing the decree of the Council is addressed only to Antioch and Syria and Cilicia, whereas it should have been addressed, according to those who raise the point, to Galatia and Macedonia and Achaia as well. Even on the assumption that the letter is being quoted in full in Acts (which it probably is not), the address really raises no problem. The letter was not addressed to the whole Gentile church, but only to those parts of it where the Judaizers had been active. If it does not mention Galatia by name, this is probably because it looks on the Galatian churches as connected in some way with the mission in Cilicia, as does Galatians itself (cf. Gal. 1:21), and there is no evidence that the Judaizers ever penetrated Macedonia and Achaia. Thus there is nothing intrinsically improbable about the address as it stands. Indeed, the account of the Council in Acts agrees with the evidence of the letters at every point where it can be checked, and those points are more significant than is usually recognized.

The Pauline letters do not describe the Council itself. They give us a clear picture of Paul's feelings just before the Council took place, however, and another clear picture of his feelings after it was over, and by comparing the two we can infer without a great deal of difficulty what had happened in the meantime. The most obvious point at which to begin the comparison is in connection with the law. The letters of the collection period are bitter in their hostility to the law. As early as I Corinthians the law is the power of sin; in II Corinthians 1–9 it is the dispensation of death; in Galatians it is the instrument by which the elemental spirits hold men in slavery; and in Romans it is the means by which sin finds its opportunity to reign in men's mortal bodies. The last three collection letters contain elaborate arguments in support of Paul's contention that the Christian who submits to the law forfeits his salvation. The letters written after the Council, however, contain no such arguments. On the contrary, they assume their acceptance. Thus, in Colossians, Paul merely states that Christ has "disarmed the principalities and powers," and he treats "regulations," such as "Do not handle. Do not taste. Do not touch," as merely "human precepts and doctrines" which "are of no value in checking the indulgences of the flesh." This is a far cry from his earlier position that the law was the instrument of slavery to the elemental spirits, and that those who pursued the righteousness of the law were "severed from Christ" (Gal. 5:4). In Ephesians he can even quote the commandment, "Honor your father and mother," though he does point out that "this is the first commandment with a promise" (Eph. 6:2). In other words, the binding force of the law for Christians is no longer a matter of controversy in these letters, and Paul is no longer concerned to warn his readers against the Judaizers or to refute their arguments. Nor is he further concerned with the specific issue of circumcision. To the Colossians he writes, "In him also you were circumcised with a circumcision made without hands, by putting off the body of flesh in the circumcision of Christ" (Col. 2:11); and in Ephesians, after reminding his Gentile readers that according to the flesh they were "called the uncircumcision" by the members of "what is called the circumcision, which is made in the flesh by hands," he goes on to explain that the two had been made one by Christ, who "has broken down the dividing wall of hostility, by abolishing in his flesh the law of commandments and ordinances" (Eph. 2:11-15). Here circumcision and uncircumcision are simply descriptive designations, and there is not only no suggestion of a continuing controversy between the two, there is the positive statement that Christ has reconciled them both to God through the cross, "thereby bringing the hostility to an end" (Eph. 2:16). This can only mean that between the end of the Collection trip and the writing of Colossians and Ephesians the controversy had been settled, and settled in Paul's favor. He no longer had anything to fear from "those of the circumcision" in the Jerusalem church. This is exactly what Acts tells us happened at the Council.

Even more revealing is the change in Paul's attitude toward the apostles. There can be no doubt but that Paul regarded the movement to Judaize the church of Antioch and its missions as directed chiefly at himself. In Philippians he writes, "Some indeed preach Christ from envy and rivalry . . . out of partisanship, not sincerely but thinking to afflict me in my imprisonment" (Phil. 1:15-17). When this was written, Paul was under great stress of mind, but it clearly reveals that he looked on the activities of the Judaizers as a calculated effort to persecute him. Nor can there be any question but that Paul believed that the movement had originated with James. He is explicit about this in Galatians, where he describes the beginning of the effort as having revealed itself in Antioch when "certain men came from James" (Gal. 2:12). To Paul this represented the betrayal on the part of James of the agreement that had been reached in Jerusalem only a short time before, when James and Cephas and John had given Paul and Barnabas "the right hand of fellowship, that we should go to the Gentiles and they to the circumcised" (Gal. 2:9). Peter's betrayal of the agreement Paul attributed to lack of moral courage, "for before certain men came from James, he ate with the Gentiles; but when they came he drew back and separated himself, fearing those of the circumcision" (Gal. 2:12). The rest of the Jews, Paul adds, "acted insincerely, so that even Barnabas was carried away by their insincerity" (Gal. 2:13).

To what extent the Judaizers may have thought they represented the real feelings of James we shall never know. According to Acts the apostles and elders asserted later that "we gave them no instructions" (Acts 15:24), and there is no reason to suppose that this is an inaccurate statement. But when the Judaizers first appeared in Antioch, Paul had believed otherwise, and the letters of the collection period are bitterly scornful in their references to the apostles. This unfriendliness is barely concealed in I Corinthians, where Paul asks whether he and Barnabas do not "have the right to be accompanied by a wife, as the other apostles and the brothers of the Lord and Cephas"; he ends with more than a touch of irony: "Or is it only Barnabas and I who have no right to refrain from working for a living?" (I Cor. 9:5-6). The bitterness is more open in II Corinthians 10–13, where Paul refers contemptuously to the Jewish missionaries in Corinth as "these superlative apostles" (II Cor. 11:5). And it is completely undisguised in Galatians, where he refers to James and Cephas and John as those "who were reputed to be pillars" (Gal. 2:6,9).

On the other hand, the Acts account of the Council not only pictures Peter and James as siding with Paul in the controversy with the Judaizers but also contains the assertion that the Judaizers had not been acting under instructions from Jerusalem. And Colossians and Ephesians, written after the Council, reflect exactly the change of attitude toward the apostles that we should expect to find if what Acts describes as having occurred at the Council did in fact take place. Not only do these letters contain no trace of the bitterness toward the apostles that is so apparent in the letters of the collection period; on the contrary, they go out of their way to emphasize the peace and unity that now reign in the church. Thus Colossians speaks of the work of Christ as "making peace by the blood of his cross" (Col. 1:20). Christ is the head of the church, "through whom the whole body, nourished and knit together through its joints and ligaments, grows with a growth that is from God" (Col. 2:19). "Here there cannot be Greek and Jew, circumcised and uncircumcised, barbarian, Scythian, slave, free man, but Christ is all, and in all" (Col. 3:11). The Colossians are to "put on love, which binds everything together in perfect harmony"; and they are to "let the peace of Christ rule" in their hearts, to which indeed they "were called in the one body" (Col. 3:14–15). Ephesians is even more explicit about the reconciliation that has taken place. There Christ "is our peace, who has made us both one, and has broken down the dividing wall of hostility . . . that he might create in himself one new man in place of the two, so making peace, and might reconcile us both to God in one body through the cross, thereby bringing the hostility to an end" (Eph. 2:14–16). The Gentile recipients of the letter "are no longer strangers and sojourners, but . . . fellow citizens with the saints and members of the household of God, built upon the foundation of the apostles and prophets" (Eph. 2:19–20). And "the mystery of Christ . . . has now been revealed to his holy apostles and prophets by the Spirit; that is, how the Gentiles are fellow heirs, members of the same body, and partakers of the promise in Christ Jesus through the gospel" (Eph. 3:4–6). This last is an exact description, from Paul's point of view, of what had happened at the Council. The Jerusalem apostles and elders had disavowed all responsibility for the activities of the Judaizers and had repudiated those who had said that it was necessary to circumcise Gentile converts and to charge them to keep the law of Moses (Acts 15:5). In other words, the agreement that Paul had reached with James and Cephas and John before the Collection trip was reaffirmed. And as far as James and Cephas were concerned (John seems not to have been present at the Council) there had never been any intention that it should be broken.

The recognition of this fact places the Council in a new light. Students of the life of Paul naturally depend very heavily on the letters for evidence about the Judaistic controversy. On the basis of this evidence the picture they draw is of a valiant struggle on Paul's part to free the Gentile church once and for all from the legal shackles which the Jewish church still stubbornly insisted must be imposed on it. It is inevitable that they should draw this picture, for it is the picture that

Paul drew of it himself in the letters that were written while the controversy was going on.

But the letters which draw this picture, although they account for about 85 of the approximately 110 pages which Paul's total correspondence occupies, all come from a single brief period in Paul's life, and the letters which were written before and after this period do not draw this picture at all. Those that come before it know nothing of any contention on the part of the Jewish Christian church that the Gentile churches should keep the Jewish law, and those that come after it reveal that the controversy had not been as serious as it had seemed to Paul while it was in progress. In other words, Paul now realized that he had magnified the controversy out of all proportion to its real importance, and not only that, but that his accusation against James and the other leaders of the Jerusalem church had been false.

It is not difficult to see the point at which Paul began to realize that this was the case. It falls between the composition of Galatians and that of Romans. The former letter is severe in its indictment of James and Peter for having, as Paul thought, gone back on the agreement that had been reached in Jerusalem. The latter is noticeably conciliatory. Not only does it contain no criticism of the apostles, but it also takes pains to soften the harsher statements of Galatians about the law. In addition, it contains an extended section, beginning with the ninth chapter, devoted to Paul's concern for the Jews. The topic is introduced in the following words:

> I am speaking the truth in Christ, I am not lying; my conscience bears me witness in the Holy Spirit, that I have great sorrow and increasing anguish in my heart. For I could wish that I myself were accursed and cut off from Christ for the sake of my brethren, my kinsmen by race. They are Israelites, and to them belong the sonship, the glory, the covenants, the giving of the law, the worship, and the promises; to them belong the patriarchs, and of their race, according to the flesh, is the Christ (Rom. 9:1-5).

This is a very different note from anything we have heard before, and it clearly reflects a change of heart on Paul's part. That the change involved Paul's attitude toward the Jerusalem church is borne out by the words with which he ends the letter:

255

> At present, however, I am going to Jerusalem with aid for
> the saints. For Macedonia and Achaia have been pleased to make
> some contribution for the poor among the saints at Jerusalem;
> they were pleased to do it, and indeed they are in debt to them,
> for if the Gentiles have come to share in their spiritual blessings,
> they ought also to be of service to them in material blessings. . . .
> I appeal to you, brethren, by our Lord Jesus Christ and by the
> love of the Spirit, to strive together with me in your prayers to
> God on my behalf, that I may be delivered from the unbelievers
> in Judea, and that my service for Jerusalem may be acceptable to
> the saints (Rom. 15:25–27, 30–31).

It is in this light that the story of the Council must be read. When
Paul came to Jerusalem it was not as the valiant champion of a freedom
which the apostles had tried to take away; it was as a man who had
charged them, in bitter terms, with an action which they had not
committed. But instead of being rejected by them, as he feared he
might be, he was received as a brother. He and Barnabas were treated
as "our beloved Barnabas and Paul, men who have risked their lives
for the sake of our Lord Jesus Christ" (Acts 15:25–26), and the very
apostles whom he had falsely accused of betraying him rose to speak
in his defense. In a word, what Paul experienced at the Council was
not merely vindication of the position he had taken during the controversy, but forgiveness from those he had wronged.

We have already referred to this experience as constituting for Paul
a new vision of Christ, and in a very real sense it was just that. Not
that it was in form like his initial vision of Christ on the Damascus
road, or even like his second, the inward "knowing" of the suffering
Christ that had come to him in the prison at Ephesus. This was a
glimpse of the human Jesus as he had lived among men, and Paul
had caught this glimpse by experiencing the forgiveness of the Jerusalem apostles and realizing that it was a reflection of the forgiveness
of Christ.

The final letters, for all the cosmic dimensions of their Christology,
are deeply colored by Paul's memory of this experience, and the dominant note in their description of Christ is as the one whose earthly
life had been an incarnation of the love and forgiveness of God. Indeed,
the principal change in the Christology of the last letters, as over
against the letters written before the Council, is in the emphasis on

the completeness of the divine nature of Christ during his earthly life. Although he wore a body of flesh, and performed the work of reconciliation "in his body of flesh by his death" (Col. 1:22), "in him all the fulness was pleased to dwell" (Col. 1:19). It was therefore unnecessary, and indeed impossible, for him to acquire a new nature by virtue of his resurrection, and nowhere in the last letters does Paul imply that such a change took place in him.

But if Christ did not need a change in his nature, man did need a change in his. According to the early letters man would undergo this necessary change at the parousia, when the dead would be raised and the living transformed; according to the middle letters he was in the process of undergoing it during his earthly life; according to the last letters he had already undergone it: he had already been raised with Christ and "come to fulness of life with him" (Col. 2:10). It is not difficult to see in this final modification of Paul's eschatology a reflection of his experience of forgiveness and reconciliation at the Council. Peter and James, as they acted there, did not resemble men in "the image of the man of dust" who would one day be changed into "the image of the man of heaven" (I Cor. 15:49). Nor were they in the process of "being changed into his likeness" (II Cor. 3:18), having acquired a partial measure of the new nature as a down payment. The change had already taken place in them; they were already like Christ. Henceforth, Paul was to speak of all Christians as men in whom such a change had taken place, addressing them as having "Christ in you" (Col. 1:27), and calling the church itself "the fulness of him who fills all in all" (Eph. 1:23). His own ministry of proclamation and warning and teaching was now to "present every man mature in Christ" (Col. 1:28), until all should attain "to the measure of the stature of the fulness of Christ" (Eph. 4:13). In spite of the strangeness of much of this language to modern ears, what Paul is saying is that the change in man's nature which is essential to the salvation of the individual, and of society, and of the cosmos itself, is the change that takes place when he becomes like the earthly Christ. The distinguishing mark of this change is forgiveness.

It is an oft-repeated commonplace of New Testament theology that where the Gospels speak of forgiveness the Pauline epistles speak of justification. Like many generalizations of this kind, this statement is at best only partly true. To begin with, only the letters of the collection period treat justification as lying at the heart of the Christian message; the Thessalonian letters do not mention it, and Colossians and Ephesians although they are aware of the idea, avoid the term "justification" and use "forgiveness" in its place. Thus both letters restate the doctrine of Romans: "Since all have sinned and fall short of the glory of God, they are justified by his grace as a gift, through the redemption which is in Christ Jesus, whom God put forward as an expiation, through faith [trust], by his blood" (Rom. 3:23–25). Colossians puts the same idea in different words: "You were also raised with him through faith in the working of God, who raised him from the dead. And you, who were dead in trespasses and the uncircumcision of your flesh, God made alive together with him, having forgiven us all our trespasses" (Col. 2:12–13). Ephesians is even more explicit: "In him we have redemption through his blood, the forgiveness of our trespasses, according to the riches of his grace which he lavished upon us" (Eph. 1:7–8); and it repeats the idea in a later passage: "But God . . . even when we were dead through our trespasses, made us alive together with Christ . . . . For by grace you have been saved through faith" (Eph. 2:4–5,8). In all of these passages, as in Colossians and Ephesians throughout, it is forgiveness with which Paul is dealing, and in the last of them, where we expect Paul to say, "By grace you have been *justified* through faith," he seems to have deliberately suppressed the word "justified" and substituted the broader and more general term "saved." Colossians and Ephesians, in other words, although they retain the substance of the doctrine of justification by faith, have given up calling it that. In these letters the work of Christ does not result in justification, but in "redemption, the forgiveness of sins" (Col. 1:14), or in the fuller language of Ephesians, "redemption through his blood, the forgiveness of our trespasses" (Eph. 1:7).

This new emphasis is particularly noticeable in the ethical teaching of the two letters. The letters of the early and middle periods do not put a great deal of emphasis on forgiveness as a Christian virtue. The earliest letters do not mention it at all, and the letters of the collection period do so only casually. Paul writes in II Corinthians 1–9 that the

Corinthians should forgive the offender who "has caused pain" (II Cor. 2:5–7) and adds, "Any one whom you forgive, I also forgive. What I have forgiven, if I have forgiven anything, has been for your sake in the presence of Christ, to keep Satan from gaining the advantage over us" (II Cor. 2:10–11). And in Romans he writes, "Repay no one evil for evil, but take thought for what is noble in the sight of all. If possible, so far as it depends upon you, live peaceably with all. Beloved, never avenge yourselves, but leave it to the wrath of God; for it is written, 'Vengeance is mine, I will repay, says the Lord.' No, 'if your enemy is hungry, feed him; if he is thirsty, give him drink; for by so doing you will heap burning coals upon his head.' Do not be overcome by evil, but overcome evil with good" (Rom. 12:17–21). This is forgiveness with prudential overtones. But in Colossians and Ephesians, forgiveness becomes the chief virtue of the Christian. There Paul writes, "Put on then, as God's chosen ones, holy and beloved, compassion, kindness, lowliness, meekness, and patience, forbearing one another and, if one has a complaint against another, forgiving each other; as the Lord has forgiven you, so you also must forgive" (Col. 3:12–13). The prudential note is sounded again, briefly, in Ephesians: "Be angry but do not sin; do not let the sun go down on your anger, and give no opportunity to the devil" (Eph. 4:26–27). But it is subordinated to what follows: "Let all bitterness and wrath and anger and clamor and slander be put away from you, with all malice, and be kind to one another, tenderhearted, forgiving one another, as God in Christ forgave you" (Eph. 4:31–32). Colossians and Ephesians, in other words, reflect an apprehension of Christ which is not found in the other letters. This is the vision of the Jesus whose message had been about forgiveness and whose life had been an example of the forgiveness which he taught. There is no sign of this apprehension in the letters written before the Council, but it is reflected on every page of those written after it. The evidence all points to the conclusion that it had come to Paul at that time.

The development of Paul's theology, therefore, was essentially the reflection of the deepening of his knowledge of Christ. His earliest apprehension of Christ had been of the exalted and glorified Lord who was soon to return to earth and establish the kingdom. This was the Lord he had seen on the Damascus road, and it is this Lord whom we find proclaimed in the earliest letters. His second apprehension of Christ had been of the one whose atoning death had brought justification by freeing men from slavery to sin and thus making possible their adoption as sons of God. This was the Christ he had come to know in the prison in Ephesus, and it is this Christ whom we find pictured in the letters of the collection period. His final apprehension of Christ was of the one who had lived an earthly life of love and forgiveness and had taught his followers to live a similar life. This was the Christ whom he had seen reflected in the forgiveness of James and Cephas when he returned to Jerusalem at the end of the controversy with the Judaizers, and it is this Christ whom he urges the readers of his last letters to imitate, praying that he may dwell in their hearts.

Paul was aware of this process of growth as it had taken place in his life, and he was also aware that God's purpose would only be completely fulfilled when it had taken place in all men. The words in which he speaks of that fulfillment make a fitting close to this study:

> **But grace was given to each of us according to the measure of Christ's gift. . . . And his gifts were that some should be apostles, some prophets, some evangelists, some pastors and teachers, for the equipment of the saints, for the work of ministry, for building up the body of Christ, until we all attain to the unity of the faith and of the knowledge of the Son of God, to mature manhood, to the measure of the stature of the fulness of Christ (Eph. 4:7, 11–13).**

INDEXES

Index of Scriptural Passages

(Page references are italicized)

Genesis
    1:26f., *65*
    2:7, *65*
    3:16, *61*
    15:6, *96*
    17:4, *97*
    17:7, *96*
Exodus
    20:1ff., *29*
    34:33, *63, 72*
Leviticus
    18:5, *97*
Deuteronomy
    21:23, *97*
    25:4, *61*
    27:26, *97*
Psalms
    68:18, *131*

Isaiah
    53, *239*
Daniel
    7:25, *159f.*
    8:25, *161*
    11:32, *161*
    11:36, *159*
    11:45, *160*
    12:1–4, 7, 11–13, *160*
Habakkuk
    2:4, *97*
Matthew
    12:28, *147*
Mark
    13:8, *149*
    13:14, *155*
Luke
    2:1–4, *202f.*

Luke
    11:20, *147*
John
    11:17, *60*
Acts
    6:1–11:30, *195, 205*
    6:9, 12, *201*
    7:1, 2–53, *201*
    7:53, *98*
    8:4–25, *197*
    8:26–40, *197*
    9:1–9, *220*
    9:3, 4, 7, *225*
    9:17, *201*
    9:20, *220*
    9:26–30, *180, 201*
    9:29, 30, *201*
    9:32–35, 36–43, *197*
    10:1–48, *197*
    11:1–18, *197*
    11:2, *199*
    11:19–26, *205*
    11:22ff., *183*
    11:25f., *201*
    11:26, 27, *202*
    11:27–30, *181, 198, 202f., 205*
    11:28, *184, 211*
    11:29–30, *184*
    11:30, *201*
    12:1, *199*
    12:1–23, *195*
    12:25, *181ff., 186, 195, 201, 203, 205*
    13:1, *191*
    13:1–14:28, *191, 194f., 205*
    13:6–12, *192*
    13:50, *188*
    14:17, *207*
    15:1, *185*
    15:1–33, *181, 185, 195, 205, 249*
    15:5, *185, 199, 201, 254*
    15:24, *253*
    15:25–26, *256*
    15:29, *8*
    15:33, *204*
    15:36, *191*

Acts
    15:36–18:22, *186, 205*
    15:36–20:3, *194f., 205*
    15:40, *204*
    16:1–3, *193*
    16:3, *237*
    16:9–15, *205f.*
    16:10–16, *194*
    16:16–40, *192*
    16:37–39, *207*
    17:5–9, *192*
    17:6f., *207*
    17:10–15, *140*
    18:1, *140*
    18:2, *211f.*
    18:5, *140*
    18:12, *211*
    18:12–17, *192*
    18:19–21, *193*
    18:22, *191*
    18:22–23, *205*
    18:23–19:8, *205*
    18:23–20:3, *191*
    18:24–19:7, *189*
    19:8–9, *189, 207*
    19:23–41, *192*
    20:1–3, *209*
    20:2–3, *193*
    20:3, *213*
    20:4–16, *206*
    20:6, 16, *214*
    20:17–38, *206*
    21:1–17, *206*
    21:15ff., *181*
    21:17–26, *206*
    21:20–25, 26ff., *207*
    22:1–21, *206f.*
    22:4–16, *220*
    22:7–9, *225*
    22:17–21, *221f.*
    22:24–29, *207*
    23:33ff., *68*
    24:5, *207*
    24:17, *188*
    24:27, *211, 214*

Acts
26:2–23, *207*
26:9–18, *220*
26:14, *225*
26:25–27, 29, *207*
27:1–28:16, *206*
27:9–12, *214*
28:16ff., *68*
Romans
1:1–6, *127*
2:15, *12, 98*
3:21–31, *244*
3:23–25, *258*
3:24–25, *101, 118*
3:27, *246*
3:31, *99*
4:13, *100*
5:9, *138*
5:12–14, 20, *245*
6:1–4, *246*
6:2–11, *91*
6:3, *14*
6:3–5, *116*
6:3–11, *142*
6:5, *92*
6:6–11, *100*
6:8, 11, *14*
6:12, *99*
6:15ff., *246*
6:16–17, 20, *99*
7:4–6, *91*
7:6, *100*
7:7, *99f.*
7:7–11, *235*
7:9–11, *100*
7:12, 22, 23, *99*
7:24, *92, 130*
7:25, *100*
8:1ff., *248*
8:1–11, *101*
8:2, *100, 246*
8:2–25, *84ff.*
8:3, *73*
8:4, *100*
8:9–13, *92*

Romans
8:18, *92f.*
8:19, *92*
8:23, *92f.*
8:25, *12*
8:29, *131*
8:35, *149*
9:1–5, *255*
10:12, *136*
11:8, *12*
12:5, *133*
12:17–21, *259*
13:12–14, *137*
15:19, *165, 167*
15:23, *171*
15:24–29, *27*
15:25, *166, 183*
15:25–27, *256*
15:25–32, *181*
15:26, *184*
15:30–31, *256*
15:31, *149, 183*
16:22, *78*
I Corinthians
1:8–9, *231*
1:11–12, *108f.*
1:13–17, *78*
1:18, *138*
1:24, *66*
1:25, *66, 109*
2:7, 9, *229*
2:10, *11*
2:12, *11, 13*
2:12–13, *57, 229*
3:1–2, *38, 94*
3:1–4, *230*
3:5, *109*
3:6–9, 9–17, *136*
3:11, *134*
3:12–15, *228*
3:13–15, *89*
3:18, *229*
4:14, 18–19, *107*
4:21, *107f.*
5:1–5, *59*

I Corinthians
  5:2, *56, 89*
  5:3, *57*
  5:5, *56f.*
  5:7f., *28*
  5:9, *24, 31*
  5:9–13, *42f.*
  6:9, *94*
  6:11, *61, 94f.*
  6:12, *62*
  7:1, *31, 42*
  7:8–9, *36*
  7:10–11, *61*
  7:12, *110*
  7:39–40, *62*
  7:40, *11, 57, 110*
  8:1, *62*
  8:1ff., *50*
  8:1–11:1, *34*
  8:8, *62*
  9:1, *89, 219, 222*
  9:5–6, *253*
  9:9, *61*
  9:19–23, *36, 62, 235*
  9:20, *94*
  10.1–11, *28*
  10:23, *62*
  10:31–11:1, *62f.*
  11:27–32, *57*
  11:28–30, *59*
  11:30, *13*
  12:1–14:40, *35*
  12:8–9, *88f.*
  12:27, *133, 136*
  13:1, *35*
  13:2, *89*
  13:13, *62, 89*
  14:18–19, *36f.*
  14:23, *50*
  14:33–34, *61*
  15:1–2, *138, 219*
  15:1–8, *40*
  15:3, *73, 238*
  15:8, *219, 222*
  15:12, 20, *40*

I Corinthians
  15:21, *72, 143*
  15:21–22, *65*
  15:23–26, *40*
  15:23–28, *228*
  15:29, *40*
  15:31, *13*
  15:35, *40*
  15:36–38, *41*
  15:42–44, *41*
  15:44, *142*
  15:45, *16, 65*
  15:45–49, *143*
  15:47–49, *65*
  15:49, *257*
  15:51, *14, 54, 142*
  15:51–52, *13, 59, 93*
  15:51–55, *42*
  15:52, *14, 54*
  15:53, *137*
  15:54, *14*
  15:56, *235, 246*
  15:58, *89*
  16:1, *169*
  16:1–11, *24*
  16:2–4, *32*
  16:6, *173f.*
  16:7, *169*
  16:8, *28, 172, 189*
  16:10, *89*
  16:12, *189*
  16:15, *183*
  16:15–16, *49*
  16:21, *78*
II Corinthians
  1:6, *11, 110*
  1:8–10, *58, 92*
  1:9, *13, 60, 69*
  1:12, *111f.*
  1:14, *56*
  1:23, *107*
  1:24, *111*
  2:1, *105f., 167*
  2:3–4, *107*
  2:4, *113*

II Corinthians
 2:5–7, *258f.*
 2:9, *107*
 2:10–11, *259*
 2:12–13, *26*
 2:15, *138*
 2:17, *64, 111*
 3:1, *111, 113*
 3:2–11, *239*
 3:3, *63*
 3:4–18, *93*
 3:6, *12, 61, 98*
 3:7, *16, 61, 63, 224*
 3:9, *61*
 3:10, *63*
 3:13, *63, 72*
 3:14, *63, 98*
 3:16, *54, 239*
 3:17–18, *54*
 3:17–5:5, *84ff.*
 3:18, *13, 54, 224, 257*
 4:2, 5, *111*
 4:7, *54*
 4:10, *110*
 4:11, *14*
 4:14, *14, 56*
 4:16, *13*
 4:16–18, *55*
 5:1–4, *55, 93, 137*
 5:1–5, *142*
 5:5, *54*
 5:6, *56, 92, 116*
 5:8, *56, 60, 92, 116, 239*
 5:11, *111*
 5:12, 13, *113*
 5:14, *14, 90f., 116*
 5:14–15, *58*
 5:16, *11, 16*
 5:16–17, *58*
 5:16–19, *64*
 5:18, *119*
 5:19, *16, 101, 131*
 5:21, *73*
 6:1–10, *127*
 6:2, *138*

II Corinthians
 6:14–7:1, *43*
 7:2–3, *111*
 7:5–16, *26f.*
 7:6–16, *106*
 7:8, *107*
 7:13–14, *106f.*
 7:14, *112*
 8:1–7, *25*
 8:3, *80*
 8:4, *27, 80, 183*
 8:6, *27*
 8:10, *29*
 8:14, *27*
 8:18–19, 20–21, *111*
 8:24, *112*
 9:1–5, *25*
 9:2, *29, 162*
 9:2–3, *112*
 9:8, *89*
 10:4–5, *109*
 10:6, *107*
 10:7, 12, *109*
 10:13, *112*
 10:14, *167*
 10:15, *108, 112*
 10:16, 17, *112*
 10:18, *111ff.*
 11:4–5, *108*
 11:5, *253*
 11:6, *109*
 11:7, *108*
 11:8, *109*
 11:9, *167*
 11:10, *112*
 11:10–11, *113*
 11:12, *108, 112*
 11:12–15, *224*
 11:13, *108*
 11:16, *112*
 11:17, *109f.*
 11:17–18, *112*
 11:19–21, *110*
 11:21, *112, 224*
 11:22, *108, 236*

II Corinthians
  11:23, *113*
  11:23–25, *68f.*
  11:23–27, *110*
  11:30, *112*
  11:33, *110*
  12:1, *110, 112, 224*
  12:1–4, *104*
  12:1–5, *220f.*
  12:7, *104, 110, 223*
  12:7–9, *223*
  12:9, *110, 112, 223*
  12:16–18, *111*
  12:17–18, *108*
  13:1–3, *104*
  13:2, *107, 167*
  13:10, *107*
Galatians
  1:9, 10, *94*
  1:11–12, *219*
  1:13–2:14, *163f.*
  1:15–16, *219*
  1:16, *104*
  1:18, 7, *82*
  1:18–20, *180*
  1:21, *251*
  2:1, 7, *82, 104*
  2:1–10, *181*
  2:2, *184*
  2:6, *253*
  2:9, *252f.*
  2:10, *83, 149, 165, 184*
  2:11ff., *83, 185*
  2:12, *252f.*
  2:13, *253*
  2:15–16, *95, 222f.*
  2:19–20, *142*
  2:20, *91, 116, 130*
  2:21, *95*
  3:2, *95*
  3:2–5, *89f.*
  3:6, *96*
  3:6–9, *241*
  3:8, *96*
  3:9, *96f.*

Galatians
  3:10, 11, 12, 13, 14, 15, 17, 18, *97*
  3:19, *246*
  3:19–20, *98*
  3:22, *246*
  3:27, *137*
  3:27–28, *135f.*
  4:1–5:17, *84ff.*
  4:3, *98f.*
  4:4–5, *101*
  4:5, *118*
  4:9, *99*
  5:4, *251*
  5:5, *92*
  5:11, *94, 236*
  5:19–23, *242*
  6:8, *92*
  6:11, *78*
  6:14, *91*
Ephesians
  1:1–3:19, *127f.*
  1:3–8, *132*
  1:3–14, *127*
  1:4, *131*
  1:7–8, *258*
  1:9–10, *172*
  1:11–14, *133*
  1:15–23, *127*
  1:23, *133, 257*
  2:1–7, *127*
  2:4–5, *258*
  2:4–6, *139*
  2:4–7, *129*
  2:6, *134*
  2:8, *139, 258*
  2:11–15, *252*
  2:11–22, *135*
  2:12–16, *173, 254*
  2:16, *252*
  2:19, *173*
  2:19–20, *254*
  2:20, *134, 173*
  2:21, *136*
  3:1–7, *127*
  3:4–6, *134, 173, 254*

Ephesians
  3:10, *133*
  3:14–19, *134*
  3:17, *136*
  4:7, *260*
  4:8–9, *131*
  4:11–13, *260*
  4:13, *134, 257*
  4:15–16, *134*
  4:16, *136*
  4:22–24, *130, 137f.*
  4:26–27, 31–32, *259*
  6:2, *251*
  6:11–17, *136*

Philippians
  1:12–13, *10*
  1:12–14, *69*
  1:15–17, *74, 170, 252*
  1:19, *232*
  1:19–24, *69*
  1:23, *70, 92, 116, 142*
  1:24–25, *174*
  1:25, *232*
  2:5–8, *143*
  2:5–11, *71, 100f.*
  2:7, *11*
  2:9, *73*
  2:12, *75*
  2:13, *76*
  2:30–3:2, *76f.*
  3:1–6, *74*
  3:2–3, *170, 235*
  3:4–11, *238*
  3:5, *185*
  3:7–11, *74f.*
  3:9, *235*
  3:10–11, *232*
  3:10–15, *70*
  3:15, *233*
  3:20–21, *71, 234, 239*
  3:21, *93*
  4:2–3, *78*
  4:4, *78*
  4:15–16, *166f.*

Colossians
  1:1–2:7, *127f.*
  1:12, *117*
  1:13, *117, 130, 138*
  1:14, *258*
  1:15–16, *131*
  1:15–17, *119*
  1:18, *133f.*
  1:19, *74, 131, 257*
  1:19–20, *11, 119, 131*
  1:21–22, *135*
  1:22, *138, 257*
  1:24, 26–27, *133*
  1:27, 28, *257*
  2:7, *136*
  2:9, *119*
  2:10, *257*
  2:10–15, *119f.*
  2:11, *252*
  2:12, *138*
  2:13–15, *131f.*
  2:16, *172*
  2:19, *253f.*
  2:20, *131, 172*
  2:20–23, *120*
  2:22, *131*
  3:1, *117, 138, 142*
  3:1–3, *71*
  3:1–4, *14, 93, 129*
  3:3–4, 5, *117*
  3:9–10, *120, 130, 137*
  3:9–11, *136*
  3:11, *254*
  3:12, *117*
  3:12–13, *258f.*
  3:12–14, *137*
  3:14–15, *254*
  3:25, *122*
  4:1–4, *5*
  4:7–9, 10, 12, *121*
  4:14, *121, 210*
  4:15, *121*
  4:16, *139*
  4:17, *121*
  4:18, *78*

I Thessalonians
1:4–5, *230*
1:10, *65, 143, 148*
2:11–12, *117*
2:14–16, *147*
2:15–16, *236*
2:16, *12*
2:17, *140*
2:17–18, *51*
2:18, *106*
3:1, *106*
3:1–2, *140f.*
3:1–8, *51*
3:6, *141*
3:12, 13, *65*
4:1–8, *144*
4:3–8, *48, 57*
4:3–17, *228*
4:9–12, *49*
4:10–12, *144*
4:13–18, *39, 142*
4:15, *147*
4:16, *65*
4:16–17, *12, 58*
5:2, 3, *49*
5:4–8, *136f.*
5:9, *138*
5:10, *64f., 73, 143, 228*

I Thessalonians
5:12–13, *49, 144*
5:19–21, *49*
II Thessalonians
1:5–8, *153*
1:6–10, *228*
1:8, *144, 228*
2:1–2, *150, 158*
2:3–5, *150*
2:3–8, *143*
2:4, *159*
2:5, *143, 158*
2:6–7, *143, 151*
2:7, *12*
2:8, *161*
2:8–9, *152*
2:9–10, *161*
2:13, *144, 153, 229*
2:15, *144*
2:16–17, *228*
2:17, *144*
3:10, *144*
3:17, *78, 159*
Philemon
15, *122*
18–19, *122*
19, *78*
22, *122f.*
24, *210*

Index of Subjects and Authors

Abraham, 96–98, 99, 100, 131, 241, 244
Achaia, 27, 49, 52, 106, 113, 165, 166, 167, 180–215 *passim*
Acts, book of, 46, 51, 68, 115, 121, 141, 149, 171, 179–215
  authorship, 5
  dating of, 5
  historical value, 5–7
  sources of, 190–211
    Hellenist (pamphlet) source, 196–205, 209–210, 211
    "Journey" source, 188–189, 191–196, 204–205, 209–210, 211
    "we-sections" ("Diary"; "Log"), 189, 205–206, 210, 211
Adam, 65, 66, 71–72, 75, 118, 245, 246
  second Adam, 65, 71–73, 76, 118, 143, 229

Aelia Capitolina, 227
Agabus, 184
Agrippa, 154
Albertz, 69
Alexandria, 154, 156, 157
Ananias, 220
Antichrist, 155–156
Antioch, 52, 83, 93, 121, 165, 166, 168, 169, 183, 184, 185, 234
Antiochus Epiphanes, 156n
Antithesis, in Pauline thought, 88
Apocalyptic movement, 227–228; *see also* Daniel, book of
Apphia, 172
Aquila, 212, 213
Arabia, 165, 180, 190, 214
Archippus, 121, 172
Aristarchus, 121, 172

Armor-of-God concept, 136–137
Athens, 51, 52, 106, 140, 167

Barnabas, 83, 121, 164, 168, 169, 182, 184, 185, 191, 192, 194, 196–215 *passim*
Baruch, Apocalypse of, 13
Baur, F. C., 17, 141
Beroea, 140, 141
Bousset,
    The Antichrist Legend, 155n
Buck, Charles H., Jr., 6n, 82n

Cadbury, H. J., 6n, 188n
Caesarea, 115, 121, 171
Caligula, 154–156, 157, 158, 159, 160, 161, 212
Celibacy, 33
    Corinthian church and, 48
    see also Marriage
Cephas, 82, 164, 168, 169, 184, 185
Charles, R. H.
    Eschatology, 15
Charlesworth, M. P.
    Cambridge Ancient History, 156n
Christ, as second Adam, *see* Adam: second Adam
"Christ party," 108, 109n
Christianity, legal status in Roman world, as seen in "Journey" source, 191–192
Christology
    in Colossians, 11, 119–121
    in I Corinthians, 53, 65–67, 228–230
    in II Corinthians *1–9,* 15–16, 64–67, 231, 234ff.
    in II Corinthians *10–13,* 103, 230
    in Ephesians, 130–132
    in Galatians, 100–102, 231ff.
    legal vs. eschatological terminology, 234
    Paul's contribution to, 231
    in Philippians, 11, 71–76, 231, 233–235
    in Romans, 100–102, 231ff.
    in I Thessalonians, 228–230
    in II Thessalonians, 143–144, 228–230
Chronology, Pauline
    Knox's approach, 9
    problem of, 8
    see also Letters, Pauline; Paul
Church, doctrine of, 133–136
Cicero, 10
Cilicia, 165, 166, 180–215 *passim*
Circumcision, 234–242, 252; *see also* Judaizers; Moses, Mosaic law
Claudius, 152–154, 157, 158, 211, 212, 213
Collection for the saints, 24, 80, 83, 149, 165–166, 182ff.
    Corinthian church and, 32–33
    in I Corinthians, 24–25
    in II Corinthians *1–9,* 25–27
    Galatian churches and, 32–33
    in Previous Letter, 149
    in Romans, 27
    see also Paul: Collection trip
Colossae, 121, 122, 123, 171
Colossians, Letter to
    Christology, 11, 119–121
    dating of, 115–122, 162
    eschatology, 115–118
    legal theory, 120–121, 251
    resemblance of Ephesians to, 126–139
Community, Christian, and world at large, 49–50
Corinth, 24, 25, 26, 27, 28, 29, 32, 46, 47, 50, 51, 52, 103, 104, 106, 107, 111, 113, 140, 141, 167, 187, 192, 194
Corinthian church
    collection for the saints, 32–33
    idolaters, 42–44
    immoral persons, 42–44
    opposition to Paul, 103, 108–114, 236–237
Corinthian Reply
    contents, 31–45 *passim*
Corinthians (letters)
    number of letters in, 4–5

I Corinthians (Letter), 9
  Christology, 65–67, 228–230
  collection for the saints, 24–25
  contents, 31–45 *passim*
  dating of, 23–29, 162
  death of believer, 13–14, 57, 59
  eschatology, 13–14, 46, 53–67 *passim*,
    228–230
  ethics problems, 13
  idols, 34–35
  legal theory, 53–67 *passim*
  marriage, 33–34
  observance of law, 61–62
  parousia, 54
  speaking in tongues, 35
II Corinthians (Letter), 9
  collection for the saints, 25–27
  eschatology, 13–14
  new covenant, 11–12
II Corinthians 1–9 (Letter)
  Christology, 15–16, 65–67, 231, 234ff.
  chronology, 84–87
  collection for the saints, 25–27
  dating of, 25–26, 29, 162
  death of believer, 13–14, 57–58
  eschatology, 13, 15, 55–67, 231ff. *pas-
    sim*
  legal theory, 8, 15–16, 63–64, 238ff.
II Corinthians 10–13 (Letter), 9
  Christology, 103, 230
  dating of, 103–114, 162
  eschatology, 103, 230
  legal theory, 103
Covenant, *see* New covenant; Old covenant
Cyprus, 148, 191

Damascus, 164, 175, 180–215 *passim*
Daniel, book of, and apocalyptic movement, 155, 159, 227
Day of the Lord, 151, 158–161
Death, concept of, 248
  of believers, 13, 14, 49, 57–60, 69–70,
    90–91, 117
  in I Corinthians, 13–14

  in II Corinthians 1–9, 13–14
  literal, 13
  symbolic, 11, 14
Deissmann, Adolf
  Light from the Ancient East, 69n
Demas, 121, 172
De Wette, 16, 17, 125
Dietary regulations, 62, 168
Dio Cassius, 212–213
Dodd, C. H.
  New Testament Studies, 15
Duncan,
  St. Paul's Ephesian Ministry, 69n
Dupont, J.
  The Sources of Acts, 190n

Egypt, 148, 156
Epaphras, 121, 172
Epaphroditus, 76, 80
Ephesians, Letter to
  armor-of-God concept, 136–137
  Christology in, 130–132
  church, doctrine of, 133–136
  dating of, 124–139, 162
  eschatology in, 129–130
  "forgery" theory, 16, 124–126
  legal theory, 132, 251–252
  new-nature concept, 137–138
  resemblance to Colossians, 126–129
  Spirit, doctrine of, 132–133
  themes in, 128–129
  title of letter, 139
Ephesus, 24, 25, 26, 29, 105, 113, 121,
  187, 189, 192
Epistles, *see* Letters, Pauline
Eschatology
  in Colossians, 14, 117–118
  in I Corinthians, 13–14, 46, 53–64,
    228–230
  in II Corinthians, 13–14
  in II Corinthians 1–9, 13, 15–16, 53–
    64, 231ff.
  in II Corinthians 10–13, 103, 230
  in Ephesians, 129–130
  in Galatians, 90–93, 231ff.

in Philippians, 69–71, 231, 233–235
in Previous Letter, 53–60
in Romans, 91ff., 231ff.
in I Thessalonians, 12, 53, 228–230
in II Thessalonians, 12, 142–143, 228–230
IV Esdras, 13
Ethics, problems of
in I Corinthians, 13
Europe, 167, 186
Paul's first trip to, 150
Exodus, book of, 64

Faith, vs. work, 89–90
Famine in Judea, 148–149, 182, 211–212
Feast of Weeks, see Weeks, Feast of
Felix, 207, 214
Festus, 211, 212, 214, 215
Flesh
Pauline classification, 41–42
transformation of, 13
Forgiveness, doctrine of, 257–259
vs. justification, 257–258

Gaius, 156n
Institutes, 82n
Galatia, 121, 165, 180–215 passim
Galatians, Letter to, 9
autobiographical passage in, 163–166
Christology, 100–102, 231ff.
chronology, 84–87
dating of, 7–9, 82–102, 162
eschatology, 90–93, 231ff.
Jerusalem visits, 7–9
legal theory, 93–100, 240ff.
Gallio, 194, 211, 213, 214, 215, 222
Gapp, K. S., 148n, 212n
Goguel, Maurice, 8
Grace, vs. law, 60–61, 234ff.
Grotius, Hugo, 141, 150, 154n
Guilt, universal, 244–245

Hagar, 99
Hatch, W. H. P.
The Pauline Idea of Faith, 95n

Hebrews, Letter to
authorship, 4
Helena of Adiabene (Queen), 148
Herod, 195
Hierapolis, 121, 171
Hurd, J. C., Jr.
The Origin of I Corinthians, 31n

Idleness, 144
Idolators
Corinthian church and, 42–44
Idols, meat sacrificed to, 34–37
Illyricum, 167
Immoral persons
Corinthian church and, 42–44

James (apostle), 82, 164, 168, 184
Jeremiah
covenant concept, 11–12, 63, 98
Jerome, St., 147
Jerusalem, 24, 25, 27, 32, 149, 154, 164, 165, 227
Council of, 8, 180, 196, 203–204, 249, 250–257
destruction of, 148
famine in, 148–149
Paul's visits, 7–9, 82, 83, 104, 163–168, 171, 180–215 passim
see also Collection for the saints
Jesus Justus, 172
Jews
Christianity and, 12
see also Judaizers, controversy with
John (apostle), 83, 164, 168, 184
John Mark, 183
Josephus, 157, 213
Antiquities, 148
Jubilees, Book of, 12
Judaizers, controversy with, 74, 77, 83, 90, 93, 95, 102, 108, 120–121, 132, 144, 165, 170, 172, 173, 180, 184, 185, 234–238, 240, 249, 250–255; see also Jerusalem, Council of; Jews
Judea, 147, 148, 154, 171
famine in, 148

Jülicher, 8
Justification, *see* Forgiveness

Kingdom, entrance into, 117, 129–130
Knox, John, 6n, 104n, 165–166
  Chapters in a Life of Paul, 8, 165n

Lake, Kirsopp, 69n
  Beginnings of Christianity, 212n
  The Earlier Epistles of St. Paul, 107n
Laodicea, 121, 171
  "letter from," 139
Last days, rebellion and, 151, 156
Law, Jewish, 8
  Feast of Weeks and, 29n
  vs. grace, 60–61, 234ff.
  see also Judaizers; Legal theory
Lazarus, 60n
Legal theory, 60–64
  in Colossians, 120–121, 251
  in I Corinthians, 53–67 *passim*
  in II Corinthians *1–9,* 15–16, 63–64,
    238ff.
  in Ephesians, 132, 251–252
  in Galatians, 93–100, 240ff.
  in Philippians, 74–76, 235–238
  in Romans, 242ff.
  in II Thessalonians, 144
Letters, Pauline
  absolute dates in Paul's life established
    by, 162
  authorship, 3, 5–6
  chronologies, 7, 68
  dating of, 146 (*see also* Letters by ti-
    tle)
  internal consistency, 16
  tests for authenticity, 17–19
Lightfoot, J. B., 7, 19, 69, 83–84, 88
  Notes on Epistles of St. Paul, 151n
  St. Paul's Epistle to the Galatians,
    83n
Luke (evangelist), 5, 121, 172, 188, 189
  account of Paul's conversion, 220,
    225–226
  chronology of, 190–215 *passim*

Luke, Gospel of, 5
Luther, Martin, 10

Macedonia, Macedonian churches, 24,
  25, 26, 27, 29, 52, 80, 81, 105,
  106, 140, 165, 166, 167, 169, 180–
  215 *passim*
Mackail, 10
"Man of lawlessness," 151–156, 157
Marcion, 139
Mark (cousin of Barnabas), 121, 172
Marriage
  Corinthian church and, 36–38
  in I Corinthians, 33–34
  in Previous Letter, 33, 48
  in I Thessalonians, 48
McGiffert, A. C., 8
Meat sacrificed to idols
  Corinthian church and, 36–37
  in I Corinthians, 34–35
  in Previous Letter, 34
Minear, P. S., 6n
Moffatt, James
  *Introduction to the Literature of the
    New Testament,* 126n, 148n
Moses, Mosaic law, 61, 63, 72n, 93, 98,
  99, 185, 200, 239, 244

Nero, 157n
New covenant
  in II Corinthians, 11–12
  fulfillment of, 11–12, 239
  Jeremiah's prophecy, 11–12, 63, 98
  in Romans, 12
  see also Old covenant
New-nature concept, 137–138
Nympha, 121, 172

Old covenant, 63, 98, 239; *see also* Abra-
  ham; New covenant
Onesimus, 121, 122, 172
Orosius, 212–213

Parousia
  of Jesus, 153, 157

of "man of lawlessness," 153, 161
in Pauline theology, 12, 47, 53–54, 117, 239
resurrection and, 70, 142
Pastoral Epistles, 3, 17
see also I Timothy; II Timothy; Titus (Letter)
Paul
absolute dates in life of, 158–162
apostolic authority, 224
arrest in Jerusalem, 8, 181, 186, 187–188, 214, 221–222
"Asian ministry," 172, 186, 187, 209–210
persecution in Asia, 58ff., 69, 169–170, 231
biographical sources, 3–9
"boasting" of, 111–113, 220–221, 224
Christology, development of, 15–16, 118–119, 143–144, 226–237
chronology problem, 8
dates outlined, 175, 214–215
events of life based on book of Acts, 179–215
events of life based on Letters, 163–175
Collection trip, 166, 169, 187–188, 204, 209–210
conversion, 82, 104, 197, 219ff.
accounts of, 219–226
date of, 8, 175
significance of, 219–260
development of thought, 9–19
eschatology, development in, 12–15, 115–117, 142–143, 226–237
in Europe, 150, 167, 186
Farewell trip, 187–190, 209–210
Foundation trip, 166, 186–187
imprisonments of, 68–69, 115, 169–170, 231–232
"Intermediate visit" (to Corinth), 25, 104ff.
legal theory, development of, 15–16, 234ff.
Missionary Journeys, 180–190

"painful" visit, 105–106, 167
view on own death, 70–72, 233
visits to Jerusalem, 7–9, 82, 83, 104, 163–168, 171, 180–215 passim
Acquaintance (1st), 166, 175, 181ff.
Acts and Letters chronologies compared, 180–190
Completion, 181–185
Conference (2nd), 166, 167–168, 174–175, 181ff.
Council, 181ff., 204–205
Famine, 181–182, 202, 204–205, 209–210
Offering (3rd), 166, 181–188 passim
see also doctrines by name; Jerusalem, Council of; Letters by title
Percy, E.
Die Probleme der Kolosser- und Epheserbriefe, 126n
Peter (apostle), 164, 200, 250
Petronius, P., 154
Philemon, 122, 172
Philemon, Letter to
dating of, 122–123, 162
Philippi, 80, 105, 192
Philippians, Letter to, 9, 68–81
Christology, 11, 71–76, 231, 233–235
dating of, 68–81, 162
eschatology, 69–71, 231, 233–235
legal theory, 74–76, 235–238
number of letters in, 5n, 76–80
Philo, Philonism, 65
Porcius, 214
Previous Letter to the Corinthians, 24, 29n, 50, 105, 106, 149, 150, 169
collection for the saints, 149
contents, 31–45 passim
dating of, 162
eschatology, 46–47
idols, 34
marriage, 33, 48
parousia, 53
speaking in tongues, 35
Priscilla, 212, 213

Qumran, 29n

Rebellion, identification of Pauline reference to, 151, 156
Renan, Ernest, 8
Restrainer, concept of, 143, 152–154, 157
Resurrection, 12ff., 55–56, 117, 142, 228
   body vs. flesh, 40–42
   Corinthian church and, 32n, 38–42
   Thessalonian church and, 39
Revelation, divine
   Paul and, 10–11
Riddle, D. W.
   Paul, Man of Conflict, 6n
Righteousness, doctrine of, 75, 96–97, 241, 246
Romans, Letter to, 23ff., 171
   Christology, 100–102, 231ff.
   chronology, 84–87
   collection for the saints, 27
   dating of, 27, 29–30, 162
   eschatology, 91ff., 231ff.
   legal theory, 242ff.
     Jewish law for Gentiles, 8
   new covenant, 12
   number of letters in, 5
Rome, 115, 121, 122, 123, 154, 156, 157, 171

Salvation, doctrine of, 73, 138–139, 238, 239, 244–246
Sarah, 99
Schleiermacher, Friedrich, 17
Schmithals, W.
   Die Gnosis in Korinth, 5n
Severe Letter (to Corinthians), 25n, 107–108, 113
Shepherd, M. H., 154n
Silas, 140, 191, 192, 193, 194
Silvanus, 51
Sin, doctrine of, 245–246
Spain, 27, 171, 173
Speaking in tongues
   Corinthian church, 36–37

in I Corinthians, 35
in Previous Letter, 35
Spirit, doctrine of, 13, 56–57, 132–133, 229–231
Stephanas, 78
Stephen, 98n, 197
Suetonius, 157, 212, 213
Syria, 154, 156, 165, 166, 180–215 *passim*

Taylor, Greer, 82n
Tertius, 78
Tertullian, 152
Testaments of the Twelve Patriarchs, 12–13
Thessalonians (Letter)
   as one letter, 6
I Thessalonians (Letter), 9, 46–52
   Christology, 64–65, 228–230
   dating of, 46–52, 158–162
   death of believers, 49, 58
   eschatology, 12, 228–230
   Judean "disaster" referred to, 146–150
   marriage, 48
   parousia, 53
II Thessalonians (Letter), 9, 140–145
   Christology, 143–144, 228–230
   dating of, 140–145, 150ff., 158–162
   eschatology, 12, 142–143, 228–230
   ethical outlook, 144
   idleness, 144
   legal theory, 144
Thessalonica, 51, 52, 106, 140, 141, 150, 158, 167, 192
   dating of Paul's first visit to, 158–162
Timothy, 25, 26, 51, 52, 140, 141, 167, 172, 193, 194
I Timothy (Letter), 3
II Timothy (Letter), 3, 17
Titus, 26–27, 29, 104, 105, 106, 107, 108, 111, 112, 113, 164, 168, 169, 170
Titus, Letter to, 3
Troas, 26, 105
Two natures, doctrine of, 66, 73, 92, 100

Tychicus, 121, 122, 139, 172
Tyrranus, school of, 213n

Van Goudoever, J.
  Biblical Calendars, 29n

Weeks, Feast of, and the law, 29n

Weiss, Johannes, 8
  development in Paul's thought, 9–10
Wellhausen, J., 8
West, J. C., 141

Zoroaster, 227

8/69